11/8 13-8 4|23

7/30

The Crowd Sounds Happy

The Crowd Sounds Happy

A Story of Love, Madness, and Baseball

Nicholas Dawidoff

PANTHEON BOOKS

NEW YORK

Pantheon Books and colophon are registered trademarks of Random House, Inc.

Grateful acknowledgment is made to the following for permission to
reprint previously published material:
Alfred Publishing Co., Inc.: Excerpt from "Sister Golden Hair," words
and music by Gerry Beckley, copyright © 1975 (Renewed) by WB Music Corp,
All rights reserved. Reprinted by permission of Alfred Publishing Co., Inc.

Hal Leonard Corporation: Excerpt from "Beautiful Boy (Darling Boy)," words and
music by John Lennon, copyright © 1980 by LENONO.MUSIC. All rights controlled
and administered by EMI Blackwood Music, Inc. All rights reserved. International
copyright secured. Reprinted by permission of Hal Leonard Corporation.

Williamson Music (ASCAP): Excerpt from "Let's Have Another Cup of Coffee"
by Irving Berlin, copyright © 1932 by Irving Berlin. Copyright renewed.
International copyright secured. All rights reserved. Reprinted by
permission of Williamson Music (ASCAP).

Library of Congress Cataloging-in-Publication Data
Dawidoff, Nicholas.
The crowd sounds happy: a story of love, madness, and baseball / Nicholas Dawidoff.
       p.   cm.
ISBN 978-0-375-40028-5
1. Dawidoff, Nicholas. 2. Sportswriters—United States—Biography. I. Title.
GV742.42.D39A3 2008   070.4'49796092—dc22   [B]   2007030525

www.pantheonbooks.com

Printed in the United States of America
First Edition

2 4 6 8 9 7 5 3 1

For Rebecca W. Carman

And for Dan Frank, Sue Halpern, and Ginger Young
Cherished friends who are family to me

"I guess everybody thinks about the old times,
even the happiest people."
　　　　—WILLA CATHER, *My Ántonia*

"Next to love is the desire for love."
　　　　—WALLACE STEVENS,
　　　　"An Ordinary Evening in New Haven"

"The secret of happiness (they say) is to live in
the imagination."
　　　　—V. S. PRITCHETT, *Midnight Oil*

Contents

The Crowd Sounds Happy

Relievers

I grew up in a city of dying elms called the Elm City, on a street with no willows named Willow Street. Uncelebrated trees shaded our part of the road, sturdy oaks and mature maples, their branches so thick with leaves that they created a blind curve just before the intersection where the street straightened past our house and made its hard line for the highway. Cars traveled at a clip down Willow Street, especially at night, and because of the curve it was impossible to see them until they'd nearly reached the streetlight glowing out beyond my bedroom window. Yet lying awake under the covers I could hear those cars coming, and never more distinctly than on rainy fall evenings when the wind had blown a scatter of acorns across the pavement. I'd be tensed against my pillow, listening to the whoosh of tires closing fast over wet asphalt, and then, an instant later, a brief, vivid flurry of noise, the rapid, popping eruptions of a dozen flattened acorns, before the whoosh receded into traceless silence as someone else hurried out of town. Long before I knew that I came from a place people wanted to leave, I saw how eager they were to get away.

Every so often a car wouldn't make it to the highway. From my bed I'd hear the familiar swelling murmur of onrushing rubber—it was like nearing a riverbank through parted woods—and I'd be picturing the car flowing through the blind curve just as the night detonated in a cry of brakes and tremendous thudding impact. I'd crawl to the end of my bed where I could peer at the window glass, but all I could see was the fine silvery mist of rain drifting past the street lamp. Retreating, I'd tug the blankets over my face as my bedroom filled with the hiss of punctured radiators and revolving flashes of hot red light. My mother would come through my door and sit by my side for a few minutes. Then she would run her hand through my hair, give me a pat, tell me to sleep tight, and the door would close. My room felt remote, bigger than usual, and every shadow playing along the ceiling terrified me. By morning, when I went outside for a look, all remnants of the accident would have been swept away so that I might have doubted that anything had truly happened were it not for the chips of headlight glass or the laciniated chunk of engine grille that I'd find in the gutter with the acorns.

But before any of those investigations, there were hours of the night still to go, and as I tried to calm myself with less upsetting thoughts, invariably my mind turned to my favorite baseball team, the Boston Red Sox. There in the dark I evaluated the feats and virtues of the players I liked best. This was the early and mid-1970s, and their names were Griffin, Siebert, Tiant, Aparicio, and Yastrzemski. We had no television, did not subscribe to the newspaper, and my bedtime was not long after the evening broadcasts of games began on the radio, so I knew very little about the Red Sox. In those days, everybody knew less about ballplayers. Yet my desire for familiarity with them was intense, and I arrived at strong impressions, most of which placed peculiar emphasis on the players' own boyhoods. Griffin, for instance, I had heard was nicknamed "The Dude," which led to my belief that he'd grown up playing second base in cowboy boots. Because Siebert was always called "Sonny," my illogical conviction was that he'd been taught to pitch by his father, out beyond the barn stalls on the family farm. The musically cadenced name Tiant led to my certainty that the pitcher had taken fife lessons as a child and entertained his teammates after games with Cuban melodies. The diminutive Aparicio, I knew, played shortstop by creeping forward on tiptoes as each pitch was released, an eccentric technique I supposed he had first employed in youth to make himself seem taller, and one that

I—tinier than he and intimidating to nobody on the playground—
sedulously imitated. I had yet to visit Fenway Park where the Red
Sox played their games, and I thought of it as a public greensward,
not unlike East Rock Park in my neighborhood, dappled with shade
trees, seesaws, basketball courts, picnickers, the ball field itself surrounded by slatted city benches from which cheering citizens took
in the game. Because very few of the player names on my baseball
cards presented challenges to pronunciation, as a Dawidoff I was
grateful to Yastrzemski. That someone had become the leader of
the Red Sox despite that less-than-sibilant thicket soothed my concerns that I might somehow be held back in life on nominal
grounds. I used to repeat Yastrzemski over and over, always with the
tongue-rolling inflection that my Russian-born grandfather, Alexander Gerschenkron, used to make a diphthong.

Naturally, I wanted the best for all these Red Sox men, which in
baseball terms meant winning the World Series. I spent a lot of time
imagining how it would feel when this baseball apotheosis happened. The Red Sox had not won the World Series in a very long
time and by now had something of an accumulating reputation for
disappointment, but I was not deterred. Like most people who
believe they are awaiting a miraculous occasion, my anticipation
took on exalted forms. As I think back now on those moments, mysterious to me is the extent to which my private worldly desires were
infiltrated by my aspirations for the Red Sox, how the team brought
up the fundamental questions of possibility. At various moments of
my early youth, the great victory was conflated with the news that a
traveling circus with clowns, trapeze artists, and a sword-swallowing
lady was coming to town to perform for an audience of one—me;
word that my younger sister, Sally, would be going off to live elsewhere permanently, with another family; a declaration of love
from a succession of adored female personages including: Mary
Elizabeth, a girl I first encountered on the swings at nursery school
and after whom I'd named my tabby cat; the haughty Claire, who
had French parents and a propensity to be "out jump-roping" when
I called up on the telephone to invite her over to play; and yellow-

haired Christine, who wore colorful jumpers and, to my sorrow, moved away after third grade. The most recurrent of my Red Sox World Series reveries made me part of a large, noisy family gathered around a laden table for Thanksgiving dinner with a cheerful father at the head to say the blessing and carve my mother's turkey.

There were plenty more variations on this theme, and on those sleepless nights, no matter what bumped and rolled outside my window, the Red Sox were there to stand by me. If things grew truly desperate, I had a fail-safe. I was no tabulator of sheep; I counted Yastrzemskis, a brief doxology that never amounted to much of a total before all anxieties faded and the terrible wakefulness was gone.

CHAPTER TWO

Game Called on Account of Darkness

ll the way from Washington to New Haven it rained, I three
years old and unsurprised to find that the sky should share
my mood. What did I know of how life worked, what was
custom or coincidence? To me, everything new that happened was
the norm. That afternoon I had gone to visit my friend Felix, a
Saturday like any other until the sudden solemnity of being told by
my mother to say goodbye to dark-haired Felix because we were
"going away." Felix lived along the crest of a hilly road out beyond
Georgetown with chips of mica embedded in the sloping street
pavement on which I concentrated while my mother spoke with his
mother, I following that shining line of road until it descended into
the sky at the end of the world. And then we were crossing over,
leaving everything known behind as we went cannonading north
along the expressway in our Volkswagen Bug while the day grew
black and water covered the surface of the window glass in tandem
with the stream running down my face.

When a child thinks, I have never felt this way before, the expectation is that now that you have, you will again. I did in the future
leave my father, Donald Dawidoff, many times, but those later
departures never in any way resembled the day we first moved away
from him. I cannot bring back his Washington face, cannot see him
as someone with whom I shared life. My first memory of him, my
first life's memory, is the feeling of losing him for good. "By the time
you were old enough to remember your father," my mother, Heidi,
said to me once, "he was a different person."

I know a few other details from my brief time in Washington, and since they were told to me a long time ago, when I was very young, not so long after I lived them, I recall them as my own memories. In our two and a half Washington years as a family, we had three different addresses, though in my recollection the trio has become fused into only one white clapboard house. Out our front picture window, across the street, was an insurance company parking lot. At the end of the afternoon it was my habit to stand on the couch in front of the window, bracing myself against the back cushions, and recite the makes of all the cars as they came in a procession out of the parking lot, the hearty Buicks and Chevys, the Morris Minors, which looked flimsy and often had dents, and especially the sports cars, the Saab with its hubcaps studded with interesting punch holes, the low, long-hooded Volvo coupé, and the spoke-wheeled British racing green MG. Our house had a front porch and a staircase inside leading up to the second floor. Out back was a spacious yard with trees and also a thick tree stump, as well as many ground squirrels that would scamper across the stump and sometimes pause to perch on it with a nut. At a certain point my father began talking to the squirrels, and he believed that even the dead ones were initiating conversations, communicating with him on urgent matters, instructing him when to strike, and whom.

Just as my changed father looked to me as he always had, my mother, too, remained the same in my eyes but appeared different to the world. The day before we were to leave Washington, she asked my friend Peter's mother if I could stay at their house while my mother packed up our belongings. I had been to Peter's house many times. Now, however, because my parents were getting divorced, Peter's mother said that we were no longer welcome inside their door. "I can't have you in my house anymore, but I guess I could meet you at a motel and look after him there," she told my mother. My mother said not to worry, she would make other arrangements. It was around the same time that my mother's mother, my Grandma Erica, fell into the habit of freckling her conversation with remarks about the unseemly ways of "divorced women." Twenty years later, when my Grandma Erica was dying, out of the blue she told my mother, "You know, when I said all those things about divorced women, I didn't mean you."

We arrived in New Haven at night. Our new house, a husky, gray, two-family structure, had only one floor for us this time, a ground-level railroad layout with a branch line to the dining room and kitchen, but there were high ceilings and not much furniture, making it feel rangy and limitless. I ran along bare wooden floors through four rooms, all the way to the very rear window, where I looked out and, unable to see anything of the backyard through the night-darkened glass, believed the unseen perimeters must be huge—big as a meadow. I was imagining a paradise of grass, bosky field, jungle gym, and fountain when my mother told me it was time to go to sleep. I still had my old crib and Sally, sixteen months old, had hers. That first floor of 292 Willow Street would be my home for the rest of my childhood.

I learned a lot of things later than most people, but something I understood early was how small a hold I would have on determining my own history. My mother says that when at first we came to Willow Street, I feared departures, didn't ever want to leave home. My mother had resumed teaching high school English at Day Prospect Hill, the private girls school up on top of the Canner Street hill where she'd worked before I was born, from 1960 to 1962, while my father was a student at Yale Law School. One day, not long after we arrived back in New Haven, an older teaching colleague of my mother's came over to Willow Street, presented her with a rocking chair as a housewarming gift, and then took me out for a short drive alone with her in her car, just so I'd see I could go away and would return.

Not wanting to empty my father's life completely, my mother had left almost all of our possessions behind with him in Washington, so initially our New Haven furnishings were mostly unwanted hand-me-downs from my mother's older sister, Susi. My mother slept in the living room on a rust-orange upholstered daybed that doubled as our couch. A skewbald rug spread over the floor. The daybed faced a nonworking fireplace that had no andirons, yet, nonetheless, was protected by a metal screen that often buckled and tipped over. A wooden mantel rose above the fireplace, while the apron in front of it was a mosaic of lacquered greenish orange tiles, several of them broken or permanently dislodged. We ate meals at what would one day become the basement laundry table, seated on heavy brown wooden chairs. My mother had a sewing machine and a radio, which, along with two or three lamps, one of them built out of an old coffee mill, were our only electronic devices.

We visited a lumberyard and bought pine planks to build cases for my mother's books. She painted the dining room floor blue—it looked to me like a calm upside-down sky—the walls were white-washed, and one day the brown wooden dining room chairs became golden yellow. Another morning, my mother appeared with an artist's palette on which she dabbed a small brush in oils as she covered the kitchen cabinets with sprays of painted flowers. For our bedroom walls she designed huge felt murals, cutting the pieces of colored fabric into shapes and gluing them into place as she constructed a farm scene with barns, livestock, and a duck pond for Sally, and for me a felt city with skyscrapers, vehicular traffic, and freighters docking down at the seaport. It could only have been inspired by New York, where I was born and lived for a year until my father was told he would "not be retained" at his job "because," said his boss, "you're a lame horse and I wouldn't keep a lame horse in my stable."

Sally and I were each given a new unfinished pinewood shelf by my father's mother, my Grandma Rebecca, which my mother painted white and then filled with our books and toys, though not my big teddy bear. Beary slept with me and I faithfully kissed him good night until his face collapsed, clots of blue stuffing leaking out everywhere. My mother made him a new mouth.

My bedroom was filled with the noises of others. It stood at the junction of three rooms, Sally's bedroom, the bathroom, and the living room, and because a fourth door opened into my narrow closet, which my mother had entirely filled with her clothes, I grew so used to the sound of turning doorknobs that from anywhere in my room I could hear the spindle threads catch and the knobs beginning to shift. Whether they rotated slowly or briskly, I knew that a moment later I would have company.

The ceiling light fixture in my room had two semi-flush bell-shaped frosted glass shades and a socket where there should have been a third bell, meaning that one bulb always hung naked. Suspended up there, the light looked to me like a three-legged stool with one short leg. Upstairs, our neighbors' passages through their apartment made all three lightbulbs flicker and wink.

Through my lone window came footfalls heading up the exterior staircase of the yellow house next door, those neighbors so close to me that if I looked out through the glass on a stormy day I could see the drops of water fall to the ground as they removed and shook out their rain hats. Drifting in from the street came music from cars, motorcycle engines, voices moving along the sidewalk in conversation. When my mother went into the kitchen, spoons echoed against the sides of metal pots; from the living room came the news on my mother's radio, the five CBS bell tones at the top of each hour reaching an appoggiatura before backfalling into resolution. Sometimes above the radio my mother sang verses of songs from her youth: "Just around the corner there's a rainbow in the sky / So let's have another cup of coffee / Let's have another piece of pie." As my mother moved around the front of the house, there was the alighting-bird flutter of shades being pulled. Sink water ran, metal and wooden drawers opened and shut, a chair scraped as my mother seated herself before the sewing machine, which whirred, stopped, and whirred countless times as she made herself dresses from parch-paper patterns. Other times she was pulling the chair up to her typewriter with keys she struck so true and fast the house rippled with little impacts. At night I could hear her removing the daybed cushions as she prepared to go to sleep. She had organized our house so that she was for Sally and me our portcullis; we were quite literally behind her, although the broader truth is that she was also behind us, always, and when all her sounds ran together and became one, I could hear her commitment to our lives. I could also hear the telephone and the doorbell, though they seldom rang.

Our New Haven backyard turned out to be the furthest thing from Elysium, though there was scarcely time to register the scatter of weeds, rusted cans, and broken glass before my mother made them disappear. Portions of the small asphalt patio near the back steps had shattered into loose pieces. Not much could be done with the patio, but beyond it my mother planted grass and flowers, built a red sandbox with a hinged, green cover to keep the stray cats from using it as a litter box, and she assembled from a kit a dome-shaped red and white climbing gym. Every clear day my shirts and socks flapped on the clothesline high above my head, while even higher, like flags on a halyard, was our neighbors' laundry. In the summer our yard was shaded by trees whose medium height meant they had grown up after the 1938 hurricane and the subsequent outbreak of Dutch elm disease that together had largely denuded the city's canopy. I had a toy dump truck and a crane that could do nothing but roll, and a real shovel with which I was digging a hole to China. When I hit a cache of broken dishes, I believed I had reached Peking.

Every night before bed we huddled in close on either side of our mother in our pajamas on the daybed, close enough to feel the warm, soft flannel of her nightgown while she read to us for hours that might have been days, so intense was the dual experience of sitting there, cushioned as a compass in a binnacle, free to enter all those big, spacious, other worlds. The books she tended to select were historical fictions with titles like *The Witch of Blackbird Pond, Calico Captive, Across Five Aprils,* and *Johnny Tremain.* The protagonists were usually young, and there were as many boys for me as there were girls for Sally. Most of the books had been checked out of the public library downtown, but the copy of *The Wonderful*

Wizard of Oz that my mother read from belonged to us, which made it possible, when I became frightened by an illustration of the Wicked Witch of the West, for my mother to go to her sewing basket, remove her pinking shears, snip the plate right out of the book, and show me that she was locking it away in her bureau, beyond my reach. That she had elected to imprison the page was better than throwing it away, because I knew that my mother was in command of that witch. The top bureau drawer, along with my mother's two desk drawers, were the only places in the house that I had never investigated. They were off-limits to me, my mother's private spaces.

My mother read with such clarity and expressiveness from those books that to this day I can bring back long descriptions from them in her voice: Revolutionary Boston stretching itself awake in morning outside as indoors, up in the Lapham family attic, two apprentice silversmiths wallow in the bed they share with Johnny Tremain, while Johnny, seething with energy, gets dressed in his leather britches, orders them to "look sharp," and then calls the lazier one "a pig-of-a-louse"; and the feel of the night when Johnny and Cilla Lapham take Cilla's feverish baby sister, Isannah, down to the wharf, where in the cool harbor air Johnny tells them about his beautiful mother, who brought him up on her own by sewing and sewing until she coughed herself to death.

But it was the many Laura Ingalls Wilder books that made the most striking impression. I liked spunky brown-haired pioneer-girl Laura so well I half thought of myself as she—until we got to *Farmer Boy,* the story of Laura's future husband, Almanzo Wilder's, childhood on an upstate New York farm. So many interesting things happened to Almanzo at ages not much more than mine. Prohibited by his stern and distant father, James, from ever handling the family's sleek Morgan horses, young Almanzo raised instead a clumsy pair of red cattle named Star and Bright, teaching them how to pull and turn together. He milk-fed a huge pumpkin that won a prize at the county fair; he saw his diminutive schoolmaster, Mr. Corse, defeat the lumpen bullies from Hardscrabble Hill with a huge blacksnake ox-whip supplied, Almanzo later learned, by his father, James; he planted corn and potatoes, sheared sheep, hauled timber, pulled molasses candy and then fed it to his pig, which got its mouth stuck shut, made ice cream in a tub using custard and ice chipped off a block by hatchet. But his favorite food, fried apples 'n' onions, sounded much better than it tasted when my mother cooked some up for us to try. Toward the end of the book, Almanzo discovered a man's ample pocketbook lying in the road to town, found a way to get it back to the owner, and was rewarded, first in a small, grudging way by that owner, who was a pinchpenny, and then extravagantly by an intervening shopkeeper who indignantly forced the ungrateful miser to give Almanzo a large sum. James Wilder disapproved of this. Then the shopkeeper offered to make Almanzo his apprentice. Back at home, over supper, James listened to Almanzo answer his question about his plans for the reward money by telling his father that he would put it toward buying a young Morgan horse of his own. In a burst of emotion at this day which had made clear that his son was both honest and hoped to follow him in life, James gave Almanzo Starlight, the family's prize colt. I made my mother read us that book several times, and whenever James Wilder smiled and said, "Son, you leave that money in the bank. If it's a colt you want, I'll give you Starlight," my throat would fill and I would feel unable to speak for many seconds.

I wanted to be a Farmer Boy too. One summer evening in New Haven, my mother, Sally, and I sat having supper as filmy beams of late-day sunlight streamed through open windows. My mother had cooked mixed frozen vegetables as part of our meal, and after separating the corn niblets from the carrot cubes, peas, lima and green beans, I grouped the corn off to the side of my plate. After dinner I announced that I would now be planting my corn crop in the backyard. My mother said fine. She walked behind me as in my palm I carried my damp yellow hoard through the back hall and down the steps. Then she advised me while I chose an arable-seeming patch of ground over by the fence where with a trowel I dug my furrow. By the time the corn niblets were evenly distributed in the dirt, they'd shriveled so much they were small and wan as baby teeth. I covered them up and watered them over the next few days until it was clear they would not grow. As I got older, I often thought about that evening, what my mother had sought to cultivate by encouraging me. I decided she believed there were things that nobody should tell you about; you had to find out for yourself.

The sidewalk in front of our house was made of black asphalt, not a smooth tar-surfaced macadam, but a cruder and more astringent hardness that to the bare knee was gritty as black sandpaper. The sidewalk was the crossroads, the railroad tracks, the big Mississippi, Yellowstone, and the Grand Canyon all together, a twenty-five-foot stretch of epic landscape; it was the whole world delimited—my territory. Close to the ground as I was, I knew every fossa and contour, and thought of them the way a surveyor does his swamps, vales, cliffs, and lakes: the sidewalk's jagged cracks, the slits of crevasse, the crumbling edgework, the volcanic eruption caused by a bulging tree root, the filmy lagoon of moss in one shallow—it glowed iridescent after a wet spring fortnight—the pale blots of discarded chewing gum that could take months to disappear, the rhododendron that never once flowered, the traces of hopscotch chalk, the dusty red berries fallen from one of the two evergreen bushes next to the porch, and deep beneath those bushes, where a rake could not easily reach, the decomposing tree leaves wadded together and smelling of mellow rot. Here on my sidewalk was the indelible cycle of life, the colored leaves that meant fall; snow and ice in all their frigid winter thicknesses and densities; a scatter of twigs and branches that were the measure of March breezes; the maple samaras that in late May came helicoptering to the ground where I searched for the longest of these winged seedlings to snap in half and stick to my nose—Pinocchio!; and the footsteps that trod to different sounds on each of these accumulations.

The windfall came from our two tall trees that stood on the dirt meridian between the sidewalk and the street. At the base of one of the trees, a gnarled round burl had formed that resembled a stool seat. I used sometimes to sit on it in summer, resting my feet on the curbstone, taking in a tableau holding the "No Parking Here to Corner" sign across the street, the stout celandine yellow fire hydrant with its valve plugs protruding from either side like hands on hips, and all the houses and sidewalks that faced me. No two houses on Willow Street had the same sidewalk. Though most sections were concrete, they were built with squared integuments that ranged from a smooth milky white to a pebbled putty color, making the block as a whole resemble a boxed assortment of chocolates. The small brass plates sunk into a couple of the concrete slabs by paving firms or city utilities were scarabs to me, and though I didn't understand why our asphalt should not be adorned in brass, I accepted it as the way of things. Likewise, on a visit to another town I saw a red hydrant and was at first horrified by the lack of uniformity in the world, and then quickly became a backer of yellow, just as I had superior thoughts about New Haven's fleet of white fire engines when taken to a strange city where I saw a red pumper go by. I was a fierce partisan of my ordered terrain.

And then something would intervene to disturb the order. One day there was a dead bird lying on the sidewalk, the bird's dark feathers limp and greasy-slick, its beak a brittle, sickly yellow. I stared at the bird, the swarming insects beginning to devour its eye. "Don't touch it" I heard my mother say even though I was alone.

Another afternoon I came outside to find a woman standing in front of our house holding a paper grocery sack out of which the bottom had dropped, leaving her feet surrounded by a turbid pool of oozing eggshells, shattered bottle glass, a splatter of fruits and vegetables. A can had rolled several feet away from her. It was spring, but a bonnet was tied tight under her chin, and she wore taut little rubber boots and a dun-colored trench coat that was too short, revealing ankles no wider in circumference than the riding stick of my hobby horse. Her pallid chin and gray cheeks stretched to a bitter point at her nose, and in her eyes was an expression of such cold, barren despair that I turned and ran without offering to help her.

In the rambling blue Queen Anne house next door, up under the eaves in the third floor garret lived a mother and her son who was about my age. His name was Lazlo. Once Lazlo came into a bulk package of Kit Kat candy bars, more candy than I had ever seen in one place. He gave me a bar and I ate it while he did the same, the smooth milk chocolate giving way to the pleasingly crinkled crepe-paper-like interior layers of wafer. It was remarkable how quickly you could eat a Kit Kat. That evening I thought of Lazlo up there enjoying as many Kit Kats as he liked, and I craved another with such ardor and pining that I became convinced that I was somehow entitled to more. The next day I hurried to find Lazlo. As we spoke, all I could think of was my worry that there were no remaining Kit Kats. My head throbbed. I hinted. He didn't offer. I couldn't hold out anymore. I asked for a second Kit Kat. "What can you give me?" Lazlo wanted to know. I had nothing. In the evenings at home we had been reading *Old Peter's Russian Tales,* which were filled with accounts of greedy fools, cunning gluttons, a collection of horn-swogglers, and a talking golden fish who offered the poor fisherman who spared him his life everything he could think to ask for. The simple, virtuous fisherman was unable to come up with a single thing he lacked, but his wife could. Everything she requested she received, and with each largess her life got worse. Old Peter had a homiletic way of speaking. He said that the fish story was about wanting more than enough, but I overlooked that part. To Lazlo, I said, "I have given you my friendship, the rarest gift of all!"

"Yes," he said, nodding like a landowner. "And I have given you my friendship *and* a Kit Kat."

My mother had a slim figure with shoulder-length brown hair the color of sunlit brook water, and she appeared tall to others although she was of no more than average height. To work she frequently wore dangling earrings, red kilts, and dark blue sweaters. With the sweater sleeves rolled up, her sinewy arms seemed poised for manual labor. So erect was her posture that her head and collar fitted together like mortise and tenon. When she smiled she looked like a prettier version of her restrained, Austrian-born mother. When she became lost in thought, she resembled her scholarly and outgoing Russian father.

In our strict household there never really were many rules. My mother's expectations flowed so logically from her own comportment that they were easy enough to understand without the aid of codes, injunctions, or prohibitions. Perhaps it was that in Washington everything had been so out of control that now everyone was grateful for routine, but, whatever the cause, Sally and I didn't have to be told twice never to begin eating before everyone else was served. In the morning, as soon as we were tall enough, we made our beds. Then somebody gave me a penny to buy a piece of Bazooka bubblegum, and that first taste was like offering a dog chopped sirloin—I would do anything for more.

The ensuing bubblegum ban was grounded in a fierce jurisprudence that led my mother to inveigh in screeds meant not only to stigmatize but abominate. Bubblegum was, she lectured, the bottomless perdition, a silent fiend scoring holes into your teeth even as it was capable of far worse, taking incisors and bicuspids within its terrible sticky grasp and yanking them right out. "You don't want to end up with real dental problems, Nicky," she warned. "Son, they'll plague you for life." The bubbles themselves were offensive to my mother ("It looks so vulgar, that bulbous thing hanging out of your mouth") as was the coloring ("that lewd pink"). Her contention that there was "something cheap" about bubblegum she buttressed with expressions of contempt for its physical nature ("You are aware you're chomping on plastic?") and abstract character ("It's a gadget-food, Nicky"). When I went through a period of swallowing the gum, she was aghast—"You can't digest that!"—and her disapproval broadened: to her it was no less than the embodiment of all that was wrong with the country in the late 1960s and early 1970s—we were a nation on the bubble, artificially sweet.

Her disapproval did no good. I was so mad for the stuff that I thought all the time about how to get some. When I came into a dollar, I committed my first conscious transgression, sneaking down to Cumberland Farms to invest all of it on one hundred penny pieces of Bazooka. You got a larger chunk of gum for your penny then, and the brown bag I brought it all home in would have held both my shoes. After I ate a dozen pieces, I hid the rest in the back-yard sandbox. I remember putting the brown bag in there and clos-ing the hinged green top as I thought about all the days and weeks I would now be in supply. Minutes later I was back for a fresh piece. Then five pieces. They were all gone by nightfall because the flavor didn't last.

Directly across from us on Willow Street in a Doublemint-green house lived an old Italian couple whose only child was a vigorous young man named Junior. Junior was beginning a life on his own on our side of the street, down the block from us in an attic apartment he shared with his slim, attractive Irish wife, and, soon enough, their infant son, also called Junior. The old father spent hours every warm day sitting watchfully on his front porch, Umbrian style. After work, Big Junior used to cross Willow Street, still in his business trousers and stripped to a white undershirt, to join his father on the porch. Over the weekend he'd wash his car in his father's driveway or meet up there with his boyhood friends. Big Junior had been a local baseball star, and as Little Junior got older, I used to observe from my burl stool as Big Junior stood him in his father's driveway and taught his son to catch and throw. Looking on, I felt oddly out-side my own self and would think, I am watching Little Junior grow up. On weekends Big Junior, his wife, and Little Junior would join Big Junior's parents for Sunday dinner, after which his wife jumped up and did the dishes. Big Junior's mother would wait for them to leave, and then she'd say "Filthy Irish thing" over and over as she rewashed every plate and fork.

Also across Willow Street from us, a little down the block to the right of the green house, was a red single-family house that belonged to the Orvilles. The Orvilles' house frequently came up in conversa-tion at our house, its mention always embellished by my mother with phrases like "sweet little red house" and "pretty little red house." Red was my mother's favorite color. Whenever I left our house, instead of looking at the green house, I used to look over at the Orvilles' red house, taking in its clean, simple proportions, studying what my mother liked.

I missed my father. When I now look at snapshots of my father and me as a young boy—in one I am sitting in a toy fire truck, my father crouched behind, his arms circling my shoulder—I am always surprised by how happy we seem. Since I didn't see much of him anymore, I tried to compensate by spending time with his photograph. It was a formal portrait that he had gone to a studio to have made. I would sit in our new rocking chair and stare at his handsome bald head for what seemed like hours.

When my father came to New Haven, he took me to George and Harry's restaurant, where I tasted fried clams and tartar sauce. After I got home my mother said she'd gone with him there on special days when they were first married, and she too had ordered clams. Over and over he brought me to see again the fire trucks at the Whitney Avenue station and, farther down Whitney, the dinosaur room at the Peabody Museum of Natural History. Once he gave me a children's book called *Little Rascal,* which was his nickname for me, and I all but memorized this story of a Wisconsin boy and his pet raccoon.

During those years I also made a few visits to Washington. My father would come to New Haven, and then drive me back down to Washington in the Rover 2000 sports sedan he'd purchased while my parents were still married. My mother had told him that now with two children they needed a larger car than their tiny Volkswagen Bug. They'd discussed a station wagon, and when my father came home from the car dealer with the Rover instead, he had, my mother said, "a funny hostile look in his eye." The Rover, with its polished wood-grain fixtures and tooled leather upholstery, had been far too elegant for young children to ride in. Now, however, it was bruised and careworn, and I could be in it.

After one of these visits to my father's, my nursery school teacher, Mrs. Nover, took my mother aside and said that "something" was happening down there "that's upsetting him." My mother explained to Mrs. Nover about my father. "You need to tell him," Mrs. Nover said. My mother said she felt she couldn't tell me because, "I don't think it would be right for me to say anything to the children against their father." As she spoke, my mother could tell that Mrs. Nover was "appalled," thought "I was a sensible person doing an incredibly stupid thing."

"When will the children find out about me," my father asked my mother.

"Don't worry," my mother told him. "Not until they've grown up."

When I was six, my father took me to Washington's National Zoo, where he got angry and walked away from me. Only by running along after him was I able to keep him in sight. He went up a sloping walkway and I followed until, finally, he slowed enough for me to catch him. My father didn't look at me, but he let me follow two steps behind. Later we stopped by an office building. I remember the closed newsstand, the immaculate marble floor of the empty weekend lobby, him waiting for the elevator, stiff with mood. The elevator door opened, he entered, and I made it too, just slipping in between the closing doors.

CHAPTER THREE

Things First

My mother, Sally, and I made frequent weekend overnight visits to see my mother's older sister, Susi. Susi lived an hour and a half away in Croton-on-Hudson, New York, with her husband, Tony, and my coeval cousin, Jody, in a small, white hillside Colonial home that we all called the Little House, although it was much larger than our home in New Haven. Typically when we drove to Croton, my mother liked to be on the road first thing, for, once we had a destination confronting us, she was impatient to be there, and a Saturday split into fragments displeased her, as did any kind of lassitude about time.

On the nights before travel, from the moment we'd eaten our supper my mother was "racing," as she put it, washing the dishes, hauling the laundry up from the basement to hang out overnight on the clothesline, caroming a dust cloth through all five rooms so that we'd return from our trip to a spotless house, setting up the ironing board for upcoming early morning duty, and at last pulling out the convertible sofa bed from the new red couch in the living room. From my bed sometimes I could hear her through the closed door to my room, gasping as she hoisted.

Before dawn she was up again, folding back the sofa bed and smoothing the cushions. By the time Sally and I were awake, there was no sign that my mother had rested. After taking in the laundry and ironing, all of it, even the dish towels, she roused us. While Sally and I ate breakfast, my mother was remaking the beds we'd stripped, with fresh sheets and hospital corners, loading the car, clearing off the table while reminding us to visit the toilet for a final time—we were not a family that willingly made rest stops—leading us out across our busy street, and pulling into the gas station just before it opened at seven.

We went to the Arco station where the proprietor's navy blue work shirt had "Vic" scripted in red within a white oval above the right pocket. That was still the full-service era, when the small business proprietors around New Haven knew all of their steady customers and, as we especially learned a few years later, during the long gas lines of the OPEC oil embargo, all of the gossip. With Vic my mother needed to do what she so rarely did, rely on somebody else, place herself in his care. Vic must have intuitively understood that for a schoolteacher with two young children in the backseat and the wedding ring gone from her finger, the open road could seem threatening. He scrutinized the oil level on the dipstick, looked carefully at our tires without being asked to, and on a hot July day might spend an extra moment saying reassuring things to my mother about the impeccable condition of her radiator. Then, when the gas tank was full and the windshield sparkling, we were off with our clean bill of transit. I often had the feeling about my mother in those years that the only two times she could relax were when she was safely in interstate motion and while visiting her sister.

Croton was less than two hours from New Haven, and, since we traveled there frequently and to few other places, I remember the details of the journey with the clarity of successive landmarks, the way the parkway narrowed, the paving surface abruptly becoming gaunt and pellagrous as we crossed over the Connecticut border into New York, a drive-in movie theater, a Carvel ice cream stand, a pizza parlor named Honey's. We never paused to inspect any of these attractions. It never would have occurred to my mother, and I knew that it should not be occurring to me. We proceeded steadily until turning onto the Old Post Road where smiling Uncle Tony, Jody, and Aunt Susi would come bursting out of the Little House to greet us.

The two sisters set eyes on one another and immediately they would begin talking. It was as though they were making up for lost conversations, which, in a way, they were. Susi was nine years older than my mother, and, in Susi's childhood, day after day her mother, Erica Gerschenkron, felt "busy" or "tired" or "unwell" and had put Susi in charge of the baby; soon Susi was all but raising my mother. It was an enormous burden for a young girl, and Susi took it out on my mother, finding ways to undermine her appearance, her abilities, her mind, habitually referring to her as "Stupid Sister." My mother was already, by nature, the more sensitive of them, and these years wore abrasions and fissures that began to mend only when the two sisters became simultaneously pregnant with their first children. In sharing that intimate experience, they began to share other intimacies. My mother tried to explain how it felt to be rejected first by your mother, and then by your sister, who was acting in your mother's place. Susi, not yet thirty-five, confessed to my mother that she now lived in a constant state of weariness: "I feel like a horse that was asked to pull too soon."

That wasn't how she ever seemed to me. Susi was short, curvy, and blond, with eyes of lapis blue and a smile so warm and wide it made me think of a sound—the midday whistle in Croton. I'd overhear her conversations with my mother, so full of lively cadences and frequent laughter, and I could tell, above all things, how happy my mother always became when she was sitting across a table drinking coffee and talking with her sister.

When you are young and living with a single parent, you are always on the lookout for the way people in more traditional families comport themselves. In Croton the rules changed, and what was frivolous or tawdry or too expensive in New Haven became acceptable across state lines, with television and restaurants and the new movie at the drive-in resurrected as "Susi things to do." Susi would lead us all upstairs to watch *The Sonny & Cher Comedy Hour* on television, or she'd strum a guitar and sing folk songs like "I Never Will Marry," "Amazing Grace," and "Daddy, You Been on My Mind" in a deep-voiced way that would make me well up with a good kind of sadness. One year, in honor of my visit in early December, she began what became an annual celebration of St. Nicholas Day, setting out our shoes along with food for Saint Nick the night before in front of their Franklin stove. In the morning, our shoes were filled with candy and dried fruits while most, but not all, of the food on Saint Nick's plate was gone. At home, in New Haven, we didn't have dessert. In Croton, midway through dinner you'd begin to wonder what day-ending flourish Susi had waiting. She thrived on the gratifications of hue, shape, and texture, was a person who, after buying Popsicles by the box for a while, decided that she could do better than Good Humor and made her own in deep, enamel colors, was a person who preferred to bake an apple strudel rather than an apple pie because everybody already knew about apple pie. Another evening she might say "Let's jump in the car and go to Carvel and get bonnets," and just like that we'd be standing in a parking lot licking soft cones of ice cream dipped in chocolate syrup, my mother happily among us, relieved from her own sense of stricture and regulation.

Uncle Tony also was a glimpse of another way of being. He was the man I saw most frequently in the world, and I liked to watch him in action, though on Saturdays the actions were delayed. Well past midday most of Tony remained supine under quilts, with only his dark hair and stubbled cheeks peeping out from beneath a ridge of newspapers. Eventually he added the paper to one of the many piles of newsprint high as my shoulder that were threatening to submerge the bed. He kept all editions, insisting on their necessity for future reference, though to locate any paper dated much past a couple of weeks would have required a messy strip-mining operation of a sort that was never attempted. One year at Christmas, Tony gave me a book of amusing headlines that had appeared in American newspapers, and after that I used to imagine how it would be reported if at last the floor collapsed taking Tony and the bed with it: "Man Succumbs to Weight of His *Times*." When Susi and my mother mentioned this bracken of information, they used to refer to "those newspapers," with an inflection that expressed equal parts horror and helplessness.

In our bookish family, because so many of his concerns were conspicuously masculine, Tony was known as the soul of practicality, and my mother referred me to him for the resolution of my technical quandaries. "Ask your uncle next time you see him," she'd say when I wondered about assembling a toy, what a secant did, or how to shave my face. He had a workshop and liked speedy cars and large cameras and safari jackets and the outdoors—was the sort of gadget-loving man who finds joy in reading maps, consumer guides, and instruction manuals. But Tony was not vigorous so much as he understood vigor; his workshop was filled with uncompleted projects, and his pragmatism was, if anything, conceptual. He was happier to explain things than to do them. Before we visited the White Mountains one summer, Tony spent a lot of time showing me how to read the Appalachian Mountain Club's guide to the trails of the Presidential Range. Then we drove up the mountains. On the day we took a sailboat out onto the Hudson, there were excellent seminars on rigging and the boom, but very little sailing. Tony worked at a think tank as a political and economic futurist, making forecasts and predictions about how Americans would one day live, and right down to the household quotidian he was a believer in capitalist technology as the source of daily progress, someone who seemed almost to look forward to his personal machines becoming obsolete, so eager was he to discover what was coming next to make his life more efficient and comfortable.

I remember many firsts. There was the first day of school at Worthington Hooker Elementary; the day I first read from a book, sounding out the name "Tip" from a paperback primer that told the life and times of Tip, a puppy, and Mitten, a kitten; the day I crouched on the floor of my bedroom and first tied my right shoelace; the day I learned to write, to add, subtract, and sight-read musical notation, skills that made the world seem like a place all made of codes; and because there I was penetrating so many of them so quickly, life seemed to promise a future forever filled with momentous new disclosures. Thinking back later, these firsts seemed crucial, the stuff of myth, and I wanted to believe that there was retrospective significance in them, and to remember all the meaningful details. Yet when I couldn't reclaim anything further from the mists, I would wonder why, simply because it was the first time, an experience should command such weight.

At home, learning some things required, in my mother's judgment, "a man to teach you," and so a succession of independent masculine contractors was called in: a high school boy to show me how to ride a bicycle—"Now, whatever you do, don't stop pedaling or you'll fall over," he warned as his steadying hand left my back; a work colleague's husband to sled with me down steep Divinity Hill (we crashed into an iron fence and saw that a Flexible Flyer would bend but not break); and even an affable stranger conveniently encountered on the beach who explained how to swim, but not when to stop—I went and went until plowing into a rock and slicing open my scalp.

Another day I hiked. Hiking turned out to be only another word for walking, but the day seemed worthy of elevation because of who took me. It was while on a weekend picnic to a state park on the Connecticut River with a man my mother dated. I became quickly attached to him, as I was drawn to all the guys who came to take her out. She was less impressed, and none of those relationships developed. "Some of them preferred doing things with you than with me," she once said.

I liked to be around men and older boys, used to visit the firemen at our local stationhouse, and to try to get Chipper, the kid brother of one of my baby-sitters, to play with me. Although he was several school grades ahead, sometimes he would, and we'd roam the neighborhood. We were both preoccupied with the people who lived in those houses along highways into whose lamp-lit rooms you could see as you drove past at night. Their existences seemed thrilling to us, possibly lurid, and there was a lot of speculating about what had brought the residents there. Chipper even slept over once, and from a sleeping bag on the floor in the dark he thought up and lobbed math problems to me in my bed to solve, lengthy equations that called for the addition, subtraction, multiplication, and division of a protracted sequence of multi-digit numbers, some of them in the tens of thousands, others in the high millions. He'd finally finish. I'd make a guess. The answer would be zero. The answer was always zero, but I never wanted to guess it because with so many numbers in the air, it couldn't all add up to nothing.

My locus was kitty-corner from our house, the fenced-in asphalt schoolyard of Worthington Hooker. Soon enough, I spent all my afternoons there. At age six, I was simply going along with time, heading out into days where everything I came upon still seemed flawless and magnificent, not its best self but its only self—the way it was supposed to be. I did not yet measure existence, only looked to it to present me with endless perfections, and one of the qualities of the schoolyard that drew me there day after day was that on blacktop, between diamonds of wire, there was just enough constraint to open everything up.

We played a lot of kickball. The schoolhouse itself was a rambling, late-Victorian structure built of sun-baked pink bricks, with jagged wall excrescences and two back porches that would pinball a cleverly placed line drive. Anything kicked over the high fence that ran from the left field foul line to deep center field was a home run, while a ball kicked over the short fence beyond the tiny right field area "Down First" was a double. The rest of right field and right center didn't exist; there were only those carom-causing brick walls and the mesh-protected windows of the school building. Drooping over the left field line behind third base was a mulberry tree whose seasonal groundfall sent many a pop-fly-pursuing shortstop skidding off course. For a while, a large tree stood incongruously at second base, but it was chopped down, leaving behind only a slight commemorative rise in the asphalt.

During the school day, at class recess time, red rubber balls were produced, and a group of us kickball players shared the field with a chaos of bouncing, skipping, hop-scotching, hula-hooping, jump-roping children. There were horse-crazed girls galloping astride phantom mounts, wild games of tag, and teachers pursuing future chemists who'd been observed concocting bizarre compounds with paste, crayon shavings, and the lunch milk. We players were eager to refine our kicking and catching to make a good showing in the ongoing, weekly, after-school kickball games between the Raiders and the Vikings. That was serious kickball, presided over by a man named Mr. Lucas, who appeared in the schoolyard each Tuesday afternoon through the fall and then again when the temperatures warmed in the spring to pitch for both teams. Any Worthington Hooker student was welcome to play. At age six, I began my career assigned to the Raiders, my first experience with the chanciness of sporting affiliations and the unswerving covenants that come with them. Immediately, I could never have been a Viking, and to be a Raider was no less than an expression of self.

Before every game, Mr. Lucas selected the week's captain for each team. When we Raiders were up, our captain created a batting order. Out in the field, we would gather around the captain and plead for positions. There was some uncertainty as to who would receive the coveted shortstop and left-center-field spots. There was no chance that I would be playing anywhere but tucked safely out of the way, alongside the near porch, Down First. Yet this was a highly ritualized process, and, like everyone else, I made a mendicant of myself, yelling "Down First! Down First!" until the magic face of destiny met my eyes, solemnly pointed and intoned "Nicky! Down First!" and away I went at a delighted scurry for another week of futility.

When I was at the plate, as Mr. Lucas dipped his arm and released the ball, the entire infield and outfield would creep toward me, converging like high tide, smothering my most vigorous dribbles and throwing me out at first. When I was in the field, if a ball was kicked in my direction I would set for the catch, only to have a teammate drift in front of me and make the play. On the whole, though, more cruising butterflies came near me than balls, so I was left with plenty of time to study Mr. Lucas and the older players.

Mr. Lucas had a taut, kinetic bearing that heightened the pulse of our games even as it kept them moving in an efficient way. He was friendly, but a little aloof, and all this, and the snappy warm-up pants striped down the side that he wore, made me assume that he was a touring kickball professional. Some of the older Raiders were more accessible, especially a tall, lean lord of the blacktop named Trem, whose line drives made thwacks when the ball glanced off the mesh window screens. Among the tips and counsel Trem gave me for success in the asphalt world was to pull my laces so tight "it hurts." Footwear being a player's only essential equipment, thereafter I scrutinized the choices of the Raiders stars, such as Zito, who was always calm and smiling as he glided around the outfield making cinematic catches in green low-tops. One winter, J.B. wore his father's high black leather infantry boots to school every day, along with five extra pairs of socks so the boots would stay on. The purpose of this, he explained to me, was to "get fast." When spring came, on the first kickball Tuesday, J.B. changed into sneakers, and then dashed around the playground bases like a hamster.

My own kickball skills languished, which I found increasingly frustrating. One Tuesday afternoon, sure that I was consigned to a lifetime of Down First futility, I began to cry. When this was noticed and people asked what was wrong, I saw that I was making a spectacle of myself and that undid me further. I ran for the schoolyard gate and, led by Mr. Lucas, players on both teams chased me down. I had long wanted Mr. Lucas to take special notice of me, yet never like this. A sidewalk conference ensued during which I was coaxed back within the fence and installed in left-center-field next to Zito. I had agreed just to end the humiliation of becoming the center of attention, but the falseness of my being out there with Zito smarted like a punishment, and I upbraided myself for desecrating the game and its natural order. I was disgusted with myself, filled with an intensity of self-loathing that I now find startling in a six-year-old. I wanted to be someone who overcame things.

There were repercussions. Trem wouldn't talk to me anymore. Ever after, when I passed him on the sidewalk, he looked away from me with contempt on his slender face. I missed him, and I hated him, and I didn't blame him.

On a late October Saturday in 1969, we visited Croton. As soon as we arrived, I jumped out of the car and sprinted toward the house as I always did, expecting the usual bountiful outdoor greeting. But not this time. The Little House had a narrow porch running below a length of picture windows, and through the glass I could see Susi, Jody, and Tony seated in the living room, two fair heads and a dusky one bent in mutual concentration. I tapped on the window. Without turning, Susi waved me inside. She appeared to be in a state of high excitement. I passed through the kitchen into the living room doorway where I saw that all three of them were intent upon a small black and white television they'd set up on a piano bench. Again, I greeted them. Nobody looked up. They were entranced. From the doorway I began to speak. "Quiet!" Susi hushed. On the television, there were men playing baseball, and to everything that happened, Susi reacted with little cries of suspense. When my aunt's heart was in something this was unmistakable—she shimmered with pleasure.

I had never seen baseball before. Susi kept directing words of encouragement and endearment toward the television, most of it for the benefit of a player named Tom Seaver. Was there some way he could hear her? Eventually, an inning must have ended, because Susi pivoted off the couch and pulled me to her in an enormous hug, dispensing her usual greetings, filling me in on what was going on. It was the World Series, the New York Mets against the Baltimore Orioles, and Susi was rooting for the Mets. Tom Seaver was the Mets' pitcher and best player. I saw now that the Mets had their nickname inscribed across their shirts in cursive letters. It was only a month since I'd learned to read, and with every pieced-together word still came the thrill of fresh possession. But what, I wondered, was a Met? Play resumed, and immediately Susi was back in the game.

I recall nothing more of the moment. There was a long time when the faintness of my memories of this day dismayed me, because it seemed vital to remember more fully my first encounter with baseball. But, of course, culturally signified experiences are frequently in themselves banal, and the true meaning often lies in what surrounds them. What I really wish I could more fully bring back is Susi showing baseball to me.

Later during that visit, Tony, with the assistance of Jody, would outline all the rules for me at the kitchen table. Tony's descriptions were precise and logical, replete with many diagrams and much attendant use of mugs, the sugar basin, stray pieces of toast, and cereal bowls to illustrate the basic functions and habits of ballplayers. By then I had grasped that kickball and baseball relied on the same template of rules, so it all made quick sense. But even before I understood the specifics, I instantly liked baseball because Susi liked it.

Baseball was a typical case of my sensual aunt's resourceful instinct for joy. She had never noticed the game until that summer, when "The Amazin' Mets," perennially baseball's worst team, had suddenly become miraculous winners. Every afternoon, Jody would come home from school to watch the games with her and add to the scrapbook they were filling with news accounts of the Mets. She was caught up in the uncomplicated happiness of the Mets story, both the surprise of all the victories, and the indulgent affection that had enveloped the team long before the players were any good. Many Mets fans were former followers of the Giants and Dodgers, franchises that had uprooted themselves from New York in the 1950s for San Francisco and Los Angeles. The spectators the teams left behind in New York regarded the 1962 arrival of a new franchise for the entire city to share, the Metropolitans (Mets), the way a family cherishes the infant born to them after the death of a previous child; sorrow and gratitude mingled and produced unconditional devotion. For years, the Mets were adored for bumbling. To see them overcoming their traumatic past and playing so successfully was thrilling for Susi. I too was immediately mesmerized by them because Susi was, by the open and uncomplicated way in which she loved them.

Susi's was an evanescent fandom, burning so brief that by the following spring she had moved on to other things. Not me. Leaning in the doorway behind Susi at the Little House that afternoon, looking at Tom Seaver and the other pixilated ball-playing figures, I felt myself experiencing such exhilaration that to this moment, whenever my mind refracts back through time into that room, I see the low ceiling, the foreshortened walls, the three heads bunched across the span of the green couch, the clean corners of the black and white screen, and the whole frame reachieves the limpid, time-frozen definition with which my memory preserves the great sentient discoveries of my childhood—archived right there beside my first pomegranate, which, with its plug ends and bulbous contours seemed hideous and unpromising, reminding me of sketches I'd seen for untenable early undersea craft, until the tough pink hide was split revealing the bejeweled catacombs of fruit and underscoring forever in my mind the tendency of sweetness to secrete itself in a bitter husk.

CHAPTER FOUR

The Killer Inside Me

In the weeks before second grade began, I had been reading crime stories. Earlier, during that first summer I could understand books on my own, I had meandered among Greek myths, Grimm's fairy tales, and Peter Pan, and all of them had put me off because I wanted to read accounts of real-seeming people, was ready, without, of course, being conscious of it, to begin to make the connections between lives out in the world and my life, to see that other people can illuminate for you and also shadow your own being. Then I came upon Frank and Joe Hardy, teen detectives. A few pages into *The Shore Road Mystery*, I was trembling with the kind of attention that eliminates sound, time, sleep. The story told of how Frank and Joe, two normal, healthy American high school boys from the city of Bayport where their father, Fenton Hardy, was a famous detective, had spent their own free time uncovering a ring of auto thieves. Cracking the case required some doing. Along the way there were high-speed car chases, frame-ups, submachine guns firing at airplanes, grenades tossed through windows, muggings, roadblocks, evil skindivers and rock climbers, a nervy ploy that involved the Hardys getting their own car stolen with themselves stowed in the trunk, and then a final flurry of capture, imprisonment (in a cave), escape, desperate hand-to-hand combat, and the arrival of the cavalry in the person of their father—disguised as a bargeman—Chief Ezra Collig and the Bayport police force just in time to slap on the handcuffs. I went through *The Shore Road Mystery* the way I consumed the canned miniature Irish potatoes that were often served that August at my Gerschenkron grandparents' New Hampshire summer house: I swallowed them down whole. "Nicky, stop that. You're going to choke yourself to death," my mother would say with alarm when she caught me bolting, but I kept doing it for that intense moment of concurrent sensation: the slick white orb shooting riskily through my esophagus as it released a frisson of damp, briny potatoeyness. Within the Hardy Boys books, the criminal milieu created sinister, suspenseful situations that were counterbalanced by the reassuring rhythms of the Hardys' daily life. Cosseted among friends and family, deliberate Frank and the more impetuous Joe went skylarking around Bayport, playing sports, dating their steady girls, trying out new electronic detective-ware, riding motorbikes and jalopies, taking their speedboat *Sleuth* out into Barmet Bay, all before coming home to dinners presided over by their indulgent mother, Laura, their proud father, and their spinster Aunt Gertrude whose cooking and conversation both featured a lot of starch. And then on with the mystery where, after numerous close calls and a penultimate moment of peril, the Hardys emerged unscathed and triumphant every time.

There were dozens of these slim hardcover books, their compact heft and freshwater-blue trim so pleasingly sized that it was a satisfaction just to hold them. They had dramatic full-color illustrations papered right onto the front cover bookboard usually depicting the brothers in a moment of simultaneous revelation and jeopardy: taking cover behind a tree from the glare of somebody's searchlight; bound and gagged on chairs as a ghastly figure crept toward them; harassed by mountain lions, tumbling boulders, Mexican bandits, or a swarthy thug wielding a boat anchor. In these portraits, the brothers invariably had about them a reliable, just, V-necked-sweater-vest sort of look—a pair of upstanders. As I began to accumulate the books, I lined them up in my new white pine bookshelf, arranging the volumes there in series order. Many of my books were purchased for me secondhand, and eventually I came into a few that were not blue but a tawny clay color and had no cover illustration save a silhouette of two boys. These turned out to be earlier, midcentury editions, when the mysteries had been published with now missing dust jackets, and I took a bibliophile's pleasure in their tactile qualities. The pages of those brown spines were printed upon thick, pulpy, moldy-smelling paper on which the ink was sometimes smudged, lending, I thought, a certain artifactual authenticity.

Part of what was attractive about the Hardy Boys stories is that they became a source of expertise. I accumulated a fund of Hardy knowledge, from the name of their chubby friend Chet Morton's yellow roadster (*The Queen*) to the phrase the frazzled wannabe detective and Hardy foil Oscar Smuff used for $1,000 ("one thousand iron men") to expressions that to me were distinctively Hardy ("Suits me!"; "That's swell!"; "lie low"; "a sinking feeling") to the spooky locales along the Bayport outskirts the Hardys' cases took them to (abandoned buildings, deserted islands, hidden inlets, swamps, and shantytowns). It was here that I first encountered everything from rune stones to pea jackets to falcon jesses to lug-sailed Chinese junks to the words "ember" and "stevedore." The series also introduced dozens of thieves, smugglers, safecrackers, counterfeiters, and nearly a kidnapper per volume, yet these were vague culprits, every one a spectral presence so faintly sketched that, once the book was done, I could never remember a thing about them.

The weather was unusually warm that September of 1970, sultry enough that most of us came to school each morning in faded summer clothes to a beautiful new teacher, Miss Swainbank. Some of the instructors in that school were older women, wool-clad duennas with rubber soles on their stalwart black shoes and student-issue nicknames like "Mrs. Crab-Apple," but Miss Swainbank wore high-heeled boots, miniskirts, and peau-de-soie-like blouses printed in wild paisley-tinted greens against which her lustrous black satin hair poured all the way down to her hips. At the front of the classroom her movements were feline, and as she turned and raised her arm to the chalkboard, shafts of sunlight from the room's high windows backlit her, the blouse rippling and glimmering as she wrote.

Something else different that September was that in the morning when I left for the schoolyard I had company. My sister was entering first grade. Sally was not quite six years old, two years younger than I and still a very small girl, but I didn't see her that way. Four years earlier, no sooner had I gone off to nursery school than she'd become highly indignant, raised such a determined commotion about the unfairness of having to stay home when "Nicky gets to go" that she'd been allowed to enroll the next fall. On school mornings, as soon as Sally and I went out of our house together, I'd go leaping down the sagging front porch steps and charge up the block ahead of her, eager to join other boys in the running races back and forth across the blacktop, eager to be on my own. After dismissal, there had begun to be baseball games on the asphalt, and they were all I could think about. In a hurry to get started playing, I left Sally to walk home by herself.

Every day after school a crowd of kids would head home up the Canner Street hill, and once in a while I'd go with them, on my way to play with a friend at his house. At first the incline was gradual, but after a crossing guard, my classmate Gordon's mother, guided us through the intersection of Canner and St. Ronan streets, the hill slanted into an almost rooflike pitch, and as I trudged, I felt the steepness of the drop. Here all the sounds of the city seemed muffled into a motionless calm, and when a landscaping van passed over a loose manhole cover, the two-tone report came loud in double time and then lingered melancholy and reverberating. That part of Canner Street was one of the most solitary stretches of sidewalk in all New Haven, and potentially among the most stirring. From the summit of the hill, the road dramatically fell away as it ran down to Whitney Avenue and the effect was like looking through a gun sight.

Among the friends I went up the hill to visit was Binder, whose family lived in a large, shingled brown house with an off-center front door on St. Ronan Street. Binder had cheerful black eyes, and, when he giggled, they would shut while his whole body bent over, gleefully bobbing and shaking. At least one of his parents was from New York, and Binder spoke with a slight Bronxian inflection. His last name was pronounced to rhyme with cinder, which meant that during roll call on the first day of school every year, when a new teacher read off Binder with the invariable long "i," from somewhere in the outer boroughs of the classroom we'd hear a pained cry of "*Binn*-deh!" He was formidably academic. During math, he went across the hall to join the third graders in Mrs. Arthur's class. I too had been invited to enlist with Mrs. Arthur for math only to be denied permission by my mother. "But Binder gets to," I had protested. Without knowing anything about her, I liked Mrs. Arthur because Cousin Arthur was my favorite character in *Babar*. "Binder's mother is pushing him," my mother told me. "You will stay right where you are." By high school Binder would be shuttling down to Yale to take his math classes with the undergraduates. During kickball, his mastery of the angled narrows of the schoolyard's short Down First doubles fence revealed something about the resourceful ways he could apply his numerical bent to a sporting competition. While playing with him up in his second-floor room, I learned that he was keeping track of the many doubles he kicked—a previously unconsidered statistic.

Just across the crest of Canner Street from Day Prospect Hill, the private girls school where my mother taught, was Whitehall, a series of two-story brick apartment buildings for married Yale graduate students. The grounds were always teeming with kids, older boys out on the main lawn playing baseball, their mothers inside changing younger siblings' diapers, those Moms preparing us snacks—bright orange longhorn cheese, if they were Levi's mother—and often willing to call mine to see if I could stay on for dinner. Back in the bedroom were the fathers trying to block out the racket and finish their Ph.D. theses. From experience I already knew that once the dissertation was accepted, a moving van would arrive, my pal and I would pledge enduring friendship, and then they'd all get into their car and follow the moving van out of New Haven, bound for a university job somewhere out in the middle of America, never to be heard from again.

One eighty-degree Tuesday morning late that September, not long after we'd repeated the Pledge of Allegiance, Miss Swainbank let a policeman into our classroom. The two of them walked to the black-board and faced us. He had on a blue uniform with a service revolver dangling at his hip. He seemed much larger than she did. Miss Swainbank introduced him and then stood back listening as he showed us a photograph of a Worthington Hooker kindergarten student. Did any of us know her? I don't remember that anyone did. Then he told us her name, Jennifer Noon. Jennifer was five years old and two and a half feet tall. She had long brown hair with full bangs and large, wide, dark brown eyes. She lived in Whitehall, but she had not come home from school the day before. Had any of us seen her? We should think hard about whether we had. The policeman told us that she had been wearing a white sweater, a checked skirt, and black shoes. She had been somewhere short of the top of the hill when she "got lost." Had any of us walked up the Canner Street hill yesterday?

In the Hardy Boys books, policemen only interrogated the bad people. The questions panicked me. I was oppressed by his suspicions, his inability to see me as I aspired to be seen. I felt myself swept into the vortex of a tremendous guilt. I had never heard of Jennifer Noon. Clearly, however, I had done something wrong. Why else was I being confronted in this way? But what had I done? It was agony not to know. All at once I understood what it was to have a sinking feeling. Then, suddenly Gordon was getting up from his seat and leaving the room with the policeman. Relief washed over me.

At the end of the day, I came outside the school onto the Down First porch, and massed there at the gate in front of me was a swarm of adults. A few parents routinely met their kids after school, but this was different. As mothers and fathers spotted their children coming down the porch steps, they burst forward and grabbed the kid into an enormous hug. Some of the adults were crying. The hysteria made the rest of us look around for our own parents. When one of us saw a mother or father, the kid invariably began crying and ran to be hugged. If a kid didn't see his or her parents, they stood there uncertainly in the schoolyard and then, very quickly, still standing there, they too began to cry. The policeman had been so deft in class that none of us yet had any full idea of what it meant that a little girl was lost. But by the time we reached that gate, we all knew.

My mother tried to shield Sally and me from what was happening, yet everywhere you looked there were patrolmen on foot, squad cars with their engines idling, roadblocks, search parties coming door-to-door, and citizen volunteers gathering down by Wilbur Cross High School in brigades of several hundred, ready to conduct sweeps for a missing child. I visited my friend Chris at his house, and standing in the living room as I arrived was a policeman talking to Chris's younger sister, Jeanie, who was Jennifer Noon's classmate. I went to the home of another friend where the television was on, and there on the screen were Jennifer Noon's weeping parents begging her kidnapper to return their daughter. Trooping into my own home came several petrified-looking kids to be taken care of by my mother while their parents joined the search parties that were now dragging the Mill River, scouring East Rock Park as well as the wooded trails that wound out toward Hamden and North Haven. We heard talk of scuba divers and of bloodhounds. Every afternoon when the school day ended, dozens of parents and concerned neighbors stood beside the crossing guard on my corner, a grim, red-eyed line, some blinking rapidly as we all approached.

The last person to see Jennifer turned out to have been Gordon's mother, the crossing guard who'd guided Jennifer through the Canner and St. Ronan intersection. Soon enough we all knew that Gordon's mother told the police that Jennifer had come straggling along alone, many minutes after the big pack of Whitehall-bound kids passed. The story we heard at school was that Jennifer's big sister had gone home to play at a friend's house after school and that Jennifer, learning of this, had decided she wanted to go home with a friend too, had hung around Worthington Hooker trying to find one, which delayed her start for home.

The authorities were said to be looking for a paunchy, middle-aged white man in disheveled clothes who'd been seen with a little girl that Monday in a far-flung perimeter of East Rock Park. On the phone with a friend, my mother lowered her voice as she described a figure seated behind the steering wheel of a gray car who'd recently made some Day Prospect Hill students uneasy by lingering out on Canner Street just beyond school property. "The girls said there was 'something peculiar' about that man," my mother whispered, and the word "peculiar" burned into my brain. There could not have been a kid in my school who was not repeatedly told that week never to accept candy from a strange man, never, ever to get into a strange man's car, never to have anything at all to do with strange men. Strange man, strange man, strange man—the strange man was all I could think about, and he began keeping me private company wherever I walked.

After days of searching in sweltering heat, word came that some socks, black shoes, and a white sweater had been found in the woods of Rocky Top, a remote, timbered section of Hamden out toward Sleeping Giant State Park. The clothes were identified as Jennifer's. But still no Jennifer. She had been missing for over a week now, and the search had moved well beyond the area of Hamden where the clothes had been discovered. Then a professional dog handler, donating his time, decided to double his rottweiler back through for a second pass. In wooded undergrowth six and a half miles from our school, the man and dog turned up a half-buried body. My perceptions, fairly accurate to this point, now derailed. Somehow I got it into my mind that Jennifer had been chopped up into pieces, which were packed into clear plastic bags and then covered with old leaves. When the man and dog swept away the leaves, I believed they were confronted by a disembodied little head with bangs gazing up at them from inside the plastic bag, the face rigid with terror. For the rest of my childhood I carried that image with me. The truth is that by the time they found Jennifer, the corpse had so badly decomposed in the warm weather that her facial features were unrecognizable and my mother said the medical examiner could make no definite findings at all about what had killed her.

As I lay in bed at night, listening to the creaking sash of my low bedroom window, the suddenly cool gusts of wind seemed as significant to me as the rain that had fallen when we left Washington. No sooner had Jennifer Noon become known to me than she was already a horrifying memory and I was left with only the strange man. The strange man had become my secret habit of dread. He was out there, close, maybe under the window. Weeks passed with no arrest, and night after night I lay there, prostrate in a membrane of fear that felt all too permeable. I wanted to save myself from him. But how would I recognize the strange man when he came for me? I became preoccupied by what he might look like. There wasn't much to go on. To the flaccid, indeterminate incubus crouching behind the wheel of a gray sedan I added a blunt, menacing brutality to his face, cold and rheumy eyes, a surly gaze. Some days he spoke in a growl; on others he rasped. I didn't want to die; I wanted someday to become a fourth grader. Had I ever stood next to the strange man buying bread at Cumberland Farms? Down toward the highway on our street was Archie Moore's, a bar where all summer a waft of stale beer had blown out of the rusted air conditioner over the door. In the late afternoon, through the haze of the tobacco-stained window you could make out shrouded men bent over glasses. I was now afraid of the Archie Moore's men, was afraid of the pharmacy up on Whitney Avenue where the bald counterman, lean and impatient in his blue coat, had a barking way of speaking. I was afraid of the mailman's large shoes. My friends' fathers made me uneasy, and I avoided them during visits, spoke only to the mothers. Threats seemed to oscillate from all directions. Late into the night I monitored the air for suspicious noises, was such an alert sentry that I could not sleep until, exhausted, I collapsed into troubled dreams.

In class at school, Miss Swainbank seemed tired and more strict, all the light daubed out of her face. After dismissal, I now came straight home, walking outside the fence past the schoolyard where stray papers blew across the empty blacktop that was transformed by our absence, a forest suddenly deprived of birds. The windy days seemed to render me motionless. I had not known that there could be an unresolved mystery; such a thing had never happened to the Hardy Boys. The uncertainty was intolerable. It occurred to me that my life was in the balance and yet I did not know what to do to save myself. At night I pulled the sheets and blankets over my head. During the day I became convinced that my survival was contingent on my acting well. To protect myself from the strange man I believed I had better be very good, that I should not make trouble or demands.

I couldn't do it. During lunch at school, everyone liked to swap and trade, dealing a bag of Fritos for a package of Devil Dogs, but nobody ever wanted to exchange anything for my bruised apples and soggy tunafish sandwiches. The complete indifference of others to my lunches was painful to me. I began working my mother hard to get me Space Food Sticks. These were the foil-wrapped chocolate treats the Apollo astronauts were supposed to have eaten aboard their rocket ship. "We are on a budget," she'd say, "and anyway I'm not going to buy you junk food."

"But they're not junk, Mom," I would plead. "Scientists made them for the astronauts." My mother was not interested in astronauts, and had a low regard for "space," which she spoke of in the tone she used when referring to things inexplicably prized by other people such as Las Vegas and hula hoops.

"No, Nicky," she'd pronounce. "And that's final."

"I hate you," I would say, and go off to my room and whisper my grievances to my cat.

Another time she told me: "When I was a child I would have given anything for somebody to make me a tunafish sandwich for lunch because my mother made me sandwiches with jam and cold butter that gouged huge holes in the bread. You could be getting sandwiches with holes."

We had these conversations over and over and then suddenly one day during dinner I noticed the beleaguered way my mother looked as I described how "sorry" other kids said my lunches were. I was stricken. I decided to punish myself by forcing myself to eat the things I liked least on my plate first, not touching the good parts until all the liver was finished. I was sure that nobody had ever thought of doing this before.

It was one thing to be a nuisance at home. My mother seemed somewhat resigned to it. I sensed that far worse, by her calculus, was any misdeed that took place in public. My dim grasp of honor and reputation led me to believe that how I behaved outside the house would influence other people's view of her. I wanted my mother to feel that the world thought well of her. There was, of course, self-interest in this concern. So often my mother seemed exhausted by the daily expense of effort. I feared that if I created further burdens, she would weaken and then I too would be vulnerable to all the bad things out there, the paunchy apparitions lingering in cars and beneath low windows. My transgressions, I knew, must not leave our dining room. Then two of them did.

One day that fall, Miss Swainbank announced that the New Haven Board of Education had created a monthlong Read to Succeed competition in which the student in our class who read the most books over the month would be declared the winner and awarded a prize. Each week for the duration of the contest, we were to report to her the titles of all the books we finished. She distributed aqua-colored stickers, one for each of us, that said in bold yellow print: "If You Can't Read You're Out of Luck." When I got home I stuck my sticker on the inside of the bedroom door where, from my bed, propped on an elbow with a book, I could see it.

Each Monday morning at school during the month of Read to Succeed, Miss Swainbank was seated at her desk as we entered the classroom. We gathered around her, reporting what books we'd read that week, and she added them to the list. I liked competition, the way it added thrust to something I would have chosen to do anyway on my own, elevating regular life into an event, and I especially liked that each Monday morning when I told her the name of a book, Miss Swainbank would keep her head down with her pen poised, confident that I had more titles to give her. I began to live for the ability to make that hovering pen descend again to the page. Once I'd turned all the titles in, I'd go to my seat and look happily around me. The great virtue of the contest was that it provided something besides the kidnapping to think about.

At the beginning, just about everyone in our class had lined up with titles. Soon, for most, interest flagged. One Monday, toward the end of the month, I stood behind Binder as he gave his titles to Miss Swainbank, and it occurred to me that only the two of us were still trying to read the most books. Miss Swainbank never distributed a running total so I had no idea how many books Binder had read. I had no idea how many I'd read either. What I suddenly knew above all things was that I did not want to lose.

Binder had always been my friend. Now I began to assess him as a rival. Binder's large, dark eyes and wiry frame seemed formidable, as did his scientist's unflappable self-possession; I feared that mathematical ability could somehow infuse reading totals, increasing his tally. That he had never really seemed to enjoy reading was intimidating; he was engaged with this in a professional way. Binder finished submitting his titles to Miss Swainbank, and it was my turn. Standing beside her, I named the books I'd read, and Miss Swainbank wrote them down. When I'd listed them all, I looked at her pen, quivering expectant in the air, and I was seized with the wretched feeling that more was expected of me than I could give. "Any others?" she said in that adored voice. Frantically I searched my memory. The memory felt blurred. There must be others. Surely I had missed one. *"Peter Pan,"* I stammered. But I had read it that summer. *"Peter Pan,"* she repeated, and pen caressed paper. I waited for something to happen. Nothing happened. "Is that all?" she asked. "That's all," I said miserably, and, when she didn't notice, I went back to my desk and sat down.

But something had happened to me; my life was ending. I was a cheat, a liar, a fraud. *Peter Pan* was right there on my shelf. I could see its cover so vividly, the washed blue background, the sea greens of Peter's broad-collared tunic, Tinker Bell in gauzy pink. I knew I could go straight home and reread the book, put things to right. But a correction after the fact could not erase the reality of the offense. A current of mortification shot through me, and then killing shame descended.

For the next week I kept to myself, reading books and spending every moment feeling pressed against a rough edge of fear. I half wanted to be found out because, if I wasn't, anybody could get away with anything. They should know what I had done. They must know. The stylus that once played "strange man" over and over in me came alive again, skipping on a perpetual groove that sang *"Peter Pan, Peter Pan, Peter Pan."* I told nobody about what I'd done. That they were not already on to me seemed impossible.

The following Monday we gave in our last books to Miss Swainbank. Sometime soon after that she announced the results. I had won by six books. *Peter Pan* would not have made any difference. No sooner was there relief than it was chased by a peculiar regret. Around and around these sensations went, swooping me up and down, unstoppable as horses on a carousel, so that I kept feeling triumphant, then ridiculous, then unworthy, and then triumphant again. I contemplated making a clean breast, reclaiming that once savored feeling of virtue experienced when I'd returned money to the corner store after they'd given me too much change. But I did not want to confess. And why must I? I had read five more books than anyone else. I felt paralyzed by incompatibilities of logic—and the desire for recognition. I had never been singled out for anything public before.

I was presented my prize by Miss Swainbank. It was a gray T-shirt with "Read to Succeed" stenciled in blue above the image of an open book. "Award Winner" was lettered below it. I pulled the T-shirt on over what I was already dressed in and wore it that way, surplice-like, for the rest of the school day. In spite of myself, I began to feel proud. That afternoon when I got home, I rang the bell, stood at the front door and when it was opened by my mother, I unzipped my coat and displayed my trophy. My mother looked surprised. That pleased me. Then she frowned. "You mean they didn't even give you a book?" she asked.

We were riding in a car driven by my friend John's mother. In the car, along with John and me were his younger brother and his younger brother's friend Jimmy. I rarely paid much attention to my friends' younger siblings. They could never seem to do very much. Then, at some point during the drive, I learned Jimmy's last name. It was Noon. As I realized that I was in a car with Jennifer's brother, my head began to whirr and buzz. I wanted to know things from Jimmy. What did I want to know? I wanted to know how it was to be he, to know if everything could somehow be okay with him, if things might possibly even be okay with Jennifer. I began to wonder how he would react to the sound of her name. This was something I knew I should not explore. But the curiosity was too powerful. It pushed and pushed as I tried to resist. Then filters failed, sluices gave way, gates swung open, and without even thinking I turned to Jimmy and out of my mouth came words: "Where is Jennifer?" I asked him. The car went silent. My face contorted into a grotesque half smile, and I felt the armrest on the door pressing hard against my rib. Nobody breathed. Jimmy looked at me. "Jennifer is in heaven," he said. From the front seat John's mother's voice cut through the air: "Nicky! You leave him alone." The remorse was instantaneous. Why would I do such a thing? What was wrong with me? Once again I returned home feeling an all-fours, face-to-the-ground shame, my premonitions of annihilation revived.

While browsing the shelves down at the New Haven Public Library, I found an oversized volume by Don Whitehead called *The FBI Story*. *The FBI Story* told of notable crimes solved by the heroic "G-men" with chapters detailing how rogues from John Dillinger to Baby Face Nelson to Alvin "Old Creepy" Karpis to assorted atomic bomb traitors were brought to justice. There was also a description of the kidnapping of a boy named Bobby perpetrated by a man and woman named Carl Hall and Bonnie Heady. It seemed amazing how easy it was for Bonnie to enter Bobby's school, explain that she was a relative, and get Bobby out of his classroom and into Carl's car. They took him to a remote Kansas field where they beat and strangled and shot him. Then they buried Bobby in a garden and planted flowers on top of him. The story terrified me. Would a body make flowers grow better? After I returned the book I couldn't stop thinking about the photographs of the kidnappers. Finally I went back to the library and checked it out again. I could barely stand to turn to the Bobby chapter and there again to behold Carl's vicious leer and his hideously scarred forehead, Bonnie's plump, pasty, sullen depravity. But over the next few months I kept looking at them, kept going down to the library stacks where I knew *The FBI Story* stood towering over the other books on the shelf about police work, withdrawing it over and over to confront again the kidnappers until gradually they didn't bother me so much.

Most gratifying of all that dark winter was the discovery of true baseball stories. Words like Great, Hero, Amazing, and Thrillers inevitably figured into titles chosen by writers whose take on the game exuded, above all else, a spectacular admiration, as though these authors saw how much I wanted to love their characters. The ballplayers were all so splendid in their actions that even when they played for teams I disliked, in the reading moment I became faithless, a baseball apostate passionately and promiscuously rooting for whoever was the subject of the chapter.

My baseball knowledge came almost exclusively from such books, so I knew far more about Edd Roush and the 1919 Cincinnati Reds than Ed Kranepool and the Mets players of my own time. Over and over I read about the Merkle Boner, the Snodgrass Muff, the Ruth Called Shot, the Wambsganss unassisted triple play, the Gashouse Gang, the Homer in the Gloamin', the Miracle of Coogan's Bluff, and all this seminal lore convinced me that baseball had an accessible significance. With the game's system of making a tangible record of every substantive event, there was a stability and an order to baseball; it had never evolved and so all of it could be known. I soon had it within my powers, on command, to repeat the starting nine for the 1927 Pittsburgh Pirates, could discourse on the swinging styles of smooth Bill Terry, corkscrewed Stan Musial, Ty Cobb, who achieved unconventional agency with his bat by holding his hands inches apart on the handle, and both Joe DiMaggio's huge cudgel swing and Willie Mays's imitation of DiMaggio, in which the lesson was that Mays only became a superior player himself when he developed his own approach. I could distinguish Wee Willie Keeler from Big Ed Delahanty, Urban Shocker from Country Slaughter, Goose Goslin from Turkey Mike Donlin, Guy Bush from Bob Feller. I had never seen any of them play; they were all long before my time—and I liked it that way.

I wanted badly to know about these men, just as I wanted to have them to myself. Nobody else I knew had heard of Rabbit Maranville or Dazzy Vance or Hippo Vaughn or Kiki Cuyler. Though I did not ever lack for companionship and got along with every kid at school, I felt increasingly like a loner, and these men filled up my room. I'd walk in, see those books with their cracked spines, and a happiness would come over me. The players in them seemed to me to come from a better time in a better America, one that was simpler, pastoral, a paradise where heaven was a ball field. If it was possible to feel no longer innocent, no longer naive, that's the way I was after Jennifer Noon. My instinct was to want still to be innocent and naive, and in that desire I experienced a peculiar nostalgia for those distant days and distant games I had never lived through, a wistful sense that it had all happened only yesterday and a long time ago. I wanted to go back. There I imagined myself in a vast, happy country connected by ball fields.

And then it was early spring, and from my bedroom I could hear the four-bar clatter of a wooden bat falling to hard pavement, and out of the house I soared to play in the shadow of bricks on days so hot the blacktop became pillowy underfoot, on days still cold enough that grape soda froze solid in the can—sometimes bursting the metal to reveal a purple chunk that tasted so good a couple of kids tried it at home in the freezer, treating whoever next opened the door to a blaze of icy heliotropes. We named captains, chose up sides, made bases with our shirts, and then time lost its interstices, hour after hour, nothing more on my mind in my elation than the thought of being there, hitting and throwing until well past the time when daylight failed.

CHAPTER FIVE

Safe Havens

That August, we arrived to spend our annual month in the country with my mother's parents. My grandfather Alexander Gerschenkron was born in Odessa, and to him it was natural, in the bourgeois Russian way, to retreat from the city during the heat of the summer. As soon as he finished the year's teaching duties at Harvard, where he was an economics professor, he and my grandmother Erica hurried up to Windswept, my grandparents' snug, two-hundred-year-old white clapboard farmhouse built on a hillside in Francestown, New Hampshire. Windswept was out of view from any other houses, two miles from Francestown's lone store, surrounded by fields and forests, tucked beside a road on which traffic seldom passed. Here, after a little morning target shooting with his rifle, my grandfather spent the day under low Colonial ceilings writing scholarly essays about European economic history and puffing on his pipe, while my grandmother gardened and wove rugs on her loom. In the evening, she made dinner and he reread Pushkin, Chekhov, Tolstoy, and Pasternak. They had met in Vienna in 1920 after my grandfather and his family fled Russia during the Revolution and always spoke to one another in my grandmother's native German though both knew many languages. For them there was no question of complete solitude since the small towns and villages of that part of New Hampshire were well sprinkled with my grandfather's summering Harvard colleagues, but most of my grandparents' days seemed to pass in contented, bucolic seclusion. The Gerschenkrons were the sort of people who relaxed by reading Dickens or Montesquieu, though they saw no point to reading Dickens or Montesquieu unless they read all of Dickens or Montesquieu, the latter, it went without saying, in the original French. Their idea of summer fun was to spend the free hours together analyzing one hundred translations of Hamlet's "Doubt thou the stars are fire" quatrain to Ophelia in languages ranging from Catalan to Serbo-Croatian to Icelandic, all in the service of an essay in which they argued that translation inevitably distorts meaning. Aside from one another, they seemed to require no other stimulation.

As a young grade school boy, August in Francestown to me felt like being marooned in the antipodes. With no other children nearby and scarce entertainments besides a tire swing and the possibility that if the weather held we'd visit the town lake around three, I spent many of my mornings in an idle torpor, staring up at those low ceilings, unable to think of what to do with myself. Getting to my feet, I'd look through the window at the thick stands of trees drooping in the heat or wander to the end of the dirt driveway to stare gloomily down the empty road and wonder where my past city life had gone, wonder how I was going to fill all the listless, rural hours. The air itself was so still that it induced strange lethargies. I was drawn to the floor, to pressing my cheek against cool wood. Once I lay down in the middle of the road just to see what would happen. Nothing did. The rustic landscapes, so compelling to the adults with the old cattle pastures overgrown in a blaze of burdock, gorse, wild strawberries, and black-eyed Susans, the abandoned barns swooning beside roads that went nowhere, the endless brooks, elderly stone walls so precisely fitted it seemed nature had rolled them into place, the mastic smells of pine sap and telephone pole creosote, the lichen-scabbed rocks, and the infrequent breezes murmuring through groves of white birch trees making them sway like disapproving fingers—it all seemed dull. Nothing lifted me; I was a coiled spring gone slack.

There were no indications in that house that anyone had ever been young. Portions of the brown kitchen floor linoleum had decayed into brittle slivers, the dining room chairs were in such

fragile condition you had to sit down carefully so they wouldn't collapse, the refrigerator chugged and listed, and on the pantry shelf
was proof that saltines had once come in metal tins instead of cardboard boxes. In the back of the hall leading from the house to the
barn, I opened a door to discover the retired outhouse complete
with the half-moon sign that had been used to display occupancy.
Spiderwebs traversed the seat. Both of my grandparents were in
frail health, so the house was overrun with the fortifications of infir-
mity: pillboxes, prescription bottles, balms, salves, extra quilts and
blankets even in summer, the need for complete silence from children during adult naptimes. My grandparents were not unaware of
how these conditions might seem to us and made efforts. I loved my
grandmother, who gave me marzipan fruits and jelly-candy slices,
called Sally and me Putzi (baby), and told me about Austria where
she'd lived until "the war," and I adored my grandfather, who sat me
astride Hoxie, his right knee, and Sally aboard Moxie on the left,
and related another picaresque adventure in the lives of Hooey and
Mooey, the two naughty children he made up. They often fell on
their heads.

One day he greeted us by saying, "Hello, GFNs." We wanted to
know what that meant. "Good for Nothings," was the answer.

"We're not GFNs," we told him.

"You most certainly are GFNs."

"No, we are not GFNs," we insisted.

"Are you not Grandchildren from New Haven?"

But a little kid held only so much interest for them; they wanted
to have lengthy afternoon grown-up conversations with my mother
and she with them. She was a different person in their company,
less available because they were always getting her to do things for
them, long lists of errands and favors that had her driving all over
the Monadnock Region. She'd get back and they'd settle in for epic
conversations touching on politics and literature and films. How
happy she looked during these sessions that could go on for hours,
how animated and unencumbered. As the three of them spoke, I
would sit on the white hassock listening to them for as long as I

could stand it. Often that wasn't very long; I had no idea what they were saying. My mother replied to their German in English because, Sally and I knew, as a child in Washington during the war against Hitler, to be the little German-speaking girl had been such a mortifying experience for her. Now, she had no interest in our learning the language, so I didn't know any German except a handful of words I heard my grandparents use frequently such as *nein* (no) and *warum* (why). As a result, my contributions to these discussions were exclusively non sequiturs. After too long a spate of *oberdeutsch,* sometimes I'd look up from my plate, feign a puzzled expression, and interject a *"Warum,* Putzi?" This was briefly endearing. More usually I'd get distracted. Once, as they talked, I examined a shelf of my grandfather's books where I found myself mysteriously drawn to the pale violet dust cover jacketing his copy of Jules Verne's *A Journey to the Centre of the Earth.* Looking up, I interrupted what they were saying to ask, "When you die, Grandpa, can I have this book?" Everyone was awkwardly silent, and then they went back without comment to their conversation. For Christmas, they gave me my own copy.

At mealtimes, in deference to Sally and to me, my grandparents always communicated in English unless they didn't want us to understand what they were saying, in which case they'd switch to German. At such times I'd listen carefully though all I could glean were the proper names. My father's came up from time to time, but it never seemed strange to me that for the duration of that month we did not call or hear from him. It was just the way of things, like the German.

My grandmother clung to spoken German as she clung to her memories of Austria. She'd left in 1938, because her husband was wanted by the occupying Nazis for having a Jewish father, for being an active anti-Nazi, and for being stateless, and her two children were in similar danger because of their Jewish grandfather. Their escapes had been harrowing, and they never spoke of them. All I knew was that my grandmother seemed to wish I was Austrian. She ordered from Vienna lederhosen for me and a dirndl for Sally that we were expected to wear upon arrival and from time to time afterward through the month. That we were so isolated up on that hill made it easier to ignore the fact of myself turned out in suspendered leather shorts and white high-tops. One of the reasons I looked forward to the annual Francestown Labor Day Parade was that it meant the summer was ending.

As I grew older, when I got home from swimming my grandfather would no longer simply ask how it had gone. Now if I told him the water had been cold, a subtle look would come into his eye and he might address me: "Nicky Boy, swimming is best when the water is too cold for other people." This sort of swaggering counterintuition had immediate appeal to me, and soon all manner of my activities were saturated with what amounted to challenges from him, many of them implied. I began to have secret accomplishments—to let only him know that I'd climbed that high in the big pine tree, that I'd descended the second floor staircase without touching any of the ten steps, that my reading pace was nearing a page and a half a minute, that I'd stayed underwater at the lake for that many seconds, meeting the lifeguard's eyes when I surfaced. The idea with lifeguards, as I now understood it, was to make them nervous, but not enough to come after you.

When he gave me a copy of *David Copperfield*, one of his favorite books, though to me it might as well have been printed in German, I read through all 825 unillustrated pages just so I could tell him that I had. As soon as I made this disclosure, my grandfather eagerly leaned forward in his white chair, saying, "Is that so, Nicky Boy," and began very seriously to talk over the book with me, a brief discussion, as it turned out, that derailed when I had no idea what a Ham Peggotty was. "Some kind of casserole?" I suggested. He sighed and shrugged. Ham was one of his favorite characters in the novel. My mother, looking on in amazement, later informed me that such a display of incompetence would not have gone so easily for his daughters when they were young. Though his rancor was notorious, I only ever knew of it by reputation. Instead, when I announced that I had broken the page-and-a-half-a-minute barrier, he said, in effect, "We'll see about that." Then, from the bookshelf he plucked a copy of Trevelyan's *History of England,* which he opened to a random page and handed over to me. Taking out his pocket watch, he put me on my mark and then sent me off. "Oh, Daddy, what are you doing to him?" my mother cried as I began frantically reading about the inept and cowardly tenth-century King Ethelred the Unready, a task my grandfather may have believed himself to be abetting by calling out my time splits. When the minute was up, the book was taken away from me and I was the recipient of an oral examination relating to the reign of the "Redeless." There was by now a considerable amount of tension in the room, so that when at last he looked at my mother and exclaimed, "The boy can do it!" I soared into the air.

He was my only grandfather. My father's father, my grandpa Teddy, had died before I was born, and although my given name was Theodore Nicholas, in his honor, the name was unused, dormant in me, just as nobody ever talked about him; I knew nothing about that other grandfather, had never seen his photograph, saw only the face of Beary, my teddy bear, when I imagined what he had looked like.

In a way my one grandfather and I were on equal footing since his difficult, unspecific Russian and European pasts were unknown to me, and I had no past, leaving us free to experience the present together. He taught me to shoot the rifle and to play chess, and always wearing his red and black plaid lumber jacket he took me to a sporting goods dealer to buy red and white boxes of rifle bullets (on the living room mantel he made castles out of the empty boxes) and, another time, to lunch at a diner in Brookline—road trips that featured a constant stream of banter and gamesmanship about who could see what marvel or curiosity out the window, and also a certain amount of suspense; he drove like a bobsledder, though an inattentive one. When we got to our destinations, his hand went onto my shoulder and he introduced me to proprietors, and to other people we met, as "my grandson," a designation that, whenever he said it, made me feel the way a corpsman must when his commission is at last conferred, and by the brigadier himself. He was fundamentally alongside me, and such was my adoration that beyond repeating his convictions and emulating his habits, it occurs to me now that I never thought of his gun as a weapon, never conceived of his tobacco as a vice.

My grandmother did not share this benign outlook on another of my grandfather's avocations to which he introduced me, listening to the Boston Red Sox on the transistor radio. She seemed to regard baseball with derision, never referring to it by name, but instead as *"that game,"* or even simply as *"that,"* and because he was susceptible to her judgments, he looked stung when she entered his study and discovered something untrustworthy in the air: "Oh," she'd say. "You're listening to *that* again." Even so, from time to time my grandfather and I tuned in together, usually on Saturdays because on weekdays the Red Sox played at night, after my bedtime. With the transistor positioned between us and the volume kept low so as not to arouse dissent, we would lean toward the speaker while the broadcasters described the unfolding events, and, when something seemed about to happen in the Red Sox's favor, my grandfather would reach over and turn up the sound a bit. Then, if the good did come to pass, he might reclaim the pronoun by saying, "Well, how about *that*, Nicky Boy?"

There he sat, an elderly professor dressed, besides his lumber jacket, in some rumpled combination of light fabrics for the heat, potentially including a gabardine overshirt, white linen trousers, or yellow cotton dress shirts that Sally, learning to embroider, had embellished on the breast pocket with initials and sometimes also farm animals. He did not look like a baseball fan and he did not speak like one; in his Russian inflection the name of his team came out as *Thread*-sooks. Yet when I was older, I would understand that baseball helped my grandfather feel assimilated into his third city within his third country. The moments before a game where the Boston crowd came together to rise as one and sing the National Anthem and then rose again before the bottom of the seventh inning to stretch while singing "Take Me out to the Ballgame," were especially affecting for someone who'd grown up in politically volatile places where many people made a habit of leaving soccer matches two thirds of the way through because riots so often broke out. Here was a happier crowd, one that felt welcoming to him even though he only joined them by ear.

I can no longer recall the particulars of those occasional games, possibly because my grandfather did not concern himself with the moment-to-moment minutiae of mingled names, numbers, and outcomes. Instead I remember the way he listened. Certainly he reveled in the dramatic crescendos, but for the most part with baseball, he preferred to take a longer view. There are men who disappear from life into baseball. My grandfather disappeared into baseball to conjure with life. He implied it was good to be a baseball fan because you became a person capable of admiring what others did well. To him Carl Yastrzemski and the other Red Sox were characters in a narrative that was theirs to create and his freely to interpret. As we listened, when he said something about Yastrzemski or Luis Aparicio or Sonny Siebert, he invoked them by surname only in the same tone of intimate masculine familiarity that he used for Copperfield and Zhivago—and for Hooey and Mooey. He told me about the prodigious Red Sox hitter Ted Williams, whose career my grandfather followed through the 1950s, speaking of Williams as a fellow man of letters and seeing to it that I read the scholarship on the subject—Williams's autobiography, *My Turn at Bat*. (My mother broadened the portrait, confiding that as a girl she'd once watched Williams play, and from that moment on "he was the handsomest man I ever saw.") And my grandfather told me the story of the muscular young outfielder Tony Conigliaro, first crumpling to the ground after being hit in the eye by a rising fastball, only to rise again himself years later, now recovered from his wounds, to face down the fastball and hit the first one he saw for a home run. My grandfather related these events as allegory. To him major league baseball was a highly symbolic world in which men like Williams and Yastrzemski and Conigliaro were knights-errant, giant killers, young men of magical valor roaming through the American League, seeking somehow to return honor and light to the northern shires of their followers, who had resided in shadow for the half century since the Red Sox had last been World Series champions. The New York Yankees, meanwhile, were horrible Gilgameshian obstacles to glory, and he detested them in a vindictive way that felt exhilarating; on my own, I was never sure that it was possible to be a good person and to hate. Listening to a ballgame with my grandfather was, in short, to hear a nine-inning fairy tale. Eventually, seated at his side, I became a little like Schiller, who once reflected that "deeper meaning resides in the fairy tales told to me in my childhood than in the truth that is taught by life."

My cousin Jody knew that the world radiated on the point of Croton-on-Hudson. Every time I visited him, Jody would remind me that Croton was "the most important railroad station between New York and Poughkeepsie," a fact that seemed all the more impressive because of the ability to gauge achievement in such a way. Croton had one-of-a-kind destinations like Silver Lake, where there was a rope swing and a legendary undertow; Pop Burger's general store with its glorious toy section; and the dark, creepy house that, suburban myth had it, inspired the ghoulish eye of Charles Addams, inventor of Gomez, Morticia, Cousin Itt, and the other members of the Addams Family. It was difficult at times for me to see how New Haven could possibly compete. In ways, it couldn't. We had no organized sports leagues for seven- and eight-year-olds that I knew of, so when I heard about Jody's flag football games on Saturdays and saw him wear the colors of the Chemical Engine team in baseball games down at the field by the Duck Pond, I found it easy to remember the names of left-handed-swinging Greg Mulhall and his other teammates, could describe their abilities with as much proficiency as Jody could.

My cousin and I had been raised to consider one another brothers and there was nobody I more looked forward to seeing. During my visits to Croton, we read *The New York Times* sports section on the kitchen floor together and then all day we played cowboys and Indians outdoors and Ping-Pong in the attic, hunched for hours

over his long work table in a cloud of paint thinner and glue assembling plastic model tanks and airplanes, listened to country music
on his radio. He was a fan of Dolly Parton, C. W. McCall, and later
the teenaged Tanya Tucker, and, because of him, so was I. At a certain point we taught one another tennis, and from then on we
played together on the town courts, long sessions never observed by
anyone, so that we alone knew one another's games, an intimacy I
treasured. At night, though there was a free bedroom for me, I
always slept on the floor of his room in a sleeping bag, perpendicular to his bed, my head facing him, the better to discuss the day just
passed, reviewing the highlights for what seemed like hours.

Three months older, Jody played with me as his equal, though we
weren't considered equals by anybody, especially me. He was a
grade ahead of me at school, lived in a bigger house, had superior
sneakers—our family's first Red Ball Jets, and then our first Adidas.
On the table beside his bed there was a sign that said "Think,"
which puzzled me, for he didn't seem to need to be told; he was an
acclaimed student. When we were eight, his sister, Liesi, came into
the family. As soon as she reached an age where she was beginning
to speak, I remember my cousin and I competing to get her to say
the name of our favorite New York Met—the pair of us on our
knees before her, I imploring "Tom Seaver! Tom Seaver!" he calling
"Bud Harrelson! Bud Harrelson!" and her tiny, alert head swiveling
back and forth in sparrow-eyed bafflement until the sudden
inevitability of "Bud!" I also remember when the demonstration of
what he was learning in boxing lessons prematurely ended with me
knocked across the room "by a left!" as right-handed Jody exulted.
On the day we got to be in a hay wagon, we had to stop our hay fight
and get out because he was sneezing and wheezing so much, and I
wished I was allergic too. At the table, he would engage the grown-
ups in their discussions of current political and scientific events
while I silently forked my food, revering him.

Croton was also, of course, Susi. Susi had a strange ability to know
what I was thinking. When Jody talked of inviting one of my friends

from New Haven to his birthday party in Croton, I speculated that the friend would not be able to travel so far, suggested that Jody needn't bother, and then Susi interrupted, yelling at me for "selfishly" wanting my friend for myself, which was true. She could be imperious, not only with me, but also, I saw, with my Uncle Tony, goading him about the sometimes indolent way he walked through life until he cried out in pitched manly outrage, "Goddamn it, Sue!" and then would come a loudly slammed door, after which the house would get very still. At first these spats upset me because I was sure the marriage was done for. But over time I saw the way the anger would subside, doors would open, small gestures of reconciliation would be made, then sheepish words, then hugs and tears, and life would play on. Theirs was my chance to see a lasting marriage, the way it functioned in and out of harmony, touching a spectrum of emotions requiring tending, compromise, reassurance, and adjustment. During one of those early Christmas celebrations in Croton, Susi and Tony each opened a package to discover that they'd given one another the same book, Erich Segal's *Love Story,* a moment of hilarity that became memorable when we saw how moved Susi was by the coincidence.

In 1970, she and Tony left the Little House and bought the Big House, an abject, gone-to-seed Greek Revival white manor house all but falling down the hill behind it. The Big House became Susi's creation. She restored it room by room, putting care into every switch, floorboard, and tile, not to mention the wing chairs, dowel-backed benches, etchings, and gold-plaited lamp tassels she carried home from the thrift shops she trawled after her duties were done for the day working with troubled children at Phelps Memorial Hospital. It was as though by will alone she could rehabilitate people and things—see them back into life at their best advantage, such as the tiny, cramped second-floor chamber at the rear of the house, which became elevated as the Pink Room.

Like my mother, Susi often had an embroidery needle in her hand, and looking at their work you could see the two sisters, my mother's creations pretty, technically precise, primary, and my aunt's bobbins holding rougher threads that she sewed at unlikely angles in browns, olive, orange, burnt reds, milky pinks and yellows. Somehow she achieved opalescence from dull colors.

In 1971, they both saw the film *The Go-Between* and argued about it. All of Susi's sympathies were with the illicit, doomed lovers, while my mother was upset about their affair's effect on the little boy whom they'd made their unwitting conduit. He was an overheated schoolboy, Susi said, drawn to their beautiful love and then selfishly ruining it. Heidi was shocked. He was a naive child, she thought, and they were the selfish ones, callously and irrevocably destroying his innocence.

There were only a few times I was alone with Susi. One of them found me sitting on her bed talking with her as she stood in front of her closet door mirror, inspecting herself in the work clothes she had just put on. Susi had long racks of costly clothes, and that day I noticed how sexy my aunt was in her crisply pleated navy blue skirt, spectator heels, and silk blouse, the thin, creamy fabric trembling over her full breasts. I remember the swish of skirt and stockings as she went through the door, leaving me alone in the room, slightly dizzy amid the stacks of newspapers.

She was not tall, but, wherever she went with her big, shining smile, she appeared tall, an inborn confidence that I misinterpreted also as peace of mind. I never knew that her blond hair was white beneath the bleach well before she was forty, and that the long nights she sometimes spent shut up alone in the Pink Room were because worry and trouble aren't far from most doors, certainly not in my family.

My mother was an intense combination of fragility and force. After our Volkswagen Bug we owned a secondhand green Volkswagen bus. On a drive north to visit my grandparents in New Hampshire, I was such bad traveling company that my mother offered to let me walk the rest of the way if I couldn't behave better. She'd said this many times before and I'd always known how she meant it. Now I decided not to know. "Okay, I'll walk," I said. My mother didn't hesitate. She pulled the Volkswagen over to the side of the road and waited, eyes forward. I hesitated. "Go on, get out if that's how you want it," she said. We were on the outskirts of Winchendon, Massachusetts. I opened the car door, stepped onto the road. My mother started up the bus and pulled away. In my mind I had instantly become a wayfarer. I began to make assessments of the terrain I would cover. I knew that on the upcoming stretches of road, hardly any buildings were visible—only woods and the occasional roadhouse with a red and white Budweiser sign and a few pickups parked out front. I kept my head down, wondering what would happen, how far I could walk before dark, where I would eat and sleep. Across the New Hampshire border there was a lot more forest before Francestown. Besides chipmunks, most of the animals I'd seen in New Hampshire were at a petting zoo called The Friendly Farm. Were there wolves in New Hampshire? I carried no money. It was dusty underfoot. I looked up and saw my mother moving at a crawl as traffic swerved around her. Fifty yards ahead of me, the bus stopped and I heard my mother shout, "Nicky, get back in this car right now." I obeyed, and when the door closed, Sally, my mother, and I all burst into tears.

Driving home late one night from a visit to Croton, I awakened from a deep sleep in the backseat to the glow of the instrument panel all lit up with little sparkles of scarlet. There was a feeling of peculiar inertia; it took me a few moments to grasp that we had come to a stop on the expressway shoulder. Our engine had seized up. I was in the middle of an event.

To my left, traffic whined past, headlamps sweeping across us, too close and too bright. My mother had switched on her hazard blinkers and now sat quietly at the steering wheel, thinking. As a parent she was usually so sure that when she was unsure it amazed me. Sally, only three, slept on in the way back. Within the stationary bus I too was still, waiting to see what would happen. It was unnerving to be at rest amid so much motion. When no traffic went by, all was silent except for the back-and-forth tick-tick-tick of the hazards. Then a huge truck would come along making the bus shudder even after the truck had roared past, a small boat rocking on swells of a bigger one's wake. After a while I canted my body away from the road and bent toward the window on the other side. Over the guardrail, the silhouettes of bulrushes and dark tree trunks fanned out before me and between the traceried lines of branches tiny lights shone in the distance. Suddenly my mother was touching me and awakening Sally and we were leaving the bus. "C'mon, kids," she said, just the way she did at night in New Haven when it was time to get out of the car because we were home. We stood beside the guardrail as she locked up the bus. I was certain I was going to have to go into those woods. My mother picked Sally up, took me by the hand, and we began walking along the highway in the night. We walked for a long time, hugging the guardrail, until finally we came to an exit ramp. We turned up the incline. Nearby there were houses. My mother chose one with lamps on, climbed the steps, and knocked while I waited one step down, still holding her hand. A door swung open bathing us in sudden indoor warmth and an elderly voice inquired our business. Soon Sally and I were drinking orange juice in the kitchen as my mother spoke on the telephone, arranging with the AAA about the bus. In times of actual crisis, she remained utterly composed. As soon as we got home, she began saving up for a new red Dodge.

Thirty-five miles down the Hudson River from Croton was my father's mother, Grandma Rebecca, in Manhattan. Every few months we drove south from New Haven to visit her. I used to experience a heightening of perception as our car crossed into Manhattan over the Triborough Bridge, passing under its gray-metal trestle towers—they looked to me like massive croquet wickets—and working our way along the East River Drive past an island of yellow buildings, a swooping aquamarine footbridge, plucky tugs nudging barges, a red fireboat, and then, after turning onto Fifth Avenue near my grandmother's building in Greenwich Village, past a church that was constructed of layered brown stones the color of German chocolate cake.

My grandmother's building on lower Fifth Avenue was tall and white, with a semicircular drive in front, doormen dressed in livery, a lobby mural of old-fashioned Dutchmen sailing into New Amsterdam, and a mahogany elevator cab staffed by an operator. Her large apartment had lavish furniture and oil paintings on the walls, scrimshaw, silver candlesticks, a dining room floor surface of alternating big black and white chessboard tiles, and a view out the den window of a garden with a fountain in which basking cherub statues sent off exuberant streams of water from between their chubby, naked stone legs. Off the dining room was a bar stocked with unlimited ginger ale.

Most of our time was spent in the living room, which faced onto Fifth Avenue. Upon arrival we'd be ushered to the pair of couches near the window where we'd usually confront several members of my grandmother's large family: perhaps her sister, Rachel, treated by my grandmother as her consigliere, or my grandmother's brother, Ben, often called Ben the Doctor, once or twice even my father up from Washington. The all-points center of the room was a round coffee table with a black marble platter covered by a spread of carrot sticks, radishes, black olives, Jarlsberg cheese, and Sally's and my favorite, marinated artichoke hearts, which we speared with tiny silver forks. There were crystal bowls of Jordan almonds, after-dinner mints in green foil, and Coffee Nips, which we weren't allowed to touch until after the brisket that was warming in the oven. To rappel into all this plenty from where I'd come from was an unsteadying experience, and every time I entered my grand-mother's apartment I would have the sensation that it looked different from last time, a certainty that the rooms were much larger or laid out in fresh configurations—though nothing about it ever changed at all.

As we ate, my grandmother would ask us about ourselves. She was then a veteran prosecutor in the downtown Family Court, and part of what made her so likable was that for a tough professional woman she had a disarming capacity for admiration—a sweetness all the sweeter because it was unexpected in someone so formidably brisk and decisive. Her father, Max, had been a Polish immigrant street peddler on the Lower East Side for whom America had eventually worked out so well that to my grandmother, his oldest child, the United States was always "This wonderful country." She aspired to feel pleased for herself, and for others, and a happy bulletin from me brought her sustained joy. I never met anybody more delighted by my good news. "That's wonderful!" she'd say, employing her very favorite word, which, with her euphonious stress on the first syllable and mild old-neighborhood flattening of the second, came out wuuun-duh-ful. "Now sit down here next to me and tell me; I want to hear all about it." Once the little triumph had been aired in full, she'd smile broadly and say, "We'll have to celebrate." Then she'd pour ginger ale into a wineglass and say, "We'll pretend it's champagne."

In my grandmother's bedroom, on the wall across from the big bed, was a sketched portrait of a rabbi, hairs billowing out from under his skullcap, his beard flowing in wispy tufts down to his robes. There was eventually something provocative to me about having a rabbi on the wall because my grandmother never talked about Judaism and gave me the impression that it was a subject that I should not ask about. If Jewish holidays were honored with family gatherings in those years, Sally and I were never included, as though our faith had been ceded to my Christian mother as part of the divorce settlement. To me, the Jewishness of my father's side of my family was an ossicle, the smallest piece of their grand, multifarious selves. Unlike my mother, who in New Haven sent us to Sunday school at the Congregational church on Whitney Avenue, my grandmother, my father, and their relatives didn't appear devout in any way that was evident to me. If there were services, feasts, or Seders, I never knew—was not invited. When I heard them mention "the holidays" it seemed like an old habit, such as spring cleaning—a necessary ritual of life, but not one anyone was interested in discussing. I had no idea then that back on the Lower East Side, although there had been a synagogue right next door, they never once went inside. Nor did I know that when anybody mentioned "the European relatives," Max became hysterical. As for my grandmother's mother, Sarah, of the murdered uncles and cousins, she said, "That's the past and we don't talk about the past." An adult might have said their faith was form rather than belief; that the faith had, in fact, disappeared, leaving only a residue of custom. They had come here to start anew, to this crowded city where you could refashion yourself and become who you now wanted to be—could make the past vanish. My grandmother took to referring to herself as "a Yankee," and her brisket she usually called pot roast. To me the implication was that New World success was contingent on obliterating that Old Country past, that in New York life was a matter of present comportment. Years later, my well-dressed grandmother astonished me by blurting out, "I was never an offensive immigrant, not one you would look down on. German Jews looked down on Russian and Polish Jews, you know."

"Who did Russian and Polish Jews look down on?" I asked.

Her face grew sad. "Ourselves," she said.

As a child, I got the sense that to be a Jew was a matter of weary obligation, a source of shame and ambivalence—a weight that even helpful America couldn't free you from. The best you could do was quietly accept it. I was glad I had another option. Later, when I was older, my grandmother said that she regretted I didn't feel Jewish.

I was given by Uncle Tony a colorful cardboard box emblazoned with NFL logos containing a Baltimore Colts football suit complete with pants, jersey, shoulder pads, and helmet. The white jersey had a blue 19 on it for the Colts' valiant quarterback, Johnny Unitas, but I did not think of myself as Unitas or a Baltimore Colt when I wore it. I was a football player, just as a few years before, in an earlier hard plastic helmet, I'd been simply a fireman. The packaging warned in several places that my football uniform was not designed for contact play, but why else would someone own a helmet and pads? I was excited by the equipment, the shoulder pads thrusting up beneath the shirt, the skintight knee britches with their voluptuous padding at the thigh and waist, the foam-lined white helmet and its big hard blue horseshoe on either side. I wanted to dive, plunge, rut around, and scrum, to have the snowy whiteness gloriously smeared with badges of dirt and sod. Every time someone called to round up numbers for a neighborhood game, breathlessly I'd ask, "Touch or tackle?" Always it was touch. Then, finally, one day through the receiver came a kid named Dave's grave voice saying, "Tackle at East Rock Park." I arrived in full regalia to discover that they were all tossing the ball around in jeans and shirts as usual. "Just kidding," said Dave, and everyone laughed. They had been waiting for me. I stripped off the shoulder pads and set the helmet aside. But afterward I went off by myself, put the full uniform back on, and rolled around in the dirt. Over and over I spun, dizzying myself enough that when I stopped, I noticed only a blurry half-present flicker of limbs and faces above me. "What are you doing?" I heard from some distant precinct. I became still. Familiar faces floated hazily into focus, one of them Dave's. I had nothing to say for myself. Finally "I'm getting dirty" came out. This was the funniest thing yet. I hated Baltimore.

One October Saturday, my father took me to watch Columbia's college football team play against Harvard in New York. My father himself had once been a Harvard athlete. He played high school football, basketball, and lacrosse with the future NFL Hall-of-Famer Jim Brown, and then at Harvard he was number 42, one of the stars of the lacrosse team. At home I had an old issue of *Sports Illustrated* he'd given me in which there was a photograph of number 42 making a crisp feed against Navy. Now we had come to see his old school team. Somehow this Harvard, his Harvard, was not the same Harvard that I saw when I visited my grandfather in Cambridge; when my father talked about Harvard, not even Massachusetts came to mind.

The game was played in a large and drafty old stadium with wooden bleachers set on a promontory overlooking the confluence of the Hudson and Harlem rivers. You could see boats going by.

Because we were part of a sparse crowd of spectators, in every direction there was row after row of vacant planks stretching out toward the river, and all the empty space and water created in my mind a sprawling sense of possibility that extended right down onto the field. Harvard's team featured many excellent players and was expected to win easily. Yet during pregame warm-up drills, after my initial surprise at the sight of football players meekly turned out in the baby blue and white of my mother's summer bathrobe, the Columbia squad began to seem very impressive to me, sleek and shifty as they ran five-yard outs in their polished white shoes. Why shouldn't they win? Swept up, I bet my father a quarter that they would. To that point I hadn't decided which team I wanted to win. My college football loyalties were to New Haven—to Yale. Now, with money on Columbia, I was pulling for them. The game began, with the home team faring so poorly so quickly that eventually I grew frustrated at the waste of it all, how inevitable the futility had turned out to be. Gesturing down toward the players, I told my father, "You should get out there, Dad, you could do better than them," and then was startled when an utterly forlorn look crossed his face.

It was baseball that I truly loved, in particular the Red Sox and Mets—especially the Mets. Only one team could be your team. I didn't know much about what the Mets looked like. There was still no television at home and never to be one because my mother believed "television is idiotic," and there wasn't a newspaper either. My mother said she wanted to read books with any free time she had and that, anyway, the newspaper was too expensive, but my newspaper-loving grandfather didn't read it anymore either, and, as I got older, I believed they both felt that as refugees they had lived through enough history. Whatever the reasons, the result was that most of my knowledge of current ballplayers came from my collection of baseball cards. In the early 1970s, "bubblegum cards" were not yet a commodity with value to anyone besides children. There were no card shops or dealers, and given the modest wherewithal of all the kids I knew, the players whose cards we acquired were a matter of pure chance. Increasing the aleatory complexion of the hobby, in my neighborhood, the one store that sold baseball cards, the Whitney Pharmacy, had an erratic stock. Local card supplies were so lean that when Binder was taken to visit relatives in New Rochelle, a town outside New York, and returned to New Haven with a wad of cards bought there for him in a variety store, I ever after thought of New Rochelle as a Land of Plenty, a spangled city of statuary, flags, gold turrets, balconies, and minarets. Meanwhile, at the Whitney Pharmacy, I'd look in the candy display beside the slender deep green and rose-colored boxes of Canada Mints and sometimes those gleaming wax-paper packages of cards were there and sometimes not. Even when I did buy a new pack, there was no guarantee I'd get any of the players I wanted, and the fickle odds against actually acquiring what I was trying to pay for suffused the transaction in suspense. I'd finger each package, trying to divine which one held Mets. After finally making my selection and relinquishing my dime at the lunch counter, I wanted right there to find out what I had, but I'd heard that patience was a virtue, so superstitiously I'd always take the cards outside the store before opening them up. This futile desire to coax fate with a display of restraint occasionally led me to hold out until I got back home.

The cards had a fresh design every year, something I never remembered until I tore open the first package of spring and saw that they were different. In 1970, the players had been surrounded by a soft gray border; a year later the thick black outline lent a starker, apertural effect. Enclosed was the regulation brittle rectangle of bubble gum and hastily I'd slide it into my mouth, feeling it disintegrate in pink shards as I began thumbing my way through Rick Auerbach, Billy Champion, and Wayne Twitchell, but, alas, not a Tom Seaver, a Bud Harrelson, or a Luis Aparicio in the deck. The many disappointments meant that when I did get a coveted card, it seemed destined, enhancing the sense of connection with the player that came with my ownership of his picture. To possess their cards was to know them a little. That illusion of interaction was fortified by the tangible qualities of the cards, how gratifying they were to hold, the surface roughened with a scrim of gum dust. A couple of packs' worth fit tight as a wallet into a rear pants pocket meaning that I could keep my favorites close to me at all times. I took them out so frequently for inspection that as the cardboard bent to the contours of my hip, the colors faded, the corners frayed.

For a while, my collection was modest. Then came a mysterious day at the schoolyard when an older boy enlisted me to help him with some spade and shovel work. He led me to a neighboring backyard where he began digging a hole in the ground in which he intended to conceal a brown shopping bag filled with what turned out to be all of his baseball cards. I think he'd been seized by the idea of creating buried treasure. I remember my ecstasy at the enterprise, the admiring disbelief I felt that he would be willing to sacrifice his entire collection for the sake of a deed. I stood by him as he lifted out the dirt, nestled the bag in place, and then began to feather the dirt back on it like a mourner at a grave. Once the hole was refilled, soon enough I forgot all about the cache of cards until, over a year later, after the boy had moved away, I suddenly remembered them. Had it really happened? I located a shovel, found the spot, and began to dig. Soon enough, I hit paper. It was like recovering Injun Joe's ironbound box of yellow coins. The shopping bag had begun to disintegrate, but once the cards were brushed clean there was Mickey Mantle, Sandy Koufax, and, far better from my point of view, the Mets' long reliever Cal Koonce paused at the end of his pitching follow-through and forever destined to smell like damp earth.

All I really knew about any of the Mets was that they were Mets, and that blue and orange imprimatur was enough to regard them with overwhelming solicitude. Unburdened by information about their lives, I could gaze at their photographs on these cardboard talismans and make them be who I wanted them to be, could believe, after a while, that there was rapport. Even today I experience a surge of well-being when I hear the name Cal Koonce, whose musty likeness I once scrutinized with enough care to remember forever the steady blue-eyed gaze and matching blue-sleeved right arm that won six games for the Mets in 1969. To love every Met was my first great act of faith, and one that made me forever understand the pull of ignorance, how seductive is the logic of tautology. They were supposed to be heroic, and so they were.

By the winter of 1971, I was an eight-year-old Mets fan of such avid dimension that Uncle Tony gave me the best day of my life to that point by taking me for my birthday to a charity basketball game near Croton in which a group of local athletes competed in a small-town gym against a team of professional baseball players, among them a couple of Mets including the first baseman Ed Kranepool and outfielder Ron Swoboda. They were all marginal major leaguers playing basketball that day, but centurions to me, especially Swoboda. He was a large, somewhat ungainly slugger, known to teammates as "Rocky," whose miraculous, full-out flopping catch of a sinking fly ball had saved a game for the Mets in the 1969 World Series. At the basketball contest, I remember the expectant buzz in the gym as we all filed in and filled the wooden bleachers. I sat one row up from the court, wearing my royal blue crewneck shirt in Metsian homage. When Swoboda, reprising his World Series turn, sprawled into the stands after a loose basketball, he came to rest on top of me, such a magical occurrence that back in New Haven I had not since permitted my mother to wash the shirt. From time to time I took it out from my dresser drawer and buried my face in the essence of great man.

One day, after Binder had been visiting me at my house, his mother came to pick him up. At the front door, I asked his mother to wait, ran back to my room, got my baseball cards, and presented the entire collection to Binder, telling him, as I pressed the cards into his hands, how much I was going to miss him after he went home. A moment later he was gone with what had taken me years to accumulate. This unplanned bestowal happened with such decisive impulsion that later in the evening, overcome by the loss of all the players, I couldn't imagine what I'd been thinking. But after that, I was more at peace when I thought about the reading contest the year before.

For somebody still new to life, the meaningful world extends only as far as you can see. Where once my view of New Haven had carried to the edges of our property, now it was as though the front sidewalk had unfurled into many sidewalks coursing out in every direction all through the city. Yet part of what made New Haven so appealing was that it had natural limits. Bounded by Atlantic Ocean estuaries and the twin russet trap rock ridges of East Rock and West Rock, the blocks of Carpenter Gothic houses lining our streets felt as self-contained as the schoolyard used to. Those houses with their cupolas and punch bowl turrets never looked better than on Halloween with all their jack-o'-lantern–filled first-floor windows aglow in the crisp October night air. Densely settled as the city was, you could move efficiently from address to address, a few steps to a fresh porch light, accumulating Three Musketeers bars at high speed. And such are the imprinted criteria of childhood, that through life, whenever I encounter a residential neighborhood in a new town my first thought is "good for trick-or-treating?"

Within four blocks, New Haven neighborhoods changed from mansions on the hill to ghetto hovels so that you knew a little bit of everybody. On our part of Willow Street alone lived laborers, pensioners, assorted professionals, unemployed single mothers, a Beacon Hill heiress, an Alexander Pope scholar, and Eleanor Estes, the author of a series of children's books about a New Haven family called the Moffats. For a succession of Christmases, Sally and I helped the author trim her tree, and then were rewarded with one of her books inscribed "From your friend Eleanor Estes." There was the Italian section around Wooster Square, the many Poles down by State Street, and an old Irish enclave up on Cedar Hill where increasingly at dusk men were welcomed home from work in Spanish. Fair Haven, Newhallville, and the Hill "out Congress

Avenue" were Puerto Rican or black neighborhoods, and riding the Yale Shuttle buses around the campus were representatives of just about every country found in my *Atlas of the World.*

My Every-City had all seasons, all weathers, climates, and temperatures. In the morning the air hung heavy with the ocean tides of the Long Island Sound. Into warm afternoons seeped the sluggish, putrid stink of the chemical-green Mill River, a surprisingly evocative smell because of all the forbidden places you could imagine that river had come through. Our brownest river was the bottom-of-Mom's-coffeepot-colored Quinnipiac, which flowed even slower than the Mill. Elsewhere there were assorted streams, rills, and freshets, the Lake Whitney reservoir with its waterfall pooling just beyond the Hamden flank of East Rock parkland, cattailed marshes, ponds, sawgrass-bordered swamp, forest glades, copses, foothills, the gas-tank-lined harbor, and Chatfield Hollow out Route 80 where you could walk on silky brown pine needles and swim in stilled amber-lit water. None of these were outsized formations. The terrain, like the city itself, was simultaneously comprehensive and scaled down, had the incipient gradations of childhood.

New Haven could not be fully experienced. Frequently we drove past the South Seas, a low-slung restaurant and lounge marked by a hot pinkish–red neon sign emblazoned with green neon palm trees promising exotic cuisine and cocktails of the Asian tropics. We never once went there, or to Blessings for Chinese, or to Louis' Lunch, the little Hansel and Gretel house on Crown Street where in 1895 Louis Lassen invented the hamburger, or to Pepe's or Sally's, the famous Wooster Square apizzas. There was no sense of deprivation, but rather the understanding that everything was not supposed to come to you at once, and that New Haven would always provide things to look forward to. It was the holding place for all of life's mysteries.

That fall of 1971, Jennifer Noon's murderer remained uncaptured—there was never an arrest—and yet my determination was to see the city as the haven it had been when I first came there, and I willed it to be so again. At eight and nine years old, such was my attachment to my hometown that it was as much a fundamental part of me as my mother and my sister. I loved the city with a pure, unquestioning affection. My early New Haven expressed itself as the powerful desire to reject experience in order to remain innocent, the compulsion to look past any obstacles to love in order to love.

Other places existed relative to New Haven. My Elm City sat positioned there at the hub of the solar system, at the heart of the universe, at the very fulcrum of the world. Everything New Haven was iconic—the one. Downtown stood Macy's department store, which remained the flagship even after I saw Herald Square. Our Broadway was *the* Broadway. It was the same way with Sears Roebuck and the International House of Pancakes. To encounter them in other places was to mark them as provincial and inferior versions. Before I'd ever been inside, I knew that the Spirit Shop was the place for wine, Kebabian's for carpets. Out near the Yale–New Haven Hospital there was Pete's bicycle shop, where the long, shiny rows of silver chrome handlebars all seemed to reach out to me. For years the prayer point for all my material desires was the jeep, tank, airplane, and war-game-cluttered shelves at Hull's Hobbies on Chapel Street. No other place had what New Haven had for the simple reason that no other place was New Haven. And so it was that we were out driving along Whalley Avenue where I saw a new yellow sign that said Subway. That we should now have a supplement to our fleet of blue and white city buses seemed unsurprising, until I discovered it was merely a sandwich shop, whereupon a bias hardened against underground transit.

A city is never fixed in time but the accumulation of all its times, except to a child. To me, New Haven was inviolate, an unalterable place forever anchored in its present manifestation. There was no old, lost New Haven; it was only I who was leaving myself behind, growing into what was. Then one day Paul Baer retired and his gloomy grocery store dematerialized into a law firm. Next, the A&P on Orange and Linden closed, whereupon Cumberland Farms abandoned our corner and its blue and white signage went up where Atlantic and Pacific had been before. A man named Hall opened Hall of Books for business at Willow and Orange.

Somehow, though, despite these disappearances and arrivals, everything remained intact. It was the perpetual rediscovering of the fixed landscape. The new installations were written on top of something vanished that was yet present—a dendrite with the old marks righteously there and still capable of explaining what was becoming of my life. The city hadn't changed because I didn't want it to change. My father had changed. That was enough.

CHAPTER SIX

Flushing

In 1971, when I was eight years old, my father lost his job enforcing anti-fraud statutes for the Securities and Exchange Commission, whereupon he left Washington, leased a garden flat on New York's Upper West Side, and opened up his own legal practice, renting a room from a small law firm that had its suite of offices on Madison Avenue between Fortieth and Forty-first streets above a Chock full o'Nuts coffee shop.

Now I saw him regularly. Once a month, on a Sunday, he'd ride the train up to New Haven to spend the afternoon with Sally and me. Then, I never thought back on any of the unhappy times with him; I only looked forward to his Sunday, anticipated it for weeks. Early on those mornings I'd go bursting into my sister's room and jump around her bed as she lay there under the covers, telling her, "Sally, Sally, Dad's coming!" until a small, sleepy smile spread across her face and her eyes opened. My mother would meet my father's train at the railroad station, bring him home, and then she'd go off on foot for the day, leaving him the use of the house and the car. He always drove us out to Hamden for lunch at the International House of Pancakes, and then we went on to the Ridge View Pharmacy for bubblegum cigars. Down the road was the Spring Glen Pharmacy. The three of us always referred to the Ridge View as the Spring Glen, a willful misidentification that my father seemed to enjoy as much as Sally and I did. That we had familiar patterns was our effort to inject a sense of circadian regularity into the relationship, our attempt to make my father seem like a normal dad.

Back at the house, my father could be a lot of fun. He invented a belly-tickling game called "So it does that, does it?," and whenever he called me Rascal I got a shiver of pleasure. He was the sort of man who preferred nicknames, perhaps because they individuated, were truer to what a person was turning out to be. My father liked absurd rhymes: "Ladies and gentlemen take my advice, pull down your panties and slide on the ice!" He was also fond of working out puns. After Zbigniew Brzezinski got a job in the government, my father's response was to ask me what a jailed national security adviser was. "I don't know," I said. "A Zbig in a poke." During those afternoons he spent a lot of time playing with the English language, frolicking and cavorting with syntax, neologisms, and unusual nomenclature the way some people I knew amused themselves with Play-Doh. When the basketball star Lew Alcindor changed his name to Kareem Abdul-Jabbar, my father was ecstatic at the possibilities. "Say it, Dad, say it," I would plead, and he'd grin and repeat the name again and again for me, lingering on the long vowels like an auctioneer. I'd always ask him to sing "It Was Sad When That Great Ship Went Down," in his beautiful tenor, and to tell me about seeing Mel Ott at the Polo Grounds. I wanted to hear all of it every time, was outraged when Sally spoke up with preferences of her own. Allegiance to the routine was essential. In fact, these Sunday visits had the quality of a long-distance love affair: each one came after such a lengthy interlude that they felt like occasions, not ordinary life.

Every time he saw me I had new preoccupations, and there was a period when my chief concern lay in road construction. One day, my father took me to visit the Leonard Concrete Pipe Company, in Hamden, where I somehow persuaded him to buy a souvenir for me: a three-foot section of gray concrete sewer pipe. My hazy idea was to submerge it in dirt and then send hose water through the tube to, well, where? That was as far as I'd planned. I have no idea how we got the thing home, but I know that when my mother saw Dad and me staggering toward her porch, she redirected us around to the cellar entrance, at the rear of the house. As my father, the pipe, and I went by, I remember the fresh powdery lime-smell of the new concrete, and then hearing our next-door neighbor, outdoors in her pink slippers, remark, "Now I know why she divorced him." Down the cellar steps we went, carrying the pipe, and when we reached the floor we set the pipe upright on its fat end. For the next thirty-six years, as long as my mother lived in New Haven, the pipe remained by the bottom of the cellar steps, exactly where Dad and I had left it. It might still be standing there.

His other gifts to me were mostly books, and looking at them now reminds me of the interest he took in my interests. Best of all there was a secondhand copy of Lawrence Ritter's *The Glory of Their Times,* an oral history of the early days of professional baseball, in which a succession of old-time players including Heinie Groh, Rube Marquard, and Goose Goslin told about all the rutted roads they had taken to the major leagues. Hall of Fame outfielder Sam Crawford was so poor that he and his friends in Wahoo, Nebraska, had to make their own baseballs out of whatever scraps of string, yarn, and cloth they could find in the streets. Then one of their mothers would sew it all together for them. I told my mother about it and she said, "That was before the Depression; almost everyone was poor then compared to now."

In 1972, Sally and I went on vacation with my father for a long weekend in Bermuda, my first time away from America. Once we got there I was fascinated by the Englishness of the place, and my father spent a lot of time standing next to me at an intersection watching a bobby directing traffic in his tall helmet. I was just getting over a bad case of mononucleosis. Thin to begin with, I had lost a great deal of weight, and when I wanted to investigate the grottoes along the shore, run on the pink sand, and splash in the quiet turquoise water, all forbidden because I'd been so sick, though my father said "No," he seemed to understand how it was to be inhibited from doing what you expected of yourself.

During school vacations there were trips to New York to spend time with my father. It was a lot like going to visit my grandmother, the same heightening of perception as our car crossed into Manhattan over the Triborough, and yet it was even better because I loved him so much, he had been so far away for so long, and now, miraculously, he was near and soon he would be pulling me into a hug: "Rascal!"

If we were in New York on weekdays, my father might take us to the office. How transporting it was to be in the middle of everything in the center of Manhattan, moving alongside the early crowds, going to work with my father. From the sidewalk outside my father's building I saw the men in business suits surging uphill from Forty-second Street, many of them carrying a folded-over newspaper and a briefcase as they went ducking into Chock full o'Nuts, emerging a minute or two later with a steaming paper cup in hand. They were all in a hurry. There was a delicatessen across the street, and at lunchtime through the window I could see them rushing in, yelling out their sandwich orders, and rushing out. It seemed to me that in these rhythms of the masculine professional day, I was watching how my father lived without me around.

My father worked on the eighth floor. Bolted to the wall in the corridor beside the entrance door to the suite were engraved, burnished-brass nameplates for each of the lawyers in the firm. There was not a nameplate for my father. Inside were the firm's lawyers with their suit jackets off and ties loosened, clients waiting to see the lawyers, a secretary, and the braying visitors paying calls to the other room that the firm rented out in the suite—a succession of enormously obese men rushing in and out from consultations with the tenant who turned out to be a parking garage tycoon, a man so wealthy he could have bought an entire office building for himself.

My father was tucked in the back of the suite, near the emergency exit and across from a wall lined with shelves holding leather-bound legal casebooks. He had a heavy desk, an extra chair, and one window with no screen that in summer was kept open a crack so that you could hear the M-1 Madison Avenue bus exhaling into second as it rumbled slowly uptown, could smell the city, which in those months had a pleasantly rank bouquet like the one that enveloped a kitchen when someone ran hot sink water into a pot after overcooking a meaty stew. Once the M-1 had crossed Forty-second Street, aside from the soft toots of horns and the anguish of a distant siren, it was quiet in my father's office. The olive green rotary dial telephone seldom rang unless it was my grandmother checking in on us, and nobody came inside, though once in a while, if we'd closed the door, I'd open it to encounter a lawyer consulting a casebook. Those lawyers would seem startled to see me, and it would take a second before they said, "Well hi there, young feller."

In 1971, for Father's Day, I built a pipe rack that I constructed by hammering lines of lost head nails into an unfinished scrap of wooden board. I'd intended the nails to fulfill the silhouette of a pipe shape, the idea being that the pipes could rest on the nails, but my hammering skills were such that some of the nails bent or got inexpertly aligned, and since a few were also rusted, upon completion they looked like the ragged prongs of rebar protruding from concrete slabs on one of the many stalled building projects you could then see around New York. After I presented the rack to my father, he tilted it against the wall on top of his filing cabinet where it became, along with a coat-stand, a clear, cut-glass ashtray, a few yellow legal pads, last week's issues of the *Times,* and loose papers on the desk, the only things in the room. "Thanks, Rascal," he told me. He said the same thing when, in August, for his thirty-seventh birthday, I ventured across the street to the tobacconist. My mother had given me money to buy my father a gift from me, and, having supplied him with storage capacity, I thought that the way you now treated a father was to give him something to smoke. My father accompanied me and then stood off to the side as I began my errand. The store was hushed and smelled of cedar. On the narrow walls hung pipes of various woodland hues made from what must have been meerschaum, briar, calabash, and walnut. They were all too expensive. I shifted my attention to the cigar cases. Gazing at the array of brown cylinders under glass, I was astonished that even something that would disappear so soon could be so costly. A feeling of consumer inadequacy came over me. I had wanted to have a triumph by finding him something that showed I knew who he was. After much deliberation, I selected four short, lean cigars that fit in their white box prim as Crayons. My father put the cigars in his desk drawer and later, during one of his twice-monthly telephone calls from New York to me in New Haven, he told me he'd smoked each after the next until they were all gone. He rented that office for seven years, and it always had the look of belonging to someone who was new in town.

His apartment over on the West Side was the rear flat on the first floor of a five-story walk-up on Seventy-fifth Street between Central Park West and Columbus Avenue, now a fashionable district but then a battered, somewhat ramshackle part of the city. People who lived in the plush apartment buildings lining Central Park West did not tend to walk west after dark. The brief lobby of my father's West Seventy-fifth Street building was gloomy and close, smelling of many pasts. Entering his apartment, you walked down a hallway, dim as an alley when he didn't change the light-bulb, past the tiny, baby-blue-tiled bathroom and then the galley kitchenette with its brown electric stove, brown cabinets, and brown refrigerator, into a living area where there was a sofa, a slat-ted coffee table, a portable Sony black-and-white television, and a table with two chairs by the window. Back in the bedroom he had a closet, a bed, and a bureau. There was exposure to the west, though the angle of neighboring roofs and patio walls meant that only a low slant of late afternoon sunlight ever penetrated. The windows had bars on them. My father, pale to begin with, always seemed paler in these tenebrous rooms. It happened with his eyes too, which became the color of the bathroom tiles and uncalm. Outside the bedroom was the garden, an urban designation since it was no more than a fifty-foot oblong cement apron. Over by the wall there were the remnants of a more agrarian-minded previous tenant, a few flowerpots with nothing in them but shriveled brown stalks in parched soil.

On a late September Saturday in 1971, I came to New York to go
with my father to my first baseball game. The Mets were playing the
Pittsburgh Pirates. I had awakened before dawn in a fever. Was it
raining? It was not raining. The game would be played. Crossing
Willow Street from our house to the car with my mother and Sally,
I had with me a pen and sheet of paper for autographs and was
dressed in the blue shirt once touched by Ron Swoboda. Swoboda,
alas, was no longer with the team, traded off to Montreal, but Ed
Kranepool remained on the roster, as did Bud Harrelson, the side-
burned Texan catcher Jerry Grote, and the two estimable Toms,
center fielder Agee and Seaver, who'd become the best pitcher of
his time. The Pirates would be challenging opposition. They had
the magnificent right fielder Roberto Clemente and so many other
forceful hitters, including outfielders Willie Stargell and Al Oliver,
that they would win the World Series that year. All the anticipated
hitting led to a last-minute inspiration: if I brought my glove I'd
have an advantage over others in catching a foul ball. The glove was
on my hand as I sat in the backseat hoping Seaver would be pitching, that he would have his way with Clemente. By the time we
reached Bridgeport I was aflame with so many expectations I strug-
gled to breathe.

The plan was that we would go to my father's apartment where
my mother and Sally would make themselves comfortable and wait
for us to return after the game. Both had books to amuse them—
Sally at six was already a formidable reader—and there was also the
television set. Once we got to New York, everything slowed down.
We did not take the East Side Drive, instead working our way west
across the width of the city. It took time to find parking in my
father's neighborhood, and then a while longer to execute the hand-
off at his apartment; he wanted to spend time with Sally. When we
finally did leave for the ballpark, my father neglected to provide my
mother with a key so that she and Sally could freely come and go.
Why I cannot say, but he didn't.

To get to Shea Stadium required a subway trip involving transfer
to the IRT Number 7 train that then made endless above-ground

stops as it trundled its way out toward Flushing, the section of Queens where Shea Stadium is. Every time I heard the name Flushing mentioned, I expected people to giggle and prepared to myself, though when they didn't, I didn't either. Outside the subway windows on both sides was such unrelenting commercial expanse that I began to despair that a green field would ever appear out of the solid seam of graffiti-smeared brick buildings with endless TV antennas crowding their flat roofs, warehouses, heavy industry, and tied-up traffic. Why had they decided to place a ballpark here? Were they right? Couldn't they have made mistakes? And what if, say, New Haven was not ideally situated? People had come by ship from distant shores to settle New Haven. Maybe its true location was meant to be somewhere else. Could the world's rigidity be resisted?

As we continued our sluggish progress, more and more people boarded the train wearing blue and orange Mets caps including many boys around my age, all of them carrying baseball gloves. Seeing this I felt thwarted and foolish—an inventor who'd dreamed up what the world already had in plenty—until then finally, on the left, rising out of a vast spread of parking lots there appeared the rim of an immense, ringed, steel structure that formed most of a circle before abruptly truncating at the far ends like an urban renewal project that had run out of funds. We left the train. From the platform, visible through the open back side of the stadium were vertiginous tiers of seats slowly filling with specklike people. All of it cupped what were unmistakably ballplayers on a ball field. Looking at them from the distance I thought of scattered leaves.

Then we were walking toward the stadium. As full as I was with anticipation, most of my recollections have faded or merged with the flow of all the many subsequent days and nights spent at ballparks across the years, but because there can only be one first game, and, because I was there with my father, there has long been the urge to recall more of it, to make it a memorable experience and a happy one. Traces of it come back the way the words do when I am trying to recall a villanelle I memorized as a child. Despite the fact that I was a boy who, without effort, remembered a surfeit of base-

ball statistics, I never was a person who recalled every line of a
poem for long. Yet if no full tercet returns, certain lines always stay
with me, as do fragments of that afternoon. I was only eight, but the
art of losing isn't hard to master.

Outside the stadium were throngs of people massing around the
ticket booths and a midway of vendors selling pretzels and hot dogs
as well as baseballs inscribed with the autograph of every Met in
identical blue ink. I pictured them all sitting there in their spikes
and caps passing around the pen to write on each ball. I hadn't
known such an item existed, also hadn't known you could purchase
miniature wooden bats or "player quality" Mets caps, but no sooner
were they seen than they were craved. My father bought me only
literature: both a Mets team yearbook and a game program with
which to keep score. Once we were at the turnstiles, an old man
tore our tickets in half and directed us toward broad concrete
ramps that took us climbing beyond the field level, the loge, the
mezzanine, and finally to our upper-level seats. Then, at last, I was
sitting in the sky looking down at the green and brown field, which
seemed to me then to be simultaneously man-made and natural—
sitting in the sky looking down at real ballplayers. They were busy
with pregame rituals, loping around the bases, ruminating together
in groups, hitting, fielding, and throwing. I remember marveling at
their distant movements, how different it all was from my prior
experience of baseball. The spectator's routine was not yet routine
to me, and I had to adjust to the compact hydraulics of swings that
sent balls tumbling into space, just as I had to get used to how fluid
and easy were the gaits crossing the grass in pursuit of those same
fly balls. The players and the descending balls usually merged into
coincident vectors, as though the hitter had sent out advance word
where his drives would fall. I couldn't distinguish their facial features, but I knew most of them by the numbers on their uniforms—
Tom Seaver was 41, Tommie Agee 20—and from my familiarity
with their baseball cards I could apply the faces myself. A check of
the program told me that the unknown 11 belonged to third baseman Wayne Garrett. On my Bob Aspromonte baseball card he was
an Atlanta Brave, but here, in the countervailing moment, the pro-

gram revealed that he was now wearing number 2 for the Mets. Not yet ready to believe my eyes, I felt toward Aspromonte the coolness one reserves for an interloper. How surreal the proximity was, how difficult to believe that of all the places in the world they might be, every Met was right there in front of me. And how jarring to realize that it was a public spectacle, that those around me also loved the Mets, and that I must share them.

The opposing Pirates lingered at the edges of the field in gray and black uniforms looking bigger than the Mets, foreign, and predatory. Among them was Richie Hebner, whose baseball card one year informed me that he worked off-season as a grave digger. When the day's lineups were announced, I learned that Hebner would not be playing. Neither would Al Oliver, Clemente, or Seaver. It was a rookie left-hander named Jon Matlack who was to pitch for the Mets. A baseball game is a long-awaited event that happens every day. When this one began, Matlack threw a strike and everyone cheered, me among them.

The Mets scored one early run against the Pirates' pitcher, Bob Johnson, the Pirates immediately responded in kind, and then nothing. Inning after inning passed with the game tied at one. How hungry a person got at a ballgame. While I stayed in my seat so as not to miss anything, my father trotted back and forth to the concession stand ferrying me hot dogs and peanuts and drinks. Overhead, jet airplanes were taking off from neighboring La Guardia Airport and passing low over the stadium lip as they gathered altitude. Ordinarily airplanes would have been only slightly less interesting to me than ballplayers and yet not here, not now. I believed that airplanes did not belong at the ballpark, but each time the day filled with engine noise, I would be unable to resist looking up to see, right there, a mammoth winged metal underbelly with the landing gear not yet retracted, the tiny rubber clusters of tires dangling plump like Concord grapes, tantalizingly close.

I remember also a trip to the restroom, standing before a stained trough beside men smelling of something sour. I remember the sight of the Mets' mascot Mr. Met, an antic figure with a swollen baseball for a head who worked the crowd between innings. And I remember my growing anxiety about Mom and Sally in their apartment dry dock as the game completed the ninth inning still tied at one, and then crossed over the Rubicon into extra innings.

The teams kept sending up substitute hitters, but nobody had any luck in his bat. A tenth inning passed, then an eleventh and a twelfth. It had become Sunday evening. People seemed of two minds about what to do. Some of those around us were giving up and heading for home, and I asked my father if we should do the same. "Rascal," he told me, "a real fan stays for the whole game." I had hated to leave, and now felt pleased to know the protocol. One of the qualities of baseball that brought me instinctive satisfaction was that fidelity to long-standing form and etiquette, how the deliberate pace of this particular game only emphasized its connection with a slower age. Many years later when I thought about what my father had said, it would occur to me that it was one of the last times he ever tried to impart wisdom to me. What to do when father doesn't know best? If you were me, quietly you stopped asking him things.

The thirteenth inning went by without a run and the fourteenth too. I had long since given up scoring the game in my program, which had fallen beneath my seat and come to rest near a puddle of soda. We had been there for hours. The field was shrouded in shadows, evening was approaching, I was far from New Haven. And then, in a sudden flurry of events, Mets second baseman Tim Foli got a single and soon was turning for home on another single by pinch-hitter Aspromonte. The throw was coming in on a line to the Pirates' catcher, Sanguillen, straddling at the plate, Foli was sliding, the umpire flung his palms wide, and the game was over— Aspromonte had won it for the Mets. I must have been thrilled. Strangely, though, I recall no ecstasy. I stooped to collect my glove, program, and yearbook from the ground. All along the row there was garbage mounding under the seats. It had all begun in my imagination as something so glorious, and now it was the furthest thing. The pages of my program were sticky and the cover had torn away from its staples. My glove held no foul ball—we'd been far too high up even to hope—and for the same reason my sheet of paper contained no Mets signatures. As we made our way down the concrete ramps, my father took me over to a souvenir man and bought me an autographed baseball. It came enclosed in a dome of clear styrene plastic and was stamped "facsimile," which I took to be a special big league kind of horsehide.

Then boarding a train more densely packed with riders than the one that had borne us out, and while the crowd must have endured these conditions well—the home team had won a satisfying game—I can recall only my sense of useless confinement standing there on a swaying floor during this return subway trudge, the fear that at any moment my face might slam into the strange torsos looming everywhere around me, the feeling of being yoked to an uncomfortable emotion I had no name for, the way my heart seemed to hurry as at last my father's key jangled at the door of his apartment and we went back down the gloomy hallway into the living area where the sight of my mother and Sally, obviously weary of captivity, filled me with shame. I had known this was happening and yet had gone on sacrificing them for my surplus of enjoyment. Greeting my sister, I was much nicer to her than I usually was, covered her in improvised enthusiasm as though we'd been apart for months and I'd missed her terribly. And then suddenly it wasn't improvised, I was desperately glad to see her. There in that darkening room, that old Susi-sense of myself as a creature impelled by greed and self-interest returned, and with it a helplessness as I wondered how I had gotten this way, the dread that I was soon to have horrible experiences because I deserved them.

They were good sports about it, though, not resentful or aggrieved at all, appeared glad that I'd had a big time, had been treated to so much baseball. It was my father who seemed injured. At that age I couldn't yet measure his moods, could only intuit them, but thinking back, it seems likely that by asking about leaving the game I had changed the day for him. My father, who found more occasion to take things personally than any man I ever met, probably absorbed the question as a rebuke, as the expression of a concern for my mother that I did not extend in kind to him, possibly even as evidence that his son was choosing between parents. So he made up a code of baseball conduct to give me what I wanted— which was to stay until the end—just as he did everything in his power to make the afternoon special for me. He did not even really like baseball.

CHAPTER SEVEN

Adventures in the Loss Column

B y the early 1970s, when I was completing grammar school, my father's alimony and child-support payments had dwindled to nothing, leaving my mother to bring us up on her annual teaching salary of $5,000. That my father was not providing for us was never something my mother discussed with me then. She still never said a thing against him. But I almost knew something was wrong. I say almost because if it is possible to force something out of your mind while also still being aware that it exists, that is what I did.

In New Haven we lived a life without ornament. Once a month we drove to the ShopRite supermarket to buy ninety meals. Under ideal circumstances my mother never would have patronized an institution that intentionally disregarded standardized spelling, but ShopRite's motto, Why Pay More?, accurately reflected its business plan. While Sally and I set off to beachcomb in the candy aisle, casing the bulk packages of Almond Joy and six-pack boxes of white candy cigarettes with the painted red-flame tip that passing miscreants sometimes tore open, making them fair game to our thinking for scavengers like us, my mother wheeled up and down the aisles, filling her shopping cart with everything necessary to make thirty breakfasts, thirty lunches, and thirty dinners. As she paid the cashier, I'd go stand by the plaza of gumball machines beside the exit door, looking through the glass at the little balloon-colored balls as my mother's cart full of brown paper bags rolled by behind me and I turned and followed her to the car. I never expected her to offer; even our loose change was strictly accounted for.

Back at home, daily allotments of hamburger patties and meat-balls, fish sticks, chicken legs, hot dogs, and stew beef were tightly packeted in foil, marked with a label, and placed in the freezer. Powdered milk was mixed by my mother in an old Cumberland Farms half gallon plastic jug with a light red handle that in the store cooler had designated whole milk. It wasn't so bad after you got used to it, though gradually the sides of the jug became so gray with use that, when friends came over and wrinkled their noses at the watery, mildly rancid taste and looked questioningly at the jug, it was no use pretending anymore that "Cumbies must have gotten a lousy batch."

Early on workday mornings when she thought I was still sleep-ing, my mother would enter my room on tiptoes, open the closet door, stand before her skirts and dresses, so many of which she'd sewn, and sigh aloud to herself, "I have nothing to wear." In winter, I ate breakfast to the predawn rasp and flutter of the twin clothes-line pulleys as my mother sent my laundry out on frozen rope. After work she'd retrieve the clothes, iron out the pale, rimed slipcover of ice now encasing the fabric, fold everything, and put it all away. At night, as out in the living room she made up her bed, hearing her struggle made me want to grow up fast. Not that she would have permitted assistance. She told us that as a girl her parents had forced her "to wait on them hand and foot," and she swore, "I'll never do that to you." My mother managed on her own, was excep-tionally good at the rigors of this kind of constricted life, in part because it suited her frugal nature.

There was no clothes dryer, no dishwasher, no air conditioner, no electric can opener or power lawnmower, not a foot scale or even an umbrella. "I won't melt," my mother used to say when she left the house on a rainy day. She was a person with categories for all of what life presented, and umbrellas were grouped under things even a careful person eventually lost. When I got older, during a down-pour I once offered to run inside a store and buy an umbrella for her. "You can get me one for my birthday," she countered. Her birthday was eight months in the future. The rain was falling in sheets, "really coming down," as my mother said. I had an old unnerved feeling. She was resisting what would make her life better. Why was it so crucial to resist?

"Mom, you don't need to wait," I told her, hearing how urgent my voice sounded. "It's raining really hard right now."

"I want to wait," she said. Now she sounded upset. "Why can't I wait? Please, don't buy me one now. I like to have something to look forward to."

Although she hated the cold, in the winter my mother kept the thermostat all the way to the left and wore two sweaters around the house along with the sealskin slippers she had received as a present long ago, before her marriage. They were luxuriantly warm and also stylish with their silvery black niello-shaded fur. Eventually, the sealskins began to fall apart, the delicate leather soles separating themselves from the furry uppers, and my mother restiched them together herself using a ball of thick white string.

The machines we did own seemed to share her stamina. They lasted throughout my childhood so that they became signature accessories, from the green push lawnmower to the dented percolator coffeepot to the brown clock radio. The one time in my boyhood when my mother bought a new car, she chose the Dodge station wagon. Tomato-sauce-red with its six-cylinder manual transmission and neither a radio nor an air conditioner, it arrived from Detroit with a piece of blank black plastic bolted across the dash. The gear shift emerged from the right side of the steering column, slim as the return lever on her manual typewriter. I never saw another car like ours; there was no difficulty locating it in even the largest parking lots. My mother seemed to associate modern conveniences with a loss of control. Machines broke, they went out of date, made those who used them helpless and dependent. "People have too many machines they don't really need," my mother would sometimes say. It was most comfortable for her to live in a simple, abstemious way that gave other people the impression that she took pleasure from making things hard on herself.

She had a lithe build and did not possess great physical strength, but she could make people believe she was strong because she had enormous willpower. She was also the most efficient person I have ever known. All the clocks in our home were set ahead on a graduated system my mother had designed to startle herself into varying degrees of urgency. The electronic wall clock back in the kitchen, for instance, glowed a panic-inducing fifteen minutes fast. On the bookshelf next to the couch, another clock warned my mother that her present was eleven minutes into her future. Nearer to the front door, the small clock on top of the bookcase told her to leave eight minutes before anyone else's clock hands would have thought it necessary. As well aware as she was of the altered denominations that were, after all, her own doing, glancing at something she knew to be untrue created in her a shadow of temporal doubt that propelled her. Not that there was any need for these spurs and stratagems. The moments of confusion that other people experienced when they forgot about the shift to Daylight Savings Time or failed to notice that a brief power outage during a thunderstorm had made mischief with the clock radio never affected my mother because she was always early, had a heightened sense of departure. Standing amidst a group of people having a conversation, she'd announce "Gotta go" in a way that could make merely punctual men and women reexamine themselves—feel suddenly dilatory. Like her father, a man willing to awaken at three in the morning to ensure that he got to the office first, before any of his colleagues, she enjoyed creating unlikely challenges for herself involving productivity, duty, and fortitude, and she found it gratifying to create and then exceed rugged expectations. Timetables were her adversaries, and she fought them bare-wristed. Although she owned a watch, she never wore it. Her contention was that watches were uncomfortable, but Sally and I knew the real truth: she didn't need one.

My mother finished every book she began and she remembered everything she read. She could tell you scene by scene the plots of dozens of movies from her youth. She was intensely interested in discussing the world of ideas. And yet she did not attend first-run films, purchase hardcover books or periodical subscriptions, or go to restaurants. I can remember very few outings. One evening, when I was eight and Sally six, she took us to the new A-frame Presbyterian church on Huntington Street to hear a free performance of chamber music featuring a harpsichord. We sat in smooth pews where I saw her excitement as she told us what to expect from a harpsichord, an eager enthusiasm in her face that I noticed again, around that same time, when she brought us down to a Yale lecture hall for a student film series screening of *The Third Man.* In those pre-video days, a revival screening was the only chance she had to watch vintage films, and in the car she prepared us, humming *The Third Man's* famous musical theme, explaining that the black market sold products of all colors, and exulting, "You kids are going to see Vienna, where I was born." The film bewildered me, just as the concert had. I had considered the sound of chamber music excruciating, and was similarly oppressed by what my mother called "a thriller"; it seemed to me that nothing was happening and half of it in a foreign language. I was disturbed by the occupying Russians and by dismal Vienna, and since now she'd told me that my family came from these ominous places, what did that suggest about us? It seemed meaningful that for these outings we went to venues that were somehow subordinated, not being used for their primary function. Yet, even as I shifted in my seat to let my mother know that I didn't understand and wanted to go home, I was aware that she was enjoying herself, and I knew that my behavior was costing her something. When I thought back on those two nights, I felt the same way as I had when I looked at that white string holding her sealskin slippers together, the despair of its coarse utility clashing with the worn but still glistening fur.

Sometimes I'd see her during one of her rare moments of leisure reading Trollope or looking at the photographs of 1930s and 1940s movie stars in the book her father had given her as a girl. She never went on dates anymore with men. On her bookshelf were the stories of Hawthorne about whom she had begun a graduate dissertation, a project abandoned when she became pregnant with me. Did she regret she could not go back and start over? When I asked her about it, she said, "All I ever wanted was to have children," and mostly I believed her.

My mother seemed to think all of life through in advance, to have a perpetual running list for everything she would do, and it was my job to be satisfied, not to propose revisions. When we went to stores, there really was a list, neatly printed in blue pen on white paper, and up and down the aisles she never deviated from it, despite me. Each time I opened my mouth I could feel the stiffening wariness spread across her collarbones, and her grip on the handle of the shopping cart tightened: I was going to ask for something. If I did, words would come bursting out of her the way they did when a dish fell to the kitchen floor: "God almighty, Nicky. I'm at my wit's end with you. You think I'm made of money. Just lay off."

But I desired so many things. I wanted to play in the youth ice hockey league down at the Yale rink. I knew kids who did. In the street hockey games we had in the schoolyard I was a better player than they. My mother said that the required ice hockey equipment was too costly for us, and, even if we were able to afford skates and gloves and pads, the ice times were prohibitively early; she could not get up before dawn, leave Sally alone, and take me to hockey. Come on! What was I thinking! I understood, and yet did I nag and pester her about it anyway? I did. And I wanted a new baseball bat, and to order from the Arrow Book Club catalogue at school, and I could not stop hankering for that cunningly detailed plastic haystack I'd seen in Malley's department store downtown, and what about a new bike? In the bounteous American way, there was not one kind of bicycle to pine after, but a whole opaline progression of them to advance through, so that no sooner did you own one model than you'd go to another kid's house where something more desirable—and more costly—made itself known. I did not get a Big Wheel tricycle with its two fat black rear racing slicks or a purple banana seat bike with a sissy bar or a Huffy dirt bicycle, and when my mother bought me a two-wheeler for my tenth birthday in 1972, it was a used red upright pedal brake model, what elderly Yale professors rode. On my birthday morning I saw it there waiting for me in the dining room and I felt my face falling and I could barely look at that bike. In a labored way I thanked her, and she could tell I was disappointed, and wondered why. I let her know that I had hoped for a new bike—and one with gears and handbrakes. She threw up her arms. When I finally grew out of that red bike, she got me the new bike with gears, a Raleigh, the brand, she told me, she herself had coveted as a child. But it was only an upright three-speed, another professor bike. Now I was disappointed because it wasn't a ten-speed racer.

My mother hated how much I hungered for things she couldn't provide. "I want, I want, I want, I want," she'd chant at me. "Nothing I do is ever enough for you," and nothing was. I could also tell that she worried that I was greedy, had a petty sense of deprivation. I remember how she'd looked at me after I'd returned from running an errand for her at the corner store and showed her that I had been given too much change. "You have to go back down there right now because it's not our money," she'd instantly said. "Someone will have to pay for the discrepancy and it'll probably be the poor cashier, the person who has the least."

I had no understanding of how money worked. As I watched my mother write checks, I didn't see why she couldn't just fill in a high enough number on the line to take care of everything. Or why not ask the drive-through teller behind the green-tinted window at the bank to put more bills in the withdrawal drawer. I decided that three of four things I desired I wouldn't mention. The fourths were still too much. If I caught my mother in the wrong mood with a request, for the rest of the day she was a fallen electric wire, emitting little sparks of rage. Through my closed door I could hear what I'd turned her into as she stormed around the house getting things done. "Ye gods," she'd tell the air, "it just never ends with that damned Nicky. It never stops. No matter how much I do for him, it's never enough. The lap of luxury wouldn't be good enough for him. I've had it. I've just had it up to here. I'm going like crazy all the time, doing everything I can for that spoiled-rotten kid, and he's sitting in there with his wants."

She gave me a pizza birthday party, kept me in baseball gloves, did so many nice things. Why couldn't it be enough for me? Why couldn't I, as she sometimes suggested, "look to your own star"? I could tell that it was because she was such a conscientious person that the idea that she was failing to do all that I expected of her was overwhelming to her. She often told me how much she wanted to be a good mother to my sister and to me, and, because I wanted to support her in this ambition, when I asked her for things she could not give, I used to feel ashamed of myself for putting her in the position of disappointing me. I wished for many things as a child and regretted wanting almost all of them. There was a gaping rictus of need.

The Orvilles' red house across the street from us went up for sale. The Orvilles were moving because they required more space, but that house had more than enough room for three. Each of us would have our own room. For weeks my mother thought aloud about how we might somehow find a way to afford the red house. "I could do extra tutoring," she mused one day. "I could teach more summer school," she proposed on another. The "For Sale" sign out in front of the Orvilles' house was like a person you are too much attracted to without knowing yet how they feel about you; you are always meeting their eyes and then jerking your head hurriedly away. There it was: privacy, sanctuary, a piece of the American Dream. Finally someone else bought the Orvilles' house. "I should have just done it," my mother said. "I was afraid I might lose my job at school." Day Prospect Hill had merged by then with the city's leading secondary school for boys, and my mother said that "they" were "firing all the women." Most unfulfilled desires are kept at a remove, but over the ensuing years, every day we would walk out onto the porch and confront the red house. It was an enduring rebuke to my mother, the inability to have the life she'd always thought she'd have, the life she wanted us to have.

The radio kept my mother constant company. It went on in the morning and stayed on until night, always tuned to the same station. That was all-news WCBS out of New York, suffusing our house in a daily thrum of elsewhere that drifted over us in the level masculine elocution of a full roster of anchormen whose voices I couldn't tell apart. This uniform, ambient presence was punctuated only occasionally by a burst of impacted rage from my mother at news of President Nixon, whom she loathed as "That stinkin' Nixon!" for being partial to the wealthy, for lying about the war in Vietnam, for being generally deficient in morals. "There's nothing worse," she said, "than someone like that who grows up poor and then when they have some good fortune, they forget what poverty feels like for other people. That man is indecent."

News radio led to some confusions, particularly regarding the traffic and stock market reports. I couldn't grasp why Neil Bush up in the Traffic Watch helicopter so frequently referred to problems involving tractor-trailers loaded with jackknives, and I misunderstood the fundamental Wall Street term to be not "share" but "chair," an error that metastasized the Dow into a symbolic operation in which the operative idiom was the four-legged chair. I imagined a man standing in a room filled with chairs that were the fungible property of each stock market company. As a company's fortunes improved, it was awarded more chairs. When things declined, chairs were taken away from them. And when the chairs declined in fractions, legs of a chair were removed, one leg chopped off, say, when a stock went "down a quarter," a leg and a half cut away for "down three eighths."

Besides the radio, another great constant in my mother's day was ketchup. She liked it with just about everything, and it was her usual practice to drench whatever meat, potato, and vegetables were on her plate with ketchup before mixing everything together into a single garnet glob that she then ate with appetite. She applied sweetness in similar bulk, adding as many as ten teaspoons of sugar to a cup of tea or coffee.

My mother always remained slender and trim, but it was a matter of pride for her to be the same weight year after year when she made her annual visit to the gynecologist. Because we owned no foot scale, this was a matter of instinct, and one year, two weeks before the day of the checkup, she decided she had gained five pounds. Immediately, she cut herself off the ketchup, the sugar, and just about everything else, and for fourteen days she followed a strict diet consisting entirely of hard-boiled eggs and grapefruit. I learned about this project belatedly, when, in my usual way, I jerked open the refrigerator to hear a rumbling sound. I looked down and saw the lower shelves entirely filled with dislodged and shifting big yellow balls. A moment later, an avalanche, and the fruits came bouncing off my shins onto my feet and rolling all over the kitchen. Sally and I survived the stench of all those eggs by feeling invested in our mother's quest. Without a scale, what would happen at her appointment was a source of suspense. Day after day I looked at her and wondered. When at last she came home from the doctor, triumphant, we ate victory bowls of ice milk, which was cheaper than ice cream.

A result of my mother's stringent economizing on ephemeral items was that she was slowly filling our house with pine furniture. Over the years, the deliverymen brought us six brown pine dining room chairs, a brown pine coffee table, a brown pine kneehole desk, and a brown pine Welsh dresser, the latter a tall hutch with a fretworked display shelf on which my mother eventually placed her set of Spode blue and white dinnerware ordered from London. It took her more than eight years to save up for that set of eight plates, bowls, cups, and saucers, and while she dusted them every week, I don't ever recall an occasion where she actually used any of it. The day a saucer chipped was one of mourning in our household.

In the living room where she slept, my mother added new red cotton upholstery for the convertible couch and a red-patterned carpet so that between them, our living room looked sunburned. My grandmother Rebecca's annual gift to her former daughter-in-law was a subscription to *The New Yorker.* On the new coffee table my mother kept a stack of back-issue magazines, four of which at night she put under the folded-out legs of the convertible sofa to protect the new rug. In every one of those *New Yorkers* was an advertisement placed weekly by The Homestead, a resort hotel in the mountains of Virginia. The advertisement featured an aerial illustration of an elegant brick building that, with its elaborate Georgian-style architecture, resembled a cross between a Shropshire estate and the administration building on a university quadrangle. People went to The Homestead to swim, ride, play golf and tennis, and to eat fine food, but what made my mother want to go was the name and the fact that guests could receive massages. "I'd give anything to go someday to The Homestead and get a back rub," she'd say.

In the summer of 1972, she took me to Cooperstown to see the Baseball Hall of Fame. I was nine. First we drove to Francestown, where Sally was to stay with my grandparents. After breakfast the next morning, we set off, driving for hours across New Hampshire, through Vermont into rolling New York farm country, my mother and I on a road trip, our first big expedition alone together. On the way she told me about Natty Bumppo the Deerslayer from the James Fenimore Cooper Leatherstocking novels, who walked beside the Glimmerglass in Cooperstown. Cooperstown was on the far shore of this Glimmerglass—Lake Otsego—and as we came near, my mother was very pleased, pointed out that it really did look as flat and silvery-clear as an enormous mirror.

Cooperstown was a one-stoplight, tree-shaded hamlet built on a scale ideal for a nine-year-old tourist. From our red-brick inn we needed only to walk around the corner to be on the three-block-long commercial stretch of Main Street where the Hall of Fame stood at the opposite end. Along Main Street there was a scatter of shops that did some trade in collectibles, but Cooperstown was the furthest thing from a baseball theme park and had, as my mother noticed, a stately, civic integrity of its own. Nonetheless, you could walk into a luncheonette called the Shortstop for a grilled cheese sandwich that tasted better because of the sign outside. Then my mother and I were hurrying down Main Street to the Hall. Because I had read so much about Ruth and Williams and Mathewson and Robinson and Crawford, to see the spikes that carried them, the bats they swung, the jerseys they wore was to add shape and color to the cloth of stories I already knew. There were early gloves no larger than a waffle, lopsided old baseballs under glass, paintings, photographs, and artifacts enough to last a dedicated patron the full afternoon, which they did.

After closing, we visited the hotel swimming pool. By the pool I fell into conversation with a boy from Ohio and his father. Quickly it became clear that the boy and I both felt sure we knew more about baseball than the other. A game was devised. We would each, in turn, name players who the other must identify. The boy's father would umpire. I went first. "Mike Corkins," I said. The boy knew he was among the most undistinguished of the San Diego Padres' many undistinguished pitchers. Now it was the boy's turn to choose a player for me to recognize. "Buddy Bell," he said. I had never heard of him. "You don't know who Buddy Bell is?" the boy said with disbelief, and the boy's father too seemed aghast, as though we were naming dictators and I had shrugged and shaken my head at Mussolini. That ended the game. I wanted to continue but, backing away, they waved off the idea with promises of trying again "another year." Buddy Bell turned out to be the Cleveland Indians' rookie third baseman, already famous because of primogeniture: he was the son of the former Reds outfielder Gus Bell. I didn't know who Gus was either. Mortified by my ignorance, I could not escape the conclusion that while I might have more baseball knowledge than any kid I'd ever met, in the end I was just local talent. I looked at the many people crowded around the pool, the bathers splashing in the water. Almost all of them, I saw, were fathers and their sons. Suddenly I felt diminished at having come to such a place with my mother.

For the next two days I was angry and sullen, sulked when I was told we were eating lunch at the diner instead of the more costly

Shortstop, had to be dragged through the Fenimore House and then the Farmer's Museum where the early agricultural implements were another rebuke; scythes and plows weren't what we had come here for. "Leave me alone," I told my mother when she asked if I was okay. Everywhere I turned there were men walking beside boys. I hated Cooperstown, hated it all the way back across to New Hampshire, where we pulled into the driveway to discover that a severe episode of arrhythmia had put my grandmother in the intensive care unit of the Peterborough hospital. My grandfather, with his own serious heart condition, had been caring for Sally by himself. Proudly they both told of how, after spending the day at the hospital, for supper every evening he'd cooked the two of them hot dogs prepared the way he said "they eat them in Vienna"—until they were black on all sides. "I made Sally charcoal," he elaborated, and it came to me that by staying home she was the one who'd gone on the adventure.

If my mother was not feeling pressed, she was the most enthusiastic person I have ever known, but each day was a succession of the needs and desires of other people's children and her own. She lived in a society that did not think well of single mothers or divorcées, and, on her own and marginalized throughout our years in New Haven, she was often, as she'd say, "just frantic." Once I told her, "My friends don't like to come over to my house because we don't have a TV, we never have any snacks, and they don't like how much you yell."

"Oooh," she said to me. "Are they afraid?" Maybe a little.

Her unhappy moods bubbled and steamed as she stalked about the house, expressing irritation and distress with noisy intakes and exhalations of breath, a symphony of sighs that in summer were supported by the beat of her Dr. Scholl's sandals slapping out their angry tempo against the wooden floors. This might have been a more irenic way of getting things off her chest than yelling or throwing things, except that the lack of explosion built and built the tension in the house. She muttered about her exertions, wondering

"How the hell can I be expected to get everything done for these damned, ungrateful, spoiled-rotten kids" as she slammed around the house getting everything done. I heard most of her discontents from the next room, through my wall and doorway, though, even if she was speaking aloud in my presence, she seemed removed to another place, to an under-her-breath existence which suggested that what was quite possibly most distressing to her was that she had nobody to share her distress with. Later, she might say, "It had nothing to do with you, Nicky," and once she told me, "I can churn up enough anxiety all by myself, it's just my awful nature." I wanted to believe her, to remember what she was like when she was my sweet mom, but in the balled-up emotional moment it was hard to.

The phrase that seeped most frequently into my room was "all I want is a little peace and quiet." I'd do my best to be still, but it wasn't only me. When our telephone did ring, more often than not it was my mother's mother calling to ask her favors, requests that my mother could never quite complete without hearing about the surprising incompetence of American teachers, how "the stupidest people all turn out to be English majors," or the "immorality" of this country where so many women had children but no husbands. It was as though having to ask her busy daughter favors was such an indignity that it required a little animus, a chaser of revenge. I used to worry that my mother was lonely even when Sally and I were at home, and it turned out she was. Neither of my mother's parents ever knew about what had happened to her marriage—"Never once did either of them ask me anything or say so much as 'are you all right'?"

My father was working the phones too, and the mails, insisting "I know my rights and I want to see more of my children," demanding the addresses of school principals and camp directors, which meant that my mother would have to call these officials and explain that if my father tried to come and get us, they shouldn't let us go. It was only harassment, for he never made good on any of these threats, but she could never be sure. After all, he was a lawyer with a lot of time on his hands. Whenever he called, I could tell who was on the line because my mother became expressionless, locked herself into a hyper-controlled state. He was so unpredictable that she didn't want to do anything to provoke him.

Even when calm, my mother's anxiety was subcutaneous; I could sense it throbbing just below the surface. Often, through some kind of wireless transmission, I'd begin to feel anxious too. Because she emanated such competence, the anxiety suggested misgivings about others, implied that the world was a harsh and entropic place, and that you had to strain against the seething disorder out there, take measures or all would come to grief. For a while she'd smoked Marlboros heavily. Then she saw Sally pick up a Crayon and mime taking a puff from it. My mother never lit another cigarette. After that she vexed more easily, would combust into screaming rages. When her anger cooled, she comforted us with deeply felt remorse.

Living with such an agitated person might occasionally be difficult, but the alternative was chaos, enough of which I'd glimpsed to feel grateful to her temperament, to regard it as my fortification, with her fits of hostility and despair, her rigid codes of order, and her sharp probity functioning for the greater good as so many merlons, spikes, and corbels. Life lived in the shade of the ramparts increases the awareness of danger, but it also makes a person feel insulated and protected, and I could not have been very old before I saw that to be perpetually on edge was her way of maintaining command of a very tenuous situation. We were not fashionably down on our luck, we were just poor, had no assets, no equity, except her. In the dominion of anxiety, it was choice that was the impossible luxury. She was a pretty, smart, decent young woman whose life had been stripped of alternatives. When, despite my mother's intricately calculated budgets, her accounts ran low two weeks before payday, she used to press her hands into her face—I remember the skin of her fingers, the veins running down them like turbulent blue rivers—and moan, "How am I going to make it through the month?" Then, because all the worry had readied her for peril, she'd wipe her eyes and find a way. Although our landlord was responsible for the repair and upkeep of the house, my mother maintained everything herself, doing her best never to call the land-lord for anything because she didn't want to give him incentive to raise the rent. That rent check was always on time, as were her taxes, paid in full.

She believed in taxes, considered everyone doing his part for the greater good the essence of a progressive society. In 1974, the year after she wrote letters to the entire Connecticut congressional dele-gation urging them to vote for Richard Nixon's presidential impeachment, she received an official letter of inquiry from the Internal Revenue Service. It is the most ethical among us who take accusation the hardest. Heart pounding, she jumped onto her bicy-cle and pedaled downtown without even taking the time to call for an appointment. By then her salary was $7,000, of which she had paid more than $2,000 in taxes. Inside the offices of Braverman and Hoffenberg CPA, she found herself on the other side of the desk from a tender-faced older man named Hoffenberg, who took one look at her and wordlessly handed across a box of tissues. After she calmed down, she described her predicament. Mr. Hoffenberg reached out, touched her hand, and said he would be glad to advise her right then. "But, you know, Mrs. Dawidoff," he said, leaning back in his chair, "there are a lot of other very intelligent people in New Haven who think it's a good idea for me to help them with their taxes because then they have me behind them." He told her how to respond to the letter, refused to charge her for the visit, and sent her home. In fact, she had overpaid, as she would continue to do annually, liking to have a late spring infusion to look forward to, liking to be on the side of right.

Seven days a week I went to the Worthington Hooker schoolyard to prepare for my life in baseball. Mostly, we kids played games, using tennis balls because the blacktop destroyed what we called "real baseballs." Even so, when one of us came into a real baseball, we never could resist bringing it along for the one or two afternoons of authentic play before the cover scuffed up so much it fell off. Soon afterward the interior yarn wrapping unraveled all over the play-ground leaving the impression of the aftermath of slaughter, with the empty cover lying over there, picked clean as a vultured pelt. Eventually, I even submitted my facsimile Mets autographed ball from Shea Stadium for use in a game, and once those inscribed surfaces gave way, I was astonished to discover a heart not built of wound yarn, but a dense clot of Chinese newsprint.

Of the kids who played in the schoolyard, the best fighter was named Jeff. I never saw him strike anyone, but such was his reputation, and I believed it. He had swept-back, sandy hair, intelligent eyes that narrowed into chilly slits as he sized up a situation, and a lupine manner of stalking down his part of Livingston Street that projected the capacity for efficient, raw-boned violence. His way of speaking was calm and supple with a measured strength, though once, when he wanted his younger brother, Peter, to come home from the schoolyard and Peter, always a handful, was resisting, Jeff barked "Peter!" and Peter was in instant motion, his feet moving before any of the defiance had left his face, so that you could see him registering both moods. When I thought of Jeff provoked, I imagined a flurried combination of direct blows punishing the windpipe and the eye socket. He didn't seem malicious, just capable of harm, the way you know a whirring fan blade is capable of harm, which is exactly what makes you, in a certain mood, want to reach through the screen and touch it.

One day, talking with my friend Vogel, I mentioned that I wasn't afraid of Jeff. What had gotten into me I couldn't have said. Nobody held any brief for my fists; I was still thin enough at the chest and arms that my future dimensions remained under seal, could not yet be foretold. Given the cosmology of our neighborhood, in which Vogel's older brother, David, was Jeff's best friend, I was as good as talking to Jeff when I said this, and I must have known it. A day later I was walking down the sidewalk near my house when a quiet, skeptical voice at my right ear said, "Hey, Nicky, I hear you're saying you're not afraid of me." I turned. The eyes were winter.

There was no time to think. I said, "I know you could kick my ass anytime you wanted to, Jeff, but that doesn't make me afraid of you. You could hit me and hit me and hit me and hit me and beat the shit out of me until you probably even killed me, but I still wouldn't be afraid of you." He stood looking at me during this little outburst with a kind of disbelief. When I was done, he seemed almost to sigh. After a moment he shook his head and walked away.

From then on I developed a great private admiration for Jeff, would have done a lot for him. Things were going on in Jeff's life, you could just tell, but there was a stoic dignity to the way he carried whatever his burden was. He handled himself, gave his best self to our street hockey and baseball games in a way that seemed to embody the heroic conception I had of schoolyard affairs. His friend David possessed a similar regal composure, and watching the two of them made me hopeful that one day I would have it too. Sometimes, late in an afternoon, I'd look out across the schoolyard and see a democracy, all of us engaged in the mutual endeavor, trying to improve, preparing for the day when at least one of us would be cheered on by tens of thousands, Jeff, David, all of them part of the hardcover story that would be written about me in some future edition of *Great Shortstops of the Major Leagues.*

When there was nobody to play with, I practiced by myself, spending many afternoons alone in the schoolyard throwing a ball at a targeted brick on the schoolhouse wall, scooping it up on the rebound and throwing it at the brick again, inventing games in which I was each member of the Mets infield, angling my throws as I moved around the defensive crescent from Milner to Boswell to Harrelson to Garrett. In the evenings, after supper, I went out to our backyard to resume my apprenticeship in the twilight, throwing now against the side of our house, forcing myself to cleanly field one hundred consecutive grounders along the chapped asphalt surface before I could go inside. I was pretty dedicated; once my underpants were soaked before I'd caught my limit. After nightfall, I threw a tennis ball against the wall of my room until I made a hole in the seaport section of the felt mural. My mother bought a can of Spackle, filled in the hole, and told me "no more playing ball in the house." The hole reemerged, and again she applied Spackle and admonishments. In time, there was a grayish abscess bulging out of the wall and various other threatening tumidities. It looked as though the whole wall might collapse on me as I slept. So my mother had to hire a man named Mr. Jackson to tear down the wall and put up a new one. When I found out his first name was Reggie, making his the same name as the Oakland Athletics All-Star outfielder, it mattered to me, seemed significant, a portent.

On the morning of my father's New Haven visiting days, I began to listen for the telephone. If it rang my mother would answer and I could hear from my room her clipped, uninflected responses: "Yes," "Yes," "Okay," "I'll tell them." Going into Sally's room, I'd announce, "Dad's not coming again." By the time my mother joined us, while she'd be saying "Your father isn't feeling well," I was seeing the whole day in front of me desolate as the scrapyards out by the highway, all the hours now empty of pancakes, empty of bubblegum cigars, empty of "So it does that, does it?" Why did I have to have a father who got the flu so often? The year after we went to Bermuda, my father planned to take Sally and me to the Virgin Islands for another holiday long weekend, a trip he then called up and canceled after we'd packed our suitcases and gone to bed the night before we were to leave.

When he did come for visits in New Haven, I watched him carefully as he arrived. Blinking uncertainly, he stood above me in the front hallway, absorbing the improvements and additions to the house and, it occurred to me one day, the changes in me. The expression that would come over his face was slack-jawed, both baffled and forsaken, and also a little pissed off. My father was the father of children for whom everything was happening without him. Partly, this was a function of distance, but there was also an unmistakable change in how I felt about him. That shift was gradual, a slow, organic conversion, but it was there, and he must have known. He spanked me once. I had that hiding coming. During one of his visits, I'd been a punk to Sally, telling her she didn't know anything, making her feel foolish, and when he called me on it, I asked him who he was to show up and start telling me how to behave. So he took me across his knees. I had begun to be afraid of him, but after he actually hit me I was in a fury, though not so much that I could miss the defeat in his shoulders as he turned away from me once the job was done. I wasn't a Rascal anymore.

During another visit to New Haven, he sat on my mother's red couch with his loafers resting on her brown pine coffee table. The sight of those dirty New York shoes with sidewalk on the bottom of the soles and their hard leather heels splayed out on the pristine varnished surface worried me. "Dad," I finally said, "maybe you should take your shoes off of Mom's new table." He turned his head toward me. A crude, slovenly glint came into his eye. "I'll do what I want, Nicky," he said. Then slowly he dragged the shoes off the table leaving a pair of long, parallel blond gashes in the wood like tire tracks across a squishy lawn.

As I grew older, in the late morning of his visits there'd be action audible from the schoolyard and suddenly the prospect of spending an entire Sunday with my father was too much to bear. So I began to do what I normally did on weekends. I said, "I'm going to go play baseball for a while in the schoolyard," and I'd slip out of the house, leaving him with Sally. Once he did come with me for a father-and-son game of catch, but only once. By the time we might have done it a second time, I'd decided that I didn't want that guy throwing things at me.

At school, a girl named Joanie brought in a mechanical family heirloom to show our class, an Edison-era phonograph that played cylinder-shaped recordings and had, as part of its apparatus, a tripod. We listened to some brief, scratchy recordings and there was a discussion of the process of invention. Later, during the rush out of the classroom for recess, I brushed against the tripod and it came apart in two pieces. Horror sliced through me. "Ooh, Nicky, you broke it," sang out pudgy Felice, who never missed anything. "No, I didn't, Felice," I said quickly, and in haste began screwing the thing back together, hoping nobody else saw, especially yellow-haired Christine with that liquid gaze of hers that remained composed and farsighted even when she laughed. Christine wore quilted jumpers and had a desert-boot-clad older brother named Steve, known to other kids only by his and Christine's last name, Berman, and revered by me because he was related to Christine, could talk to her every day, a privilege he seemed to handle with remarkable composure—I had seen him consulting with her in the school hallway. I used to imagine myself in his place, seated at supper in the Berman house on Everit Street, asking her to pass the peas.

Joanie brought the phonograph home and the next few days went by without any mention of the tripod. But maybe it had simply been placed in a closet, the damage still waiting to be discovered. Joanie had been in my class every year, a kind, understated, knee-socks sort of girl with black hair and a smile that made her seem unprotected and shy because she half closed her eyes and hung her head when she did it. Nobody could have had a thing against her, except now me. I feared and avoided her. I avoided Christine too. I was unworthy. For many months I tried to resolve the situation in my mind, some days standing by the front window in our house and agreeing that if, say, seven cars went by before I took another breath, all was well with the tripod. If that was too easily accomplished, it became seven cars with out-of-state license plates. Tripod. Tripod. Tripod. Tripod. I reviled the sound. When Uncle Tony happened to mention his telescope's tripod, at the word I startled, felt something wormwoody in my belly. Finally, after the school year ended, I confessed to my mother. She walked over to the telephone and called Joanie's parents. The tripod was fine. But now Christine's family was moving away from New Haven. More than anything I wanted to say goodbye to Christine, to talk to her, to tell her . . . tell her what? I hadn't the words. Falling back on my bookshelf for guidance, I thought of Tom Sawyer doing handstands in front of Becky Thatcher's house after which she tossed him a pansy. Soon enough Tom had proposed and Becky had accepted. I left our house and walked over to Everit Street. That I did not know how to do a handstand failed to occur to me then. When I reached Christine's white house, I slowed a little as I passed by. Nothing happened. At the corner, I reversed course for a second lap, and this time, feeling braver, I stopped in front of the picture window. No lights were on, all was still in there, and the lawn, I noticed, wanted cutting and weeding. Christine, it turned out, had already left town. When I got older, I used to find myself awakening from pleasant dreams in which my head had rested on a lap of quilt.

All day I was hungry, wanted to eat everything. During school I buried my nose in the purple chemical scent of freshly mimeographed classroom assignments and was also drawn to dipping my licking finger into the sultry, fragrant murk of the paste jar. At home, where there were no snack foods, I resorted to drinking pickle juice and eating uncooked egg noodles—they crunched down to a tasty mulch. Visiting my mother's friends the Pollaks over on Everit Street, I sampled everything the older Pollak girls said was good, including dog biscuits. That a dog would enjoy them made sense to me; I did too, especially the green ones.

To pay for better snacks, I began to work. Through my grammar school years, I mowed grass, raked leaves, and shoveled the snow off walks in my January boots, and with my take went hurrying down to the corner commissaries along Orange Street where I spent everything I'd earned on more bubblegum than ever— pounds of it—and now also Creamsicles, fruit pies shaped like my grandfather's tobacco pouch, Slim Jim sausages with their list of ingredients filled with long words I could not pronounce, coffee cakes, Good & Plenty, Red Hot Dollars—quarter-sized and not hot at all—Danish pastries laden at the center with enormous ponds of sweet cheese, honey-flavored cough drops, milk-chocolate-covered shortbreads, a radioactive-orange-colored cheese puff called Jax, and barbecued potato chips, unbearably delectable with their blackened edges and fiery-red-dusted surfaces. All of it was washed down with bottles of red cream soda—identical in flavor to regular cream soda, yet somehow superior—and then, in an instant, everything was gone, leaving a moraine of empty bags, bottles, wrappers, and split plastic straws.

It was an itch, a yearning, a voracious, insatiable desire for salt and sugar that could be truly satisfied only when I discovered a source that seemed in some mysterious way to modify those cravings—a little store we called Cheap Joe's. Cheap Joe's was beyond our neighborhood, down past Orange Street at the end of a long block of resigned little green and off-white houses with their curtains pulled and oil spots in the narrow driveways. The faltering porches smelled of old cooking, and many of the people I passed outside on the sidewalk were edgy, dead-eyed. Behind locked back-yard gates, barking dogs strained on rusty chains. I used to feel excited going along the route, thinking that there was an unexplored world out there that had a truthfulness entirely its own.

Cheap Joe's was all ramshackle integrity and vague disrepute, had the corn-syrupy, cheap commercial glamour of a crossroads grocery in the rural South. On the shabby sign outside was painted a bottle of 7-Up, and a jumble of other garish advertisements were plastered up on the washed-out interior walls. As I came through the door into the dim, mildewy room, I could make out all manner of groceries crowded right up to the ceiling, from rolls of chicken loaf to cans of coffee, bottles of Wink soda, and faded boxes of detergent. No doubt they sold milk and all the other staples, though I never saw anyone buy anything there except candy. Why would they? A scarred wooden counter was to the left of the entrance and behind the counter were sagging shelves jammed with a sugary convergence, a florid, glittering display of tantalizing confection that was so much in contrast with the dank surroundings that it transcended what it was, bringing to mind an arcade or a holiday carnival. Guarding the treasure was Joe, a well-fed man in a beef-stained white apron with a pecuniary glint in his eye, who must have won his nickname by taking his place in the lineage of kid-hating candy store owners, though I always admired him: all this was his. There was a conformity to the candy sold at most stores, a selection of the same brand-name mints, gums, and chocolates. Nobody went to Joe's for Life Savers or a Hershey Bar. What he offered was louche, decadent, original. There was Gold Rush and Rain-Blo, crystal chunks of rock candy, enormous, confetti-colored jawbreakers, wax lips, wax soda bottles filled with colored goop, and the flat, round, soda-flavored Bottle Caps. You could buy Mexican Hats and Hot Tamales, Mike and Ikes, Now and Laters, Squirrel Nuts, Tart 'n' Tinys, Ice Cube chocolates, which were misleading because there was nothing cold about them, and long dowels of bubblegum wrapped in colorfully striped plastic. Over here were Kits and down there Tangy Taffy and Sky Bars and Pixy Stix and Lemonheads and Boston Baked Beans and giant SweeTarts, which made your tongue bleed when you licked them, and, speaking of licking, Lik-M-Aids, a high-concept, labor-intensive operation involving the use of the applicator, a chalky white candy stick you dampened in your mouth and then plunged into the sleeves of sour fruit powder before sucking off the clinging filaments. There was candy named after cows and weapons, and candy-shaped jewels and candy-shaped pacifiers. There was more, much more, new varieties on every visit, and, though I could never try it all, I wanted to: the fundamental attraction was the excitement of becoming a connoisseur of my own particular vice.

There was a time in my life when I put every cent I had into the pinguid palm of Cheap Joe right down to the silver Kennedy half-dollars my Grandma Rebecca had given me for an early birthday with instructions that "you should save them because they will be worth something someday." The ache for candy really was semi-hysterical—beyond reason.

Unexpected things had begun to occur with some frequency during my visits to my father in New York. One weekend we went to the circus where my father drank a large green and white paper cup of beer and a few minutes later we had to leave right in the middle of the elephants, excusing ourselves down the row. It happened again when he began nodding and shaking partway through a Knicks basketball game. On the way home, in the frigid winter air outside Madison Square Garden, I smelled the sweet char of roasting chestnuts and pulled on his coat until he bought me a paper bag–full from the vendor. Once shelled, they were mushy and sour, cold at the center, nothing like what they promised.

One time, in a summer before I was ten, my father and I went to visit some guy at his house out on the edge of the countryside. There were fields, space, beating heat, bugs. It felt like I was exiled on an atoll, far away from anything, but probably it was just a new subdivision outside a New York or Connecticut town. I was put in front of a television by myself where I watched *The Electric Company* while my father talked with the man in another room. I thought something called *The Electric Company* would have men climbing poles and construction trucks and cranes. It didn't; the show was educational. It got dark. Sequestered in there, I was bored, then restless. I began to wonder if I would ever get home. Through the window I could see lights way out across the fields. Much later, we left.

My father was putting on more and more weight, his belly now a globe straining at his shirts, and whatever he was eating wasn't agreeing with him because at his apartment, after he used the bathroom, the stuffy air told of his gastric distresses. Otherwise it had the stricken smell of unwashed clothes. My life slowed down within those suffocating rooms, and a creeping paralysis would come over me. I can remember little of what we did or what we talked about. I knew never to mention my mother, and increasingly I told him as little as possible about myself or my life in New Haven. He, on the other hand, told me more than I wanted to know about himself, especially on the occasions when I stayed overnight. It was as though he couldn't resist the little eruptions of inappropriateness that came over him. Out in the main room he would make up the sofa with sheets and blankets, giving me his bed in the back room, and then, as if in recompense for my putting him out of his room, he served up disturbance. Lying next to me he'd tell me about swimming nude with other men at the Yale Club swimming pool, and he would talk about women. Once, when I was nine, at my bedtime my father was sitting on the bed next to me, and he wanted to recount his youthful experiences with Italian prostitutes. I managed to put all the details out of my head except for a description of a Roman bordello decorated in red velvet. For years, every time I entered his apartment, I winced, expecting to see red velvet.

Another day, my father related the story of his mugging. He said he'd seen a group of black guys coming toward him and made a break for his apartment building, trying to get away, but they cut him off halfway down the block, grabbed him, roughed him up, and took his wallet. There seemed to be no point to the story other than that he'd been victimized, was prey.

Unless he was telling again about his old high school teammate Jim Brown, my father didn't seem to like black people very much. One night we'd been visiting my father's sister, Judy, and her husband, Bob, gave me a treasure, a real baseball signed by Jackie Robinson, Duke Snider, Roy Campanella, and every other member of the 1955 Brooklyn Dodgers, the only Brooklyn team ever to win the World Series. It was an incredible gesture, but Bob knew how much I loved baseball, and, as we left, he took me aside and presented me with the ball. I was nine. We rode in a taxi back to my father's, and, after we got out of the cab and it drove off, I realized that I no longer had the Dodger baseball. Horrified, I told my father. Looking down at me, my father said, "Well, Nicky, you've made some little nigger kid up in Harlem very happy."

Now I was afraid of New York. On our way in from New Haven in the red Dodge, nearing the city the expressways grew loud and smoky with the exhaust clouds that came spurting out of trucks in rapid belches. As we drove through the Bronx, the highway shoulders were cluttered with abandoned cars that right there in full view had been stripped clean of their hubcaps, tires, and anything else that could be moved by thieves who then often set the bare frame that was left on fire. After emptying out the engine cavity, the thieves didn't bother to lower the hoods, making the cars look as though they were calling out in pain for a dentist.

The roadway swung up high, right alongside the heart of the South Bronx, a bleak, leaden moonscape of rubble-strewn lots and shattered apartment houses with skeletal fire escapes zigzagging up the facades, many of them, like the cars, burned-out, deserted, cratered. Seen from our car, all the broken windows looked like chapfallen eyes staring back at me. There in the Dodge I became convinced that my luck was about to change. Horrible things were going to happen. I would soon end up down there in the abyss.

On my father's West Seventy-fifth Street block, at one end was a news and soda shop with a rickety gumball machine outside that was chained up so nobody would steal it. Behind their little window, the gumballs were losing color. Down at the other corner were the soot-brown walls surrounding Central Park, a place created for the mingling of classes where my father said nobody went because it was full of muggers. At night the whole neighborhood was dark under a sulfurous sky. Plumes of steam rose from the streets making everything seem part of a night never to become day again. Was something burning under there? Korean delis had not yet come to light up New York's evening corners, and, as we walked down my father's block, I held his hand tight so as to feel less vulnerable.

Being in that city was like being thrust into some other side of the world that looked to me like a ransacked room, every drawer hanging open, belongings scattered, spilled, broken. None of the usual rules or considerations applied: things were expected to be dirty, dented, bashed in, and not to work. Everywhere there was trash strewn around, garbage swelling out of cans, a veneer of dog shit so you had to be vigilant about watching out where you were stepping. When I looked at other people, the faces I saw along the sidewalk seemed to be up to no good and angry with me for noticing. Nothing was ever going to get better for anybody in my father's city, and because in my New Haven life I did not share this outlook, here the people resented me, might set upon me at any moment. What did madness look like to me? This harsh, putrefying, spookily shadowed place was madness.

I didn't want to go there anymore. And yet I did want to. That was where he lived, and without him I would be without any father at all. Down into the subway we'd go. The stations were filthy, the wall tiles dripping with moisture, the express banging past us waiting on the local platform, the express's lights flickering manically on and off, its gray-metal sides coated in spray-painted graffiti, overdrawn ganglions of green, pink, orange, hot red, and purple that were more evidence to me that New York was mayhem, a place where people could get away with whatever they wanted. My insides would freeze up as our train arrived and a crowd massed at both sides of the doors. I knew I would have to be quick to get on or those doors would slam shut and I would be left behind. I tried to make an emergency plan with my father, to decide what to do if we were separated, but one could never get worked out.

The night in 1974 when Hank Aaron of the Braves was likely to hit his 715th home run to break Babe Ruth's all-time record, the game against the Dodgers was nationally televised, and I was upstairs on the second floor of our New Haven house, at the Sullivans' apartment, watching with Mr. Sullivan. He was a retired aircraft engine factory worker who had fought during World War II, which I knew although he wouldn't talk about it. Mr. Sullivan didn't care for baseball, but here he was with me, wearing a V-neck white undershirt, his feet in soft shoes on which he'd used a knife to cut away the portion of the top covering the toes so I could see white-sock-covered toes protruding. His unshaven face was bristly, his fingers yellow from the cigarettes he rolled by hand and smoked, and he smelled of man. Hank Aaron hit the home run, but the picture of the slumped Dodgers pitcher Al Downing made me sad that everyone was celebrating his humiliation, until Mr. Sullivan started talking. I don't remember what he said, just the realization that he was sensing my mood, and in that moment, in an unspecified and inchoate way, I became aware that somebody who was not your father could briefly feel like one, might even want that as much as you did, and that it might be okay to reveal yourself a little.

Another day, Mr. Sullivan suddenly gave me some of his battlefield souvenirs from the war, including a Nazi officer's Iron Cross, an eagle breast patch, some kind of artillery projectile. He still wouldn't discuss any of it. Was there ever a truly heroic veteran who liked to tell his war stories? When I was too sick to go to school, I went up and watched television with Mr. Sullivan all morning. I was also welcome in the evening.

One night when I climbed the back stairs to visit him, Mr. Sullivan was sitting at his kitchen table with his outdoor nylon jacket on. He was unshaven and raving, talking wildly and nonsensically, calling me "Mick," trying to hug me, his voice slurred and his breath reeking of whiskey. After that I liked him less; for all his kindnesses, I couldn't quite forgive him. It wasn't just his weakness. It was that with people like him, like my Uncle Tony, like my baseball coach, all the nice moments weren't sufficient. I always wanted more from them, and when inevitably I touched their limits, the disappointment was outsized. I wasn't theirs.

In my neighborhood, though almost every boy I played baseball with wished to be a professional, I believed I was different, that of all of us I was the one who had it. The reality was that it mattered most to me; I was unique only in the intensity of my affection for the game. I crouched there at shortstop thinking Hit it to me, Hit it to me, really wanting the ball, but also influenced by my knowledge that these were the exact words that went through the mind of the old Dodger Pete Reiser when he was out in center field. Had someone told me then that those who made it to the major leagues were a drop in the ocean compared to all the boys in America who'd hoped to play for a living, it wouldn't have dampened my ambitions; part of childhood is the ease with which you can see yourself as the future exception. So many American men spend some portion of their youth aspiring to be major leaguers, making the stories that become the biographies of real major leaguers the few completed drafts of narratives begun by countless boys contemplating how the world will look back on them when they are a Phillie, a Brave, or a Detroit Tiger.

Among those whom I envisioned someday testifying to my ten-year-old promise was a high school athlete named Bambi, who'd one day let me join the big kids on the schoolyard infield as he hit them ground balls for fielding practice. I made play after play on harder and harder-struck balls until Bambi began hitting only to me, trying to make me miss. I didn't miss. Suddenly he stopped and alerted the entire schoolyard to what was happening, calling out, "Hey! Hey! Look at this little kid! Look!" and then they were all watching as I became a seine net, floating before every ball, allowing none to avoid capture. Another afternoon, during a summer softball game at Erich's Day Camp, the camp director, Mr. Brown, passed by the ball field just as I, on a dead run from shortstop, crossed to the second base side of the bag to stab a grounder, transfer, and throw out the runner at first. Mr. Brown looked out at me and said, "Nicky, that's as good a play as I've ever seen made on this field." I replied, "You should've seen the one I made yesterday." I meant that the historiography needed to be accurate, that he should know the truth, that the pop fly I'd caught from shortstop all the way out near the small basketball court in left field after the softball fell through a tree had caused me much more difficulty, but before I could launch into a full corrective, Mr. Brown gave me a funny look and resumed walking.

One summer, my cousin Jody came to New Haven to join me at day camp. For two weeks he would be the one to sleep on my floor next to my bed. Our counselor that fifth grade year was a tall, dark, splay-legged man named Frank who had a little Broadway Joe about him with his mod tumble of black curls, mustache, Bermuda shorts, and pair of old white step-in loafers that he always wore without socks. Frank was a man of spontaneous actions, and I could tell that he thought it was good to be up for anything. Because around him I was, he seemed especially to enjoy doing things with me. When he proposed going for a trek out across the island toward the haunted house or cliff diving off the high rocks at the far end of the long beach, sometimes only the two of us went. Frank had once been such a promising young catcher that he told me he was approached by the San Francisco Giants. He still carried the scout's business card, which he showed me. During the school year, Frank was the coach of the varsity baseball team at the public high school in my part of New Haven. At Erich's Day Camp he paid a lot of attention to our softball games. One day Frank brought in some baseballs and announced a camp-wide contest to determine the camper who could hit and throw the farthest. First, on the diamond, I hit one off a center field tree, and then, down on the beach, my peg made the farthest mark in the sand. Frank then added a third element of competition, a pitching accuracy contest, open only to me and the kid whose throw had gone second farthest. Frank would umpire. I hummed one in. "Ball!" cried Frank. Then the other kid wound and threw. "Strike!" cried Frank and awarded the other kid the baseball.

Frank took an increasing interest in me after that contest, and his way of doing so was to tweak me about my fielding errors, to act loudly unimpressed by anything I did well, even critiquing how much Beefaroni I ate at lunch, telling other kids I'd be three hundred pounds at thirty if I kept up eating so much. This all seemed to be his way of urging me to improve myself, and I went along with it. He even came to one of my Little League games. No man had ever come to watch me play before.

But after a while, all the attention from Frank began to make me feel like it was hard to breathe. It got so oppressive that I confided in my cousin how much I hated it. Jody also liked to play shortstop. Cousinhood, said Tolstoy, is a dangerous neighborhood. The next day Frank came up to me and said that he understood that I hated him. I was horrified, couldn't speak. It was okay if I felt that way, Frank continued, but he wanted me to know how much he still liked me. Numb, I just nodded. Later I asked my cousin why he'd done this to me. "We were talking and it just came out," he said. Then he added, "I wanted to help you." It felt as though in one day I'd lost both of them.

In the aftermath I believed what had happened could have been avoided, that there would have been no problem if I hadn't complained. I was increasingly attuned to what authority figures wanted of me, my wish to be responsive far exceeding anything else. I was no sycophant, but I never crossed any of them, no matter what. I didn't have it worked out why I was so committed to pleasing everybody. I notice now that the stranger my father grew, the more bewildered and powerless I felt in the world, to which my impulse was to try as hard as I could to mollify any potentially unsettling forces around me, making myself impervious to them by being attentive to what would smooth all roads. Back then there was the vague, pressing feeling that if I left the straight and narrow, I risked more than what anybody else would.

The fall of 1973 had begun what was to be the last year of Worthington Hooker kickball. Down by the highway exit, the new East Rock Community School was nearing completion, and kids from all the local school districts would go there. I was now almost eleven, a fifth grader, and had been looking forward to what I imagined as the lordly feeling of being a Worthington Hooker sixth grader, to enjoying the run of the place, savoring the admiration of the young, the confidence of authority, and maybe even acquiring a real nickname. We all wanted one. "Call me Red from now on," Vogel told me one day. Ballplayers and boys in adventure stories always had nicknames.

The one looming change spurred many changes. I'd arrive in the schoolyard with my fielder's glove to discover spray paint on those previously sacrosanct red-brick walls. Somebody lit the trash bin on fire, and local stores began to put up signs warning about the consequences of shoplifting. For the first time my mother locked our car door after parking for the evening. People just passing through our neighborhood didn't think to do that. Standing next to a car one day, a kid tried to get me to rob it. The car was a tannish green sedan, American-made. Looking through the window, on the back seat I could see books, papers, clothing, and a fresh can of white Spalding tennis balls. "The door's unlocked," he suggested. "You could get those tennis balls easy." I looked inside. The thought of it had an intimate appeal. It was as though I was about to enter someone else's life for a moment without his knowing.

"You do it if you want them so much," I said.

"Just take them, Nicky. It's easy."

"Why don't you take them if it's so easy?"

"Because I want you to."

"But why does it matter to you what I do?"

"It just does. Come on." The voice was pleading now, but there wasn't ever any question.

Walking along Livingston Street with my good friend Brad not long after he'd confided in me that he, like every boy at Worthington Hooker, thought strawberry blond Nellie was a fox, Nellie glided by on the opposite side of the street. "Hey, Brad," I told him, "there goes your girlfriend!"—which inspired him to take my hockey stick and sail it into the middle of Livingston Street; which caused me to give him a shove; which led him to grab me around the throat and throw me down; which led to an astonishing event. A yellow Volkswagen screeched to a halt next to my hockey stick. The Volkswagen's door flew open, a man got out and ran toward us yelling that he was an off-duty policeman and we'd better break it up right now. We were instructed to keep out of fights in the future or we'd be getting ourselves into a lot of trouble. I gaped at my savior. He was telling me how to stay on the lighted path.

One weekend that same year, Mom, Sally, and I went to spend a day in Hamden, where a favorite colleague of my mother's lived. The colleague had a son named Ricky who was three years older than I and an ice hockey player. Hamden was a big hockey town. Everywhere you went in Hamden you saw kids wearing jackets with crossed sticks patches and their names embroidered at the breast. When we arrived, Ricky told me that I was needed for a street hockey game he and his friends were getting up nearby against a group of boys from another neighborhood. We walked to a playground where the members of the other team were shooting

around as they waited for us. All of them were teenaged meso-
morphs, big mothers with lots of biceps and acne, except for the kid
I was assigned to cover, a chesty little guy for whom the score didn't
seem to matter. He was in it for agitation, poking at me with his
stick, ragging and chipping, filling every interaction with accumulating tension. I had listened to Marv Albert call enough New York
Rangers games on my transistor to know what "Gentleman" Jean
Ratelle, the classy Rangers center, would do. Ratelle had recently
been presented the Lady Byng Trophy, awarded annually to the
most sportsmanlike player of the year, precisely because he could
disregard invitations like this one. I tried to ignore and outplay the
kid, but here these were negative integers that only emboldened
him. Now he was telling me "I could beat your butt" and wanting to
know whether I agreed. Suddenly I became conscious that the
progress of these communications had been followed with interest
by all the others. The game stopped and everybody looked at me.
I felt as though I had been thrust alone into a circle of light; the
others on my team seemed now to be standing far away from me. I
had an idea of what was expected of me. I began to think my way
out of it. Was I really supposed to show up for somebody else's
hockey game and start swinging? Why would I want to fight this
kid? I wasn't even sure how to punch, whether my thumb should be
tucked inside my fingers when I made a fist or wrapped along the
knuckles. Was I trembling? Could the kid tell? What made him so
confident about challenging me? What had he detected? It would
be humiliating to lose to someone smaller. The kid, fully energized,
bouncing loose with certitude, his breath avid, inflamed, level with
my chin, told me he would make me swallow my teeth unless I
admitted that he was tougher. Well, wasn't he? Choosing my words,
I said, "I guess so if you say so."

A low, sickly groan traveled behind me and the day seemed to
hang its head and fall away. Whooping with scorn, the kid turned to
his teammates, who welcomed him back to their ranks, patting and
congratulating him as though he'd scored his tenth goal of the day.
The one thing worse than finding out that you are scared is seeing

that others know it too. Ricky and his friends were looking at the ground, flicking at pebbles with their stick blades. The game started up again, but halfheartedly—the score was no longer of interest. On the walk home, the others on my team all avoided me, keeping ahead, talking with one another in low tones, except for Ricky, who kept shaking his head, repeating the fatal words every few blocks until I finally burst out, "But what was I supposed to do?" Ricky stared at me so flushed with outrage it took him a long moment to get control before finally, in a spasm of affliction, he cried, "But we were all there right behind you." Up ahead there was a curse and somebody battered his hockey stick on the sidewalk. I had disgraced them.

Walking down Livingston Street, I saw two flaxen-blond heads crawling out from under a front porch. It was a boy and a girl who lived on the block. Grime smeared their faces and clothes, and spiderwebs clung to their hair, filmy against the whiteness. I thought they had been playing Hide-and-Go-Seek except that we hadn't played that in years, and, besides, nobody ever hid together, especially a boy and a girl. Then it occurred to me that where they had just come from was a place I knew nothing about.

One afternoon, on my way down Orange Street, eleven-year-old I came upon a pair of garbage cans at the curb beside which someone had placed a stack of *Penthouse* magazines bound neatly together with twine. There must have been a couple of years' worth. I circled around them. Yes, they were all *Penthouses*. I had no idea what a naked woman looked like and didn't have any clue what I would see if I opened the magazines except that it was what boys were supposed to aspire to see. I checked the sidewalk and the windows of the house. Nobody was watching. I took the *Penthouses*. All heated with upcoming experience, I moved from block to block. As I walked, I began to feel a strange remove in which I was aware of myself as a person to whom things were on the verge of happening. All the way home I carried the bundle of magazines, until I was climbing the steps of our house, passing through the front door, greeting my mother, and then the spell was broken. I was carrying something I should not have, and I was extending my arms as I said, "Mom, look!" Almost in the same motion, as though we were partners in a relay and it was now her baton, I handed the magazines to her and she went through the house and out the door, holding the bundles away from her slightly the way a cat owner does while walking to the trash after being presented with a dead mouse. When she came back inside, the magazines had never existed.

On a hot day Brad and I decided to go fishing out by the falls at the foot of the Lake Whitney reservoir beyond East Rock Park. We had rods and a gun-metal-blue tackle box filled with fresh- and saltwater lures and plugs between which I couldn't tell the difference, as well as red and white plastic bobbers, snell hooks, purple fake worms, and my multi-bladed red Swiss Army knife recently given to me by Tony and Susi. Brad and I were full of the optimism that has yet to be complicated by expertise; neither of us knew a thing about fishing. When we got out to the falls, I put a fake worm onto a hook and began casting. In the clear water I could see my worm; it looked very purple and very alone. Alongside us appeared a group of several kids I didn't know. Quickly they began to cast advice our way, one kid in particular. "Come over here, it's better," he said after a little while, motioning to the far side of the falls. When I followed him around, the kid began offering rapid counsel while the others drifted away. Soon I heard laughter and saw them riffling through the tackle box. Moments later they were all running off toward the park with my Swiss Army knife.

Brad and I walked back to his house where we told his father what had happened. Brad's dad was a Yale professor, and, while not a large man, he had a blunt mustache and, I now saw, a decisiveness to match. "Brad and Nicky, get in the car," his father said. We drove out to the reservoir, turned onto the park road in the direction the kids had been taking when we'd last seen them, and began to retrace their route. The road circled the base of East Rock with wooded escarpment on both sides. Not many people walked around here; it would have been hard for anyone to miss the kids if they'd continued in this direction. Which they had. Every time we came upon someone, Brad's father would stop the car and we'd describe the kids and they'd nod and point down the road. Brad and I were getting very excited. We knew we were on to them. The road wound around and finally emptied into a dead-end huddle of houses on Cedar Hill. Brad's father kept up the procedure and soon enough we had a name and an address. Then we three were walking up the front steps of a weather-beaten white house and knocking on the door. With Brad's father beside me I felt expansible in my righteousness. The kid who'd been advising us about fishing opened the door. "You want your knife," he said to Brad's father, as though he had been waiting for us. He disappeared from the door, returned a moment later, and wordlessly handed it back to me. The knife had been out of my hands for no more than an hour.

The last time people had been looking for something they'd lost around East Rock, it was for a little girl, and they had been too late. The difference, as I saw it, was Brad's father, how quickly he'd mastered the situation, how calmly he'd decided on the best course of action and proceeded. I'd always liked him; now I liked him more. I hoped he liked me, wanted him to.

Another day Brad's father got out a baseball and bat and took Brad and me into East Rock Park for some fielding work. He hit us grounders and we did our best to stop them. On lawn littered with divots, stones, roots, bark, Johnson grass, and fallen branches I acquitted myself well enough that Brad's father said, "Nicky, if you can make those plays here you can make them anywhere." He did not say such kind words to Brad, never talked that way to Brad around me. Later I wondered if it bothered Brad how well I got along with his dad.

Visiting my father in New York, at times we took the bus instead of the subway, and once, on our way up Madison Avenue, an older woman boarded and came walking down the aisle. Her hands were filled with shopping bags, so I stood up and offered her my seat.

When I looked over at my father, his face was vibrating with rage. "You didn't have to do that," he hissed, and then he refused to speak to me for the rest of the ride.

We were probably on the way from a visit to my grandmother's. My grandmother was unfailingly pleased when Sally and I came over with our father, sitting everybody down and fussing over the three of us, feeding us carrot sticks and black olives and Jarlsberg cheese, artichoke hearts, and ginger ale or Sacramento tomato juice, and then, at dinner, looking out from her place at the head of the table to announce how "glad" she was "that the family is together." My father would glare or make a noise in the back of his throat when she said that, and she'd refuse to notice, would steadfastly go on in jaunty tones, describing how "wonderful" it all was. He was the only person I knew who didn't seem to think well of her. It was like encountering someone who hated the smell of a bakery.

I don't know when I realized that she had become my father's primary source of income. Eventually, when he took me to Polk's hobby shop to buy me a model Tiger tank or a Big Bertha rocket kit for my birthday, I understood that my grandmother was paying for them, just as I knew that the same must have been true about Bermuda and when he brought us to a Connecticut inn for a lakeside summer vacation. He also had a girlfriend named Lois along for that trip, and they spent a lot of time behind a closed door. Between ourselves, Sally and I referred to her as Lo-down Lo.

Another time we borrowed his friend's home in Rockville Centre, Long Island, while the friend was away. My father took us to a movie with lots of violence and killing in it and then slept most of the next day while Sally and I watched television. Had we been with my mother, I would have been jubilant at these activities. Here it concerned me that my father was doing the wrong thing, and I had the impulse to let him know about it, to tell him how to be with us, just as I did when the friend came home and we went out to dinner at a restaurant with him and his kids. The check came, and the friend picked it up. My father loudly insisted on contributing his share. I watched as he put five dollars on the table.

What was going on with him? I'd wonder and then I'd try not to wonder. He'd become a paunchy, middle-aged white man in disheveled clothing—and very strange. All my mother ever said was "It's important for you to have a relationship with your father." So when he did odd things, I just tried to look away and ignore it all and pretend I'd seen nothing until I could go home. By then I was no longer talking with anyone in New Haven about my father.

One day at school, I did take up the matter obliquely with my baseball friend T.J., telling him how much I hated going to New York. T.J. wore a plastic hair pick that rose out of his afro like a stick in the garden with a seed packet on top. He had a reputation for fearlessness and for being a good fighter—for "going off" on people. Now a look of anxiety crossed T.J.'s face. He said he'd been to New York himself. Rapidly nodding his head up and down and widening his eyes, he told me, "Nicky, it's different down there. New York is different. They do not fuck around in New York and they will fuck you up." That he was frightened too was such a relief to me I wanted to hug him for saying it.

In 1974, before my sixth grade year when I was eleven, my mother brought me to Fenway Park in Boston to watch Dick Drago pitch for the Red Sox against young left-handed Andy Hassler and the California Angels. The Red Sox were thrashed 12–1 that day and earned it. The regular catcher Carlton Fisk was not in the lineup, replaced by Bob Montgomery. While speedy Angels such as outfielder Mickey Rivers went flickering around the bases like moths, Montgomery plodded so slowly that I was chastened for the Red Sox. We left the game early because we were expected at my grandparents' in Cambridge for dinner, and I didn't object. My grandfather was unwell and Hassler, a tall, rangy Texan, was dominating the game. He was that rare baseball commodity, a large and talented left-hander, who was expected to emerge as one of the league's best pitchers. His performance that day must only have made people more certain that he would become a great star. Baseball has a long,

162-game season, and this was only one date on the schedule, but because it was the lone Red Sox game I'd been to, it achieved a significance. They were losers.

At our new school, Brad and his friend Simon began to have it in for me. It began with nicknames, "Pricky Dawidick," "Dicky Dickedoff," "Jack Dawidoff." Ridicule of me seemed to electrify them. Every day they worked up a new means of torment, for the way I dressed, for whatever I said in class, taking ravening pleasure when others, encouraged, joined in. If they discovered that a dog had pissed in the schoolyard, they rolled a tennis ball through the puddle, picked it up and threw it at me. Even when they weren't around I felt them in league, out there plotting. During homeroom one day, the door opened and something was tossed inside. Simon's leering face flashed by the closing door as whatever it was arced through the air, fell on the classroom floor, and the door snapped shut. The thing lay there like an unexploded shell. Everyone looked at it. I sank in my seat. The desk of a girl named Cindy was closest. Getting up, Cindy frowned as she walked over to the object and bent down. She was the last person in that classroom any prepubescent boy would have hoped for sympathy from; she seemed to hold it against us that she had grown large early and towered over everyone else. Disgust now covered the part of her face that wasn't hidden behind a hood of bangs as she held up in her hand the most obscene and terrible object I had ever seen. It was underpants with no pants, only a crotch. Worse, the crotch was spread with a wide urine-yellow stain. Cindy announced, "This is yours, Nicky." My name sounded degenerate to me as she said it. She walked over to hand the thing to me. I shrank away, but she pressed it on me. The yellow on the crotch was obviously Magic Marker. Across the waistband they had written my name in black ink. Everyone was staring at me. "No, it's not mine," I said. I got up, went to the trash can, and threw the jockstrap away.

One morning at the breakfast table, I looked at my foggy glass half full of orange juice and thought, These are the times that people tell you you will look back on and laugh about one day, but I know I never will.

It did not occur to me to seek revenge. Instead, I devoted a lot of time to trying to understand what I had done to anger Brad and Simon. It wasn't simply that I was unaware of the time-honored male code—a boy doesn't have to win, but he has to fight—it was that, more than ever, I believed I had to remain in full control or far worse would happen. Always, I saw enormous risks, the event of worse, future possibilities I couldn't handle. This I could handle.

On an afternoon when I was out biking with Foltz, my closest friend that year, I rode off the sidewalk into Edwards Street, and then behind me I heard a thud, the sound of something falling and a cry. A car had hit him. A few bad bruises were the extent of his injuries, and soon Foltz was all right. But where had that car come from? I'd looked both ways and had seen only a clear street. It was my fault. But how could I have known? The world felt ever more full of unpredictable sources of harm.

I did not tell Sally about Brad, and I never knew until years later that during those months he and Simon were tormenting me every day, some girls in her class, one of them Brad's sister, were giving my sister a very hard time. I remember breakfast then at our round table, both of us silent as we ate, neither aware of what the other was going through.

At home at night, I reread my favorite books, the pages turned so many different times, they slowly disintegrated, the bindings collapsing, losing their grip, releasing the yellowed, crumbling paper. One of those books was *My Turn at Bat,* Ted Williams's autobiography, a small volume that seemed somehow to have absorbed the sensations of my own life; more than any other ballplayer's story, this one felt like mine. I liked to hear about Williams's big home runs, his feuds with sportswriters, and how, after the game, he would head off by himself, find a movie theater and watch two or three Westerns alone, and then go have milk shakes—two or three of those too. But what I liked best was the way the book had seemed

to grow with me, remaining so responsive to my developing preoccupations that it all combined indissolubly with my existence. That
Williams had endured a messy and troubled boyhood in San Diego
was to me a great consolation. Growing up, he lived in a shabby
bungalow filled with busted furniture, and rarely saw either his
father or his mother; the two eventually divorced. His brother was
always in trouble with the law. At my age, twelve, Williams was finding refuge from loneliness and shame about his family in baseball
games at the local North Park playground where he was always the
first to arrive and the last to leave. He tried to share other kids'
dads, drove himself furiously, cried a lot. All of it later made him
both moral and flawed, a frantically motivated self-made man who
decribed himself as "all bottled-up," both exuberant and enraged,
sulky, high-strung, and persecuted—and honest about all of it,
frank even about his problems getting to know girls, his sense that
other people disliked him, and his envy of Red Sox teammate
Bobby Doerr's closeness to his father. He said he hated the
Yankees, and also hated New York, thought the city was an ugly and
inhuman place. I loved that voice of his, how intimate and masculine and older it sounded, a heroic man talking to me in a way that
was affectionate and tough, had high standards, but was there for
me in my struggle to meet them. Williams's story was moving in its
sadness, a person living such a magnificent life who had to try so
hard to enjoy it. I felt grateful to him and nostalgic for his times as a
player, for times I had never lived in. Maybe I kept reading about
Williams because I couldn't do what I really wanted, which was to
watch him play, and then be with him, have him tell me more stories, tell me that it would be all right in the end for me, that he was
there for me and why don't we clear out of this little room, Nicky
Boy, and go catch a couple of cowboy movies together. Three milk
shakes after.

Another book I read over and over was *My Ántonia*. The main
character was named Jim Burden, an orphaned boy from the East
who was brought up by his grandparents on their farm in Nebraska.

After he finished high school, Jim found himself filled with great, conflicted feelings about his duty to head back East and go places in the world, and his yearning to remain forever on the wide, grassy Nebraska prairie where under the huge skies there were houses filled with beautiful Bohemian and Scandinavian girls named Tiny, Lena, and especially Ántonia, whose eyes were large and full of light, whose feelings outran language. When you danced with Ántonia, each step was a new adventure, a fresh outlook. On the wall of my room there was a map of the country, and looking up from *My Ántonia* I wanted more than anything to go to Nebraska, where there were beautiful Bohemian girls and Wahoo Sam, a place a person wanted to be from, a place with no Brad and Simon.

And yet, though I hated some of what had become of my life, I also wanted to stay right where I was and endure it. It was my life as it was supposed to be. All that sixth grade winter I walked to school closing my eyes for long seconds to squeeze away the threat of tears on my eyelashes, waiting to get back to kilter, waiting, as it turned out, until April, when the baseball season began.

With a glove or bat in my hand I felt free and powerful. The physical actions particular to the game appealed to my limbs, the binary torsion of hips and shoulders unfurling into perfect geometries: a low line drive, a strong throw from the shortstop hole. They were motions you could refine, make distinctly yours, and that I *was* my swing had powerful resonance to me. I spent hours improving it, adjusting my rear elbow, the placement of my feet, the tilt of my chin, how high I held my hands before at last engaging my wrists— all the while thinking of Ted Williams, who told in his autobiography of doing the same thing, even in hotel rooms where, late one night working in front of a hotel mirror with a bat in his hand, he miscalculated and connected with his sleeping roommate's bedpost, taking the roommate, in effect, deep.

That spring in Little League, on the day of my games I'd lie in bed watching for the morning play of sunlight creeping across the wall from behind the shade to tell me there was no rain. Even on

rainy days I always believed we had sufficient light to play. The year
before I had been treated as a Little League liability all the way up
until my team's final game of the season when my coach told me I
was pitching and I nearly threw a no-hitter.

I thought baseball would always be that way, a progression of
expectations where first you only aspired to make the team. Once
you'd accomplished that, you wanted to receive a starting position,
and then, secure in the lineup, you hoped to bat third, be a star.
This was a year all that came true. I hit third, batting .500 while
pitching and playing infield for Latella Carting—The Garbagemen,
as the *New Haven Register* referred to us when they wrote up our
games. On the field, between white chalk lines, within boundaries
of logic and order, aggression was my natural state. The day burly
Mark Perez and I hit consecutive homers, our whole team was
elated, all of us embracing as the beaming Perez yelled "Back to
back" at me and pounded my arms. As I walked home up Willow
Street, the whole sidewalk looked different; even the chemical
whiff outside Edward's Cleaners smelled pretty close to perfect
after you went four-for-four. At school all the best players began to
talk shop with me, including the dominating Munson Auto Body
pitcher "Mutsy" Anderson, who, like a lot of other black guys, came
to school with one of his pant legs rolled up close to his knee expos-
ing the borax whiteness of his tube sock. Fashion had begun to
interest me. "Hey, Muts, why do you do that with your pants?" I
asked him.

"I don't know," he said.

"Muts," I said, "it's because you want everyone to see how good
your sock is, right?" That was it and he blushed. The year before he
had been divinity to me.

At the end of the season I was selected for the league All-Star
team, and then also, when an All-City roster of players was chosen
from New Haven's four baseball leagues to play in the annual East–
West Game, for the first time I heard my name announced over a
PA system, leading off and playing second base for the East under
the lights before a huge twilight crowd at Blake Field. Walking to

the plate to begin the game was all that I could have asked out of life. If I was a good enough person, I believed, these were the things that would keep happening to me until someday I would become a great ballplayer and therefore a great man. There would be many more tribulations and, as in the books, they would be overcome. My belief in the hard skin of self-determination had become complete.

Somewhere in those years between 1972 and 1974, I began switching from being a fan of the Mets to the Red Sox. I don't know when this happened or how the decision evolved, only that somehow it did. I was giving up a long-standing cause, and I wasn't proud of that. I did my best not to notice that I was abandoning the Mets. But looking back, I realize that it was not the Mets or the Red Sox, those objects of my affections, that truly mattered, but rather the desire to feel affection, the intense childhood longing to be close to something. So instead of thinking about or admitting what I was doing, it was easier just to drift away from my New York team and quietly migrate to Boston—which I associated with my grandfather. I began to love the Red Sox because I just couldn't love the Mets anymore.

And so in October 1975, during a visit to Croton, Jody and I sat in Susi and Tony's bedroom watching on television the Red Sox play the Cincinnati Reds in the World Series, I pulling for the Red Sox with everything I had. I remember all the Red Sox players from that time, and, for some reason, recall many of them with avian characteristics: the magnificent rookie center fielder Fred Lynn, whose left-handed swing had a quality of motion (I thought of tacking swallows) that seemed more graceful than those who batted from the other side (I tried replicating it right-handed in Susi's floor-length mirror—it could not be done); the Red Sox shortstop Rick Burleson, known to his teammates as "Rooster," who pursued ground balls as though he intended to impede their progress hen-like, by descending on top of them; the tall, slender catcher Carlton Fisk, a proud eagle of a man from a small New Hampshire town;

and pitcher Luis Tiant, the ebullient Cuban who seemed to be starting every World Series game, and in each of them throwing hundreds of pitches, all delivered with a complicated terpsichorean prelude of bobbing plumage and cantilevered tail feathers; on one leg, with his bearded head swiveled and tucked, he was a flamingo. I also remember how it felt when they did magnificent things, most especially Fisk, whose game-winning home run in the twelfth inning of Game Six, a veering clout he willed safely off the foul pole with ardent waves of both arms, little bounding two-footed jumps and then an ecstatic leap. Watching him in full semaphore made you sure that, if you cared enough, you too really could make the world the way you wanted it.

Except that he couldn't and neither could you. The Red Sox lost the Series the next day when, with the game tied in the ninth, manager Darrell Johnson brought in a rookie relief pitcher with the melancholy name of Burton to replace sturdy Jim Willoughby. I was still imploring Johnson to reconsider, to go with a more senior reliever, when Reds second baseman Joe Morgan flicked a short single over the infield, scoring Pete Rose, so that when I later read Roger Angell's account in my mother's *New Yorker* of a November scene in a quiet Boston bar featuring an elderly man who looks down into the depths of his drink and mumbles "we never should have taken out Willoughby," I heard my own inconsolable self.

Or did any of it happen that way to me? It was Fisk himself who many years later said that he had never once watched film footage of his famous home run and never would because memory is so delicate, so easily stripped or altered, and film is such a powerful usurper of truth. Ordinarily I would have felt the same way as Fisk did about retaining the integrity of my own experience. But something had come over me, and I wanted more from those events, wanted them to matter enormously, to have lasting symbolic force. And so into my own memory I welcomed the perceptions of Roger Angell and all other infiltrators, waved and jumped and leaped into great personal moment all the tragic details I could collect of those games, from Ed Armbrister's crucial uncalled interference with

Fisk on a bunt play to the hegiric flight of Tony Perez's home run off Bill Lee's "Leephus" slowball, willing into truth the larger distortion, which was this: in October 1975, at age twelve, I was a lifelong, long-suffering Red Sox fan. As for the Mets, they had never meant a thing to me. How could they have? Being good meant remaining loyal and true to those who were close to you—especially when they were down.

CHAPTER EIGHT

Parade's End

One evening in early 1976, when I was thirteen, the telephone rang on the wall behind me while we were eating dinner. It was Dad on the line. He always asked how I was, how school was going. That year there was plenty to tell. I had begun attending, on the full scholarship given to faculty children, a private school up on a hill across town, and I liked it. My classes had the grave weight of subjects long studied—Latin, geology, and Shakespeare—and I played sports that also had classical rigor, first football and now wrestling. Always I made the team and was its smallest member. After classes, athletics, lunch, and then more classes, at the end of the afternoon a history teacher led a model-building club. He was an elbow-patch and vinegar sort of man, brimming with imperatives about making boys into men and famous for his sesquipedalian vocabulary and his signature methods, such as flunking students on their early assignments on the theory that it would create a sense of urgency about learning. This late in the day, though, with his Oxford-cloth sleeves rolled to his elbows, he was more easygoing. "Take your time," he told us as he applied sand-colored paint to an Afrika Korps armored car. "I've been working on this one for a year." There were many nice kids at that school who invited me to birthday parties, bar mitzvahs, beach clubs, and to visit them on weekends at homes spread in all directions around the city. When I developed an early reputation for unreadable handwriting, one of them presented me with a pen he said would cure it. I had the feeling that I'd stepped into a fresh chapter of my life.

After a couple of minutes I handed the telephone receiver over to Sally and returned to my meal. Sally also went to a new school, and she had never seemed in better spirits. During those rare afternoons when we were both at home in our rooms, a lot of fun seemed to be going on behind her closed door, especially when her friends, tall Carey with the brown pageboy hair, and Sarah, whose last name sounded to me like "dress-up," were visiting. They both were very pretty in a lanky, foal-like way and I began to look forward to their passage through my room. I was rarely allowed in Sally's room. Gradually it occurred to me that I went through my childhood scarcely knowing the sister who slept just on the other side of the wall, that there was so much going on in the world I didn't know about even though it was all happening right there in front of me, that I knew nothing of my times, and I'd wonder why that was, for I thought of myself as an inquisitive person.

Now Sally was mentioning to Dad that she'd just had a bad day. "You come by that naturally," he told her. Sally hung the phone up on the wall, looped past me back around the table, and sat down. "Dad says he's mentally ill," she announced. My mind filled with images of horrible things going on inside the skull, a miasma of wet, rusted infrastructure, malarial fluids, disconnected wires and faulty parts, bats winging around. Nobody talked about mental illness then. I didn't know what mental illness was. But I knew what it meant. I can't remember any more of that evening at all, but my mother says that at this disclosure my whole body went slack before collapsing like a washed-out bridge—"You cried and cried for months."

After my parents divorced in 1966, there had never been a conversation about why our family was breaking up. You cannot do that with a three-year-old and a one-year-old, and by the time we were older, it was too late, the moment had passed. My mother's decision was to look forward, pouring all of her resources into making our new lives as happy as possible. Now we did the same thing, tried to believe the phone call had never happened, didn't pursue it.

On one level, that wasn't so difficult, because my father never again made any mention of his problems, and no one else in my family talked about them to me either. My mother never discussed any of it with us because her sense of justice made her believe that she shouldn't say anything against her ex-husband to his children. Here was the rare instance where she was unsure of how to handle a situation. She felt sorry for him, didn't want him to be cut off from his kids, and she also feared what he might do if she refused to let us go to New York and see him. There was a legal agreement, and he was a lawyer demanding his rights who she thought wouldn't hesitate to go to court to get them. She imagined an unfolding disaster. His family would then support him, putting us against relatives we loved. That he was ill intimidated her; how do you deal with an ex-husband who nobody thinks can control himself? She always insisted that we have our visits with him even when I didn't want to go, telling me many years later, "I was thinking more of him than of you because he was so sick."

For most of growing up, I had no idea what she and all the other adults knew, that after proceeding through high school as a Long Island rendition of the All-American boy—intelligent, handsome, musical, athletic; the avatar of his immigrant family's dreams—as a Harvard junior he'd begun to see everywhere around him huge faces with green ears. The creatures told him to give away all his possessions and he did, right down to his graduation watch. I met one of his college classmates years later who told me, "I knew your father then. I didn't understand what he was talking about, and he didn't understand what he was talking about. He was nuts." Later, there was another massive breakdown at Harvard Law School. Again he pulled himself together, completed law school at Yale, came to New York, and seemed to be enjoying life, buying art, paying my mother's grad school tuition, until he was let go from his job. Then on to Washington where he made it those few more years until becoming more violently unhinged than ever.

The past unremembered figures so much in your life, has such bearing on your existence, that it has an inevitable way of asserting itself even if you don't want to know about it. Occasionally I over-heard a relative making behind-the-hand references to "Donald" being "in the hospital again," and before I could hurry something else into my mind, I'd be imagining him on the island of the yellow buildings in the river below the Triborough Bridge, which by now I knew were wards for the insane. Behind one of the barred windows I saw my father strapped down, staggered bands of light flickering and dilating across his face. Or I saw him standing high up there in his sallow tower, framed by light and bars, visible to all, staring out at the cars on the roadway, staring at me as I rolled past in the red Dodge on my way to see my grandmother and not him, his haggard, stricken mouth agape, his thin-wristed hands with their copious black hairs clenching the iron shafts the way the chimps had those times we went to the Washington zoo together. I heard him calling out to me.

No doctor ever knew how to help him, nobody knew what to do, how even to talk about "Donald's troubles." All was inscrutable, a futile mystery, and yet now this new vivid knowledge of him from the telephone overwhelmed me. Through all these years I'd known that once we'd been a family like any other, until something awful happened in Washington. As I'd grown older, for many years I had felt myself in the presence of crucial information that would explain what had transformed my father, a cuneiform truth hovering right there in front of me that left me both curious and also glad for my ignorance, aware that there were things out there in the world I would be unhappy to know about. Now that the curiosity had been fulfilled I felt scalded by it, right to have been wary. That I had such a dad was so shocking and upsetting and also shameful that I shoved all the implications out of my head. I wanted no part of this knowl-edge, didn't want to come from that, and definitely didn't want to think that it might one day be me. Better not to know, to carry on, seem normal, appear to be a person who wasn't sick, wasn't going to get sick. I fled.

My new school had been founded as a Latin grammar school in 1660, "For the Breeding Up of Hopeful Youths," according to its benefactor, a Colonial governor, and only in the past three years since the merger with my mother's school were female youths welcome on the hilltop. It was still mostly men drinking coffee in the wood-paneled faculty lounge, and boys dominated the enrollment in each of the six junior high and high school grades. The place rippled with physicality, achieved its ligature from the assertion of muscle and strength.

On the first day of seventh grade, a tall, lanky eighth grader shoved a seventh grader named Stanley into a row of lockers. Stanley was good-looking, had lustrous ebony skin, but what it covered was a lethal sureness of purpose that galvanized so quickly that Stanley became a blur of recovered balance as he spun and came slashing back at the eighth grader, inflicting blows before other eighth graders could pull him away, the boy more startled than injured, protesting as he backed off that what he had done was his right as an eighth grader, Stanley shouting, telling him, "I don't care what you are. Do not ever fuck with me again." Other eighth graders milled around in confusion like ants whose hill had been disturbed—they had been waiting a long year for this day. All of us seventh graders who looked on must have been aware that the eighth grader had chosen the wrong man, that Stanley was way ahead of all of us.

I was never close to Stanley. Instead I watched him then from a distance, wishing that I could somehow still be myself and yet be like him. I can see him ambling around the old brick campus, sometimes breaking into a lope or a curvet, but never a full sprint, for, although he was fastest among us, the point was not to show it. There was a certain coldness about him that could seem aloof, even insolent, yet it meant that when he decided to be amiable it disarmed people. One delightful female teacher used to become so slack-jawed and adoring in his presence she'd coo, "Oh, Stanley," when he offered just about anything in class, the rest of us shifting in our seats as he grinned that mirthless smile of his. Yet he was never vindictive, was often genial to a subaltern, had the ability to make you feel special, chosen, even when he was only involving you in connivance. He was powerful in that he made others powerless without trying to; he didn't recruit or advertise, he didn't ask—he didn't need to. Stanley's presence alone made kids fall in line. By the time we were juniors he captained the basketball team and if I encountered him working alone at a basket in the school's gym, he always accepted my challenges for a game of one-on-one, chortling from the back of his throat as his shots poured through the rim like milk into a glass. He discussed sporting matters with great serious-ness and was willing to be teased, to a point, especially about his farts, which were legendarily plangent and could clear a room. Once, as we encountered each other on a walkway, an inspiration came into my head and I greeted him "Gassius Clay!" At the same time we both saw that I'd crossed a line. I had only a moment to wonder what would happen before the fist thudded hard into my shoulder. Then he nodded once and strode wordlessly away leaving me with my numb arm to marvel at that decisive ability to assess. The kids who were masters of that time in life were the ones who seemed nonchalant about experiences the rest of us couldn't yet conceive ourselves having. They knew what to do.

Stanley was probably first in our class to have a girlfriend. She wore Tretorns, a white canvas tennis sneaker with a trademark blue, V-like emblem on the side. Tretorns, along with clogs, were the exclusive footwear of the pretty girls in that school, and I was so shy about all girls that it took only the distinctive, hollow, horseshoe-on-cobblestone clip-clop of the advancing clog for my eyes to go to the floor. I used to wonder how the borderline types knew on which side of the divide they fell, and what might happen if a less attrac-tive girl, an aspirant, appeared in clogs or Tretorns, what delicate taxonomic balance it might disturb, whether she would be rebuked by a true member of the phylum or perhaps reclassified, but it never happened. I could be sure because in that first year when I studied the rules of grammar in three languages, I also learned from memory what every kid in my class wore on her feet.

This attention to footwear was some residue of kickball days, per-haps, though it had also become natural for me to look downward, and knowing that Dave T. came to school in Puma Baskets, Dave G.

in blue Specs track sneakers, Mark in dark blue suede Pro-Keds low-tops, Horace in compost-brown Clarks Wallabees, and Randy in Top-Sider deck shoes was a feat I accomplished effortlessly, without conscious intent. There was much, however, I failed to notice—that, for instance, you never wore white crew socks with brown or black shoes. This wisdom was passed along to me by Randy, the same Randy who showed me how to calculate my batting average, introduced me to Led Zeppelin, and who helpfully clarified that the brown Top-Siders I had on over my white socks were actually Docksider knock-offs, not the authentic Sperry. That fashion relied on a system of inflexible canons was his point, and I was receptive, was all for orderly systems. When I raised my eyes, I took in everywhere around me Lacoste sport shirts with their trademark alligator lying in wait at the breast. I too wanted to walk with reptiles. For the first time ever, from my grandmother I requested garments for my birthday—asked for and received two Lacoste shirts, a blue and green rugby-striped long-sleeved model and a second long-sleeved solid red one. On the evening of my birthday party, when my guests assembled at our house to be taken out for a movie at the Strand, I brought the earlier arrivals into my bedroom, pulled open my dresser drawer and proudly displayed my acquisitions. I was beginning to relate how I'd picked them out myself in New York, with my grandmother, when I noticed the blank, quizzical looks on male faces taking in a boy who still played Show-and-Tell—and with his clothes. I shoved the shirts back in the drawer, having achieved exactly what I was out to avoid: I was not like them.

I was old enough to go on the train with Sally to New York unescorted to see my father. Once a month on a Sunday morning we boarded the second car of the 9:00 A.M. local, took a seat on the right side, and, as the train pulled out of New Haven, I'd watch the city's roofs vanish above the track-side walls, and then look out at the crazy fencing atop the embankment, the strew of bottles, clothing, auto parts, toys, and old basinets and washing machines discarded along the frontage, wonder how it all got there, and then my city was gone and we were on our way, moving from town to town down the Connecticut shoreline. From Stamford, it was express to 125th Street and on into Grand Central Terminal, the end of the line. As we departed 125th Street and the train slid out of the morning down under the city streets for the eight-minute tunnel approach to Grand Central, I'd put away my homework, press my face to the window, the tiny tunnel lights twinkling by as I'd brace myself for what was coming.

I never knew which Dad would be meeting us. He was almost always punctual, but sometimes there'd be a weird defective look in his eye, a tremor in his hands, a bandage over an injury. A couple of days his glasses were broken. I'd look at his large head in a phrenological way, searching for clues so as to assess his mood. They fluctuated through various forms of turbulence: often he was sullen, restive, or agitated, either way an unpromising sign. My goal—it quickly became a policy—was to have my nerves sheathed in distanced calm by the time I reached the information booth, took his hand, and said, "Hi, Dad." We always met at the information booth, though there were days when he was so up for it, so eager to begin the visit, that he was waiting at the gate grinning a wide grin, and my shoulders would drop at the sight of him there so happy to see me that he was depriving me of those extra seconds I relied on to prepare myself for him.

His voice always sounded the same, but his speech was often not lucid, his behavior erratic. When he got into altercations with people we encountered on sidewalks or in restaurants, when he told me things I knew he shouldn't—he liked to describe new women he wanted to "lay"—when he suddenly lashed out at me, I didn't know what to do. Your father is supposed to protect you, and mine was scaring the hell out of me.

On the way to his apartment, we'd often take a route passing through Times Square where the raw neon of the peep shows and porn palaces lit up the hustlers and derelicts and shell-game barkers swarming outside on the Forty-second Street sidewalk, lit up all the disappointed faces ducking into all the lousy doorways and dives and the crappy souvlaki joints we ourselves visited once or twice. Smells hung listless, and several times I saw a single shoe abandoned on the pavement, which made me fear for its former occupant; was somebody hopping out there? Even at this hour, on this day, the sidewalks were raucous, noisy with unconcern, the stacks of Sunday papers at the corner newsstands telling about how New York was going bankrupt, telling about Son of Sam, and the murder rate, and strikes and blackouts, telling about a city in manic conflict with itself.

Even then, at its nadir, New York was still the place that drew so many people from all over America to make their way, where they played in the low-roofed streets of downtown, where everyone from back home came through at least once, because New York was the center of life in America, was, in the just-invented phrase of the time, the Big Apple. I never knew that city. To me, it was a fallen place, only to be endured, gotten over, like a case of food poisoning.

Up in my father's neighborhood, the grainy, water-stained light of late Sunday morning on Columbus Avenue seemed to weaken him; even on those days when he was abloom with enthusiasm, he couldn't sustain it for long, and the visit would droop into a lugubrious procession of dejected hours. Sometimes he'd telephone my Aunt Judy, and if he could convince her to leave her own young family and come over, he was relieved, calling his sister "Jude," as good-natured she strained to salvage the afternoon for his children.

Across one lunch table, when I was thirteen or fourteen and the Volkswagen Rabbit was a new and popular car, my father declared his intention to buy one. Thoughts of how he was going to pay for a car like that ricocheted through my head as he spoke. Somehow, he'd remained a member of both the Harvard and Yale clubs, "for business," he said, and once or twice we sat at the Harvard Club on old leather couches under stuffed animal heads, though we didn't eat anything besides the free pretzels, Ritz crackers, and orange spreading cheese. I saw the way people he greeted there had sized him up, began to edge away at the sight of him, thinking of ways to avoid an interaction. Out in public, with new people, he never spared an opportunity to mention Harvard.

He was full of a grand past and a grand future, yet undefined in his present. He did no more regular law work that I knew of, yet to all he declared he was an "attorney," maintaining that august ordinal truth through his refusal to take on any other source of income even as his sparse flophouse furnishings and shabby clothes unmistakably suggested he was on the way down. To look at him standing on a New York street corner was to confront a man with little more status in the city than his street-peddling grandfather.

By now I knew about many stories of squandered youthful promise, but I never thought of my father that way. In Hemingway or Faulkner the failures were romantic, had the ache of beautiful demise. My father's was a story nobody wanted to tell. The situation remained so troubling for all concerned that, out of his presence, members of my father's family hardly ever introduced me to another person as Donald's son. To those who met me with my grandmother and asked her whose child I was, she always first ignored the question, capitulating only when pressed. I was the same. When I did have to admit that Donald was my father, I felt expression drain from my face.

With him in New York, there were many meals at a local Chinese restaurant called the Cherry, where no cherries were on the menu, or anything else sweet or fresh. We ate greasy fried rice scattered with red, fat-veined cubes of pork and bowls of wonton soup the temperature of standing water. My father came there frequently, he said, which burned at me as an injustice. Why should he dine out while my mother, counting pennies in New Haven, had never been to Blessings to eat Chinese food, had never been to Louis' Lunch to try a hamburger? All I was capable of doing then was begrudging him. A long time later it occurred to me that at this place where he claimed to be a regular, nobody on the staff ever seemed to recognize him.

I didn't ask him how he was going to pay for the Rabbit, didn't let him see me flinch when he said he was soon going to open up a savings account for our college education. I just nodded and said, "That's good, Dad." I sought never to say anything provocative. When I was talking with other people in a room where he was, I tried not to look as though I was enjoying myself too much, so he wouldn't feel bad that I never looked like that anymore talking with him. He prickled with sensitivity, and I feared his lack of control, of which I was reminded in even the most tranquil moments by the loud, panting way he took in air, by his laugh, a guttural gooselike honk that erupted in salvos of three; by the third one, I wondered if it would ever stop.

What more did we talk about on all those Sundays? What did we do? I have no photographs, scant recollections. They were days disowned by memory.

Sally was listening to Paul Simon's early solo records in those years, and at the time I dismissed them out of hand as younger sister music. Now when I hear Simon's overcast outer-borough baritone singing "Still crazy after all these years," singing "Anyway you choose you're bound to lose in New York City," I hear the desperate, sad, and ravaged Ratso Rizzo city I knew, I hear my old times with my old man, and I am back inside that dim and bedraggled West Side apartment with the bars on the windows, confronting my father's listing posture, the relentless, inexorable, unflagging deathlessness of the afternoons.

I wondered what my mother did on that single day a month when Sally and I were not around, and once I asked her. She said she spent the morning sitting down at the dining room table slowly drinking a cup of coffee and having a good feeling that the day was spread out before her. She perceived the day in terms of space. The apartment, the room, the table, they all seemed large to her, and she felt that suddenly the space of her life was enlarged across that table. After a while she would catch up on chores. I thought it seemed a shame that on her one free afternoon she was dusting and doing the laundry, but she explained that she liked doing chores. Then she admitted that she always wanted to tell somebody what

she'd done. "That's the fabric of life," she said, "all those tedious little things that add up to a story that's almost fun when there's
another grown-up to share it with."

When November came, kids at school clothed themselves against
the cold in puffy ski jackets made of down-filled pouches that
encased the body in plump, tubular layers. The first time I saw a
couple of people wearing them I thought they looked like larvae.
When everyone began showing up in down, I wanted such a jacket.
More than anything I wanted one. My mother didn't see why I, who
didn't ski, needed such apparel, and, the third time I tried to convince her, she informed me I was "a fop" and "a conformist."

"What's a fop?" I asked, and she told me about the French and
the English, that the French were obsessed with clothes and food
and as a consequence the English repeatedly had to rescue them
from rout during wars. "What about Lafayette?" I pointed out. "He
rescued us."

"Honestly, Nicky," she said.

Just the same, soon we were on our way out to a winter sports
shop in Orange. I'd heard about the shop from kids at school. My
mother didn't like Orange because it was a suburb, a word that
when she said it sounded lascivious with misplaced values. "I hate
the way suburban people live out there in little segregated tribes of
their kind only, with their lower taxes and insurance rates," she'd
say. "America is supposed to be a more vital and complex place than
that." To get her to go to Orange I must have spoken about the shop
with great authority, conveyed the pressing necessity of going only
there, implied that the jacket qualified as gear. Gear was Vibram,
drill bits, the Texas Instruments calculators that regular people
were just beginning to own. My mother didn't know a lot about
gear. At the ski shop, chalet-like in my memory, with a lot of
Colorado-style open-beam work and wide panes of glass, the jackets the salesman showed us cost more than my mother said we
could afford. But come over here, my mother was waving. She had
discovered a rack of cheaper ones. They had the essential tubular

armature, but flatter pouches. Sounding happy that we would not go home empty-handed, my mother said expansively that I should choose any of them, whichever one I liked. "Look, they even have hoods," she discovered. None of the expensive coats had a hood. Could more mean less? I was also suspicious about the pouches, wondered why they weren't puffy. I consulted the label inside the collar. These pouches were "fiber filled." "Mom," I informed her. "They have polyester in there, not down." My mother sometimes spoke about polyester as though it were the suburb of fabrics. Tonight, however, she said only "Nicky, come on," and I could tell that she was suddenly weary in the way exhaustion flooded over her when she took off her sunglasses at the end of a long, hot, summer car ride. It was getting late. The salesman had abandoned us long ago. What was it about clothing that such small variations made all the difference? I went back to the cheap rack, selected a blue coat, and wore it to school the next day, wishing hopelessly that it would look like where it had come from. Each time a kid mentioned my "fake down" jacket, I felt more ludicrous, and by the weekend, which we were to spend visiting in Croton, to have it on my back made me want to flop around in pain. "What's the matter with him?" Susi asked in Croton, and when my mother threw up her hands and explained, Susi pulled back her chair and went to the coat closet. "Nicky, come here," she said. Opening the door, she produced a down jacket she'd recently bought herself. "Try this on," she said to me. "It's not a girl's jacket, it's unisex!" The jacket fit perfectly. "He can have it," she said to my mother, "and I'll wear his."

The one thing every other kid had that I could not even aspire to was a television in the house. So opposed was my mother that the year somebody sent us one for Christmas, she packed it up and sent it back. Since TV shows formed such a large part of the American conversation, not to have one at home marked me as the boy who didn't know. I'd begun to notice on the bedroom walls of several pals the identical poster of a woman in a red swimsuit with an ultra-brite smile and a waterfall of frosty blond curls. I didn't think she was that pretty, kind of elbowy and having a shampooing problem, and perhaps that's why it took me a while to ask who she was and finally become aware of Farrah Fawcett-Majors, star of *Charlie's Angels*. Not to have lusted after what all of American boyhood had been fantasizing about implied that for me there would be deeper consequences for not having a TV; that I would be left out in big, life ways; that I wouldn't have the information. Over me swooped a completely new kind of inadequacy—the sort of potent, confusing sensation I would have liked to ask my mother about, except for a further realization: I now had subjects a boy definitely could not take up with his mother.

Thanksgivings I dreaded. We'd stay Wednesday nights at my father's, and then on Thursday we'd go over to my grandmother's or to Judy's to celebrate. My grandmother never lost her immigrant enthusiasm for Thanksgiving, the only holiday I ever knew her to care about. Yet this day, which demanded only that we be grateful for what we had, invariably confronted us with what was lacking, and nobody felt the family disappointments more acutely than the most disappointed of us. My father was at his worst from Thanksgiving Day until after New Year's, and while Christmas and New Year's Day tended to leave him lonely and hopeless, Thanksgiving infuriated him. The enforced levity in overheated rooms seemed to make him think the relatives were laughing at him, the family stain, for he often excluded himself, searching out a slight and leaving early, his voice bellowing threats as he retreated: "I'm warning you, I'm not going to take it much longer." All these episodes passed without comment from everybody else, though, after one of them, two different older relatives pulled me aside, withdrew their wallets, and wordlessly handed me money.

A couple of times, my father refused to come at all, and everyone seemed relieved except my grandmother, to whom the perfect algebra of a fully present family meant everything. It was usually late in November that she, who the rest of the year told me never to criticize my mother, who never otherwise failed to underline "the great respect I have for Heidi," fell back on lamenting to me my mother's decision "to leave him." Speaking to me, my grandmother would then refer to him pointedly as "your father," emphasizing my filial obligation, emphasizing that you can't escape your past and you can't escape your family. I ascribed some of this to her desire to have me share what I was sure she must be feeling, the constant worry that the telephone would ring to tell her he was in trouble again. He was her lifelong responsibility because she was his mother, and, as she soon began more emphatically to explain to me, he was mine because I was his son.

My birthday came right after Thanksgiving, and from my grandmother I'd receive my card in an envelope inevitably addressed to "Master Nicholas Dawidoff." In what way at eight, eleven, or fourteen was I master of anything? Enough to master the knowledge that there was something unseemly in the family "we don't talk about." My grandmother told me, "life isn't supposed to be easy," and I accepted that, but at a certain point I, who ate everything, became suddenly unable to stand yams or cranberry sauce and never could stomach them again.

One Thanksgiving, my father showed up at my grandmother's dressed as a rabbi and carrying an old black King James Bible in both hands, the book outstretched like an offering. The strangeness of this entrance, with its twining of faiths and assertion of doctrine in a family that didn't talk about religion, didn't talk about creed, didn't talk about madness, cut through the room. Everyone winced. As he made his rounds, his hands convulsively shaking, each person he greeted just said "Hello, Donald, happy Thanksgiving." When he approached me, I studied the fibers of the rug fabric. After he finally left, a great-aunt collapsed into an armchair with a huge glass of gin.

The pain he caused could never keep pace with the pain he felt, no matter how vigorously he expelled it. He emanated pain, and it crackled through him like a shorting circuit, crushing him and also keeping him alive. With his infected brain he broke everybody's heart, because it was as though he wanted all of us to be as wretched as he was so we could feel for a brief time, on this special day, what he always felt.

Eventually there were two Thanksgiving dinners. Early in the day, Sally and I would meet Dad at our grandmother's for turkey. Then, in the late afternoon, he'd go home, and the three of us would head off uptown to join everyone else for the real party. We never told him that we had further plans, but he must have known.

All conformists are the same; they think they're not conformists. It seemed to me a cruel and cynical turn of chance that my mother, who cared not at all about fitting in, could have a son who cared so much. When my mother talked about conformists, I shared her cutting opinion of them, agreed that people of worth went their own way. Yet when I watched the conformists at school, in them I saw the confidence and composure of people who knew that they wanted what the world wanted. I thought of the conformists' lives proceeding at a steady velocity, their always knowing what to do because it was time, having jobs and families and dining rooms that nobody ever set foot in, were left fallow and immaculate in favor of the cozy eat-in kitchen nook right up to the move to Florida, where they'd play golf and drive white Oldsmobiles through the changeless weather. There was an attraction to how naturally everything came to them, would always come to them, how they blended without effort. Because it was tacit that I was not going to have a life like that, the future Floridians I went to school with came to represent a standard against which I tested myself. I knew now what I'd been fearing, that I might well be mutilated at the core, peculiar, some kind of invisibly palsied freak-boy. As simultaneously I tried to sort out whether something devastating had already happened with my own chemistry or whether I might still fend it off, my tireless efforts at assimilation were a gambit whereby, if others thought I was okay, more or less like them, I too could believe it to be so. It never would have occurred to me that those others around me might be exercising some variation of this same logic, and I wouldn't have liked it if I had known they were. I was invested in everybody else's stability, couldn't handle any more deviance. I was out to convince myself of who I wasn't, to fit in with myself, to be certified right in the head, to feel like an American boy.

That thirteenth year I got a new orange and white cat and I named him Teddy after Ted Williams. By this time we'd had so many cats I had trouble remembering them all. We got them as kittens and raised them as indoor cats. For a while they were content to roam the house, to sleep on my bed and be petted. But then, as they grew older, they would sit in the window and mew so pitifully that eventually my mother would succumb and announce that it was "inhumane to prevent an animal from going outside." She'd let them out the back door and once they'd tasted the fresh air, they could never be denied it again. Two months or half a year would pass before brakes would squeal on Willow Street and we'd have no cat. Each death was so upsetting to us that my mother would eventually give in and allow Sally and me to have another cat, vowing never to let this one go outside. Teddy lasted longer than most, in part because he was tough. The first time he was hit, my mouth fell open as I saw him come streaking along the side of the house and accelerate out into the street where he bounced headlong off the right front hubcap of a delivery van, went pinwheeling into the gutter, and survived. Half a year later, he darted back into the road for the last time. It was a brutal thing all that cat death, and the only way I can explain its recurrence is that my mother felt there was so much she could not give Sally and me, and because a new kitten was something she could give us, she did.

On the way home from visiting my father, back in the Grand Central tunnel, I'd look in the window at my reflected face, checking to make sure there were no resemblances. Then Sally and I, unwinding, relieved, might burst together into giddy laughter. My sister and I spent a lot of time going our separate ways, staking out our own territory. Yet these rides home from visiting our father were some of the best moments of my childhood, the relief we shared, the way she liked me to make her laugh—some days I had only to look at her and move an eyebrow, and she'd dissolve into giggles, and then I would too.

We had a private system of communication. Our hometown was Na Have. Somebody dishonest was a cheat bomb. She herself was Allende, the end of a nominal progression that had gone from Sal to Salvador to the surname of Salvador Allende, the leftist Chilean politician whose name was often on the radio during our childhood until after he was martyred in a military coup. People then had recently begun to exchange high fives, and Sally and I sometimes greeted each other by holding open a palm and saying, "Slap me five!" When the slap came, the recipient would avoid it by turning the waiting hand over and saying, "My dog's that high!" This amused us endlessly. At other times, when we sensed the other really needed a laugh, we'd meet eyes, one of us would say "Hein-hein! Nurl-nurl!" and we'd both crack up. Relatives who gave us a hard time were called "Tives," which rhymed with hives. During especially stressful family moments, we'd meet eyes and quietly mouth, "Tively Times!" We had a name for all this: we called it Nerd Lingo.

Even though it was already evening when we got to New Haven, because New York seemed to ferment under a coat of grime, I always changed my clothes, washed away all the accumulated fetors and distillations. As I held my palms under the tap, dark water flowed into the drain. Then for three weeks I wouldn't think about New York until, on a Sunday or Monday, I'd remember the upcoming Sunday and feel glum, and then I'd put it out of my mind so successfully that later in the day I'd try to remember what had made me glum, and it would come back to me and I'd feel glum again.

To me my father was easiest just to ignore. He was confusing in a way that I did not want to work out because nothing good had ever come of those calculations. Very rarely, in spite of myself, he did spring into my head. On the highway we passed a warning sign, "Falling Rock Zone," and I had the image of him, as I did when I read in a news magazine about foreclosed farmers, heard someone describing what ends up on the bottom of the harbor. As I puzzled over how he occupied himself through the day, the impossibility that a man could remain forever inactive with no purpose made it seem inevitable that he would become a criminal, disgrace us all. My expectations of him were completely random; at any time he might do anything. Though my father never hit me in New York, as the day of the visit approached, my fantasies were filled with scenes of him going berserk and I fought to obliterate them. What would keep a man like that from lashing out at everyone? Why wouldn't he turn to crime? I feared him with a mortal dread. To me he was a speckled person, my unlucky draft number. I could see that my mother and just about everybody else was at least a little afraid of him too and I sensed he could see this—made use of it. He was so sick, and because of that so strong. He used his weakness as a weapon.

Many times I told my mother I didn't want to go see him, but she never made our visits optional. "It's important for you to have a relationship with your father," she'd say over and over. On the appointed Sunday morning, before she put us on the train, my mother would call around New York to get reassurances about what kind of shape my father was in and, as far as I know, nobody ever told her "Don't send them." I was shackled to him. From the time I'd been a small boy I was bothered that he was my responsibility, and not the reverse. It was my duty to go, in the same way that I must do my chores, attend church. Only he could get out of our visits—and anything else he wanted. Since I didn't want to go, and had to, the clear implication was that I was doing it for him, that it would be hurtful to him if I failed to show up. As I got older, I saw that my grandmother was right; it was my moral obligation to spend time with this person I had begun to loathe.

A friend from my school came along with me once to New York and met my father. We had become close midway through that seventh grade year. My friend was very intelligent, jovially sarcastic, and filled with a range of interests unlike that of other kids I knew at our school: together in his basement we watched the endless procession of college football bowls during Christmas vacation, played board games reenacting Napoleonic battles, used to trade each other the black-spined Penguin paperback classics we bought and read for fun, dealing a Froissart's *Chronicles* straight up for a Bede's *A History of the English Church and People,* and bought records by America and Queen, groups we adored one day and disowned the next. It seems to be true that we briefly formed a club we called the WORM Association. With his family I went to the shore, to the mountains, to the Yale Bowl. For a time we spoke on the telephone every night in a heightened state of eighth grade consciousness, discussing for hours Horatio Hornblower's rise through the British navy. These conversations persisted until, right about the time it began to seem funny to be talking so much to another boy, he had his first girlfriend and the calls all but ceased. By then we had known each other for years, and when someone else in our class told me my friend was adopted I refused to believe it, could not imagine that he would have withheld such fundamental information. There was a developing uneasiness, a sense I would have explained then by saying that a best friend should have everything in common with me and that my friend and I were on diverging paths. Maybe it's that out-of-it kids always half resent those willing to become their companions. For years my friend's running joke had been that I was a simpleton, but now all at once I didn't think it was funny anymore to be "Nick the Nerd," didn't think birthday cards on which he drew a picture of a bomb and wrote "This card will self-destruct in five seconds. Unfortunately, I didn't have enough T.N.T. to blow you up with it" were amusing. My friend had grown mordant, unpredictable, and that his temperament seemed to have shifted alienated me, as did his new interests: listening to him talk with enthusiasm about anarchy or the virtues of the Soviet Union, I felt horrified, like a matron clenching at her stole as she hears bright talk from a back-door man. During those years I was always attracted to and then worried by high-strung, vulnerable people. In a published photograph taken of our high school newspaper staff working on the Thanksgiving issue, my friend and I are seated beside one another in the foreground. I am looking straight at the camera and haven't noticed that my friend is holding up a picture of a turkey in one hand and with the other he is pointing at me. He seemed increasingly strident and bizarre. I was afraid of what was happening to him, afraid he would snap. Every morning before school assembly, leaning against the hallway wall, I would speak guarded sentences to my friend until my teammates from baseball came up, whereupon I would greet them with affection as my friend relinquished his place and walked away. One Friday night, following a screening in the school auditorium of the Hitchcock film *Psycho,* I needed a ride home. My friend offered me one. I got into the car feeling I had to, even as I thought that he was the second-to-last person in the world I wanted to leave that particular movie with. Soon after that, one evening he tracked me down by telephone at a house where I was baby-sitting, said he was in trouble, needed my help now or he didn't know what would happen to him, what he would do to himself. I wanted to help, to take care of my friend, and I wanted no part of whatever was happening. In a panic, I telephoned my mother, who said, "You are not to leave those children." Back at school, there my friend was, unscathed. Back when my friend met my father, Dad was having a good day and there was an instinctive warmth between them. After that, my friend occasionally asked after Dad, and my deflecting answers eventually led him to burst out, "Why do you hate your father?"

Besides that friend, I never talked about my father with anybody in New Haven. I hoped people would assume that I just didn't have a father. To casual queries about him, I left it that he was a lawyer in New York and a bachelor. "Like in *The Odd Couple!*" someone said. I'd seen that show, and the idea that my father could be taken for a charmingly neurotic Upper West Side bon vivant with an interesting job, a regular poker game, wit, charisma, and attractive girlfriends in go-go boots momentarily stunned me. I'm not sure what I eventually replied—something deprecating. Rarely were there questions about him. It never seemed to occur to anyone to ask, and those that did found the subject unfruitful. I was sure that if anyone knew of my background I would be as ostracized as he was. I put my secret father in a compartment of my brain and locked it up tight.

I'd begun to come home from New York more terrified than ever that what had happened to him would be my fate as well. After one upsetting visit with Dad, my mother and I came as close as we ever did during my childhood to really discussing the situation. She looked me over and asked me if I had read Virginia Woolf's novel *Mrs. Dalloway.* I hadn't. She told me about Septimus Smith, who is mad and constantly destroys life—"makes everything terrible" as his wife, Lucrezia, says. My mother showed me the part where Septimus lolls on a bench in Regent's Park and gazes at the clouds, the leaves, and the trees that he believes are signaling to him. Then my mother looked at me and said, "You don't do that, Nicky. You don't distort things." I understood what she was trying to tell me, but nothing ever completely convinced me.

As a fourteen-year-old junior high school student, I now felt antipathy for everything I associated with my father—from the city of New York to lacrosse to womanizing. I made sure that I breathed noiselessly and vowed never to be fat, bald, or a loud laugher. When my father told me his favorite novel was Ford Madox Ford's *Parade's End,* and urged me to read it, I ignored him, feeling that, if I did read it, somehow he would rub off on me. People from time to time assumed I was Jewish—"your last name"—and I quickly explained that I was a churchgoer, and then I took further measures. Until then I had been the child my mother had to drag to Sunday school. Now I allowed the church to baptize me and I joined the confirmation class, was the class member to give the confirmation sermon to the full congregation, whom I informed that "As Simon went to Jesus, we come to you to join the family of the Christian church." Following the service, I was presented a Bible by Reverend Bradley with my name embossed on it in gold. I never attended services again. Sally, meanwhile, without saying a word to anyone, scheduled a private appointment with Reverend Bradley, explained to him her doubts about the existence of God, and came home afterward to tell us at dinner they'd agreed she should not be confirmed.

My sister, I slowly discovered, had qualities that were redoubtable and unique. Intrinsically she was organized in creative ways, understood foreign literatures, music and poetic meter, designed and made everything from cakes to wrapping paper to sweaters from scratch; she could sing, had wit and an instinct for cutting through cant. She also persevered. When given the choice, most people in high school tend to seriously engage only in their strengths. Sally, gifted at so many things, also took on difficult endeavors that didn't come naturally to her. She was not a fast runner at all, but she joined the cross-country team, and stuck with it despite finishing last in races, always completing the course, always improving her times. Then one summer she up and decided to run three hundred miles. Every day I watched as she set out to log her daily total, saw her run through storms and heat waves. Sometimes my mother would be out there with her, accompanying Sally by bicycle. There was a sheet of paper on which her distances were tallied. What made it all even more admirable to me was that she did not give the impression of being very impressed with herself and the many unusual things she could do. I thought, How can she not know?

After dinner Sally and I went to our rooms and closed our doors. Living just a few feet from each other, my sister and I each became skilled at creating privacy, especially Sally. One year at Christmas someone gave her a silver Cross pen, the sort of luxury item that neither of us had ever owned. When I wondered who it was from, she refused to tell me. Quickly I was desperate to know, worked every maneuver I could think of to wheedle it out of her, offered to cut deals, tried to tempt her with my own secrets, but she had me and she knew it. All she did for months was laugh and shake her head until I forgot about the pen. Once in a while, I'd remember. "Nope," she say, and around again we'd go. More than a dozen years later, at Christmas, I opened a slim package for me from Sally to find inside it a tarnished metal pen and a slip of paper on which she'd written the name of one of my friends from the neighborhood. I'd always assumed he came over so much because he liked playing Dungeons & Dragons with me.

On the telephone I didn't want my father to know me, and parried his questions with monosyllabic evasions.

"How are you, Nicky?"

"Fine."

"What's new?"

"Not much."

"How's school going?"

"Okay, I guess."

Soon he'd resort to telling me in detail what he'd had for dinner that night or he'd feed me anecdotes, some of which later sounded familiar when I read a book he'd given me of Theodore Roosevelt's letters to his children, rafts of words I listened to with a mixture of disbelief and queasy alarm, the way I did the first time a telephone drummer called the house with a new product to sell. Did this person really think we would buy anything from him? Eventually my father would give up and ask for Sally.

Then one night he said he had been offered a job teaching law in Cleveland. A miraculous hope lifted in me. I told him how wonderful this was, told him he had to take the position, told him that Cleveland, where I'd never gone, where the downtown river had been on fire, was the land of possibility, the city of dreams. As I spoke, he was pretty quiet. After that I never heard anything more about Cleveland. He would never leave New York, and our conversations soon reverted to the familiar pattern. Occasionally, however, after saying "Goodbye, Nicky," he'd add also "I love you." Nothing anyone ever said to me upset me more. I'd want to tell him to prove it, tell him how cheap his words were, tell him to leave me alone, tell him that I despised and detested him, but I never said any of this and I never lied either. "Thanks," is what I'd reply.

When I finally did read *Parade's End,* I discovered this memorable line: "It is probably only God who can, very properly, devise the long ailings of mental oppression."

CHAPTER NINE

Grief

I was at home one evening in eighth grade when my mother came into my room to tell me that we were leaving immediately for Croton, that Susi, only forty-eight, had suffered one heart attack at the wheel of her car, and then a second, more serious episode back inside her house and might not live through the night. When we drove up to that big white house where I'd spent so many Christmases and vacations, Susi's green Plymouth station wagon stood right outside where it always was, looking nothing like an accomplice. The telephone kept ringing. When my grandparents arrived from Cambridge, I was even given a present, a book about Napoleon. I slept that night, as I always did, in a sleeping bag on the floor beside Jody's bed, and I slept soundly. I had no experience with the death of someone I knew, did not yet fantasize about death and loss in the way that provokes the troubling sense of déjà vu when the outcome eventually comes to pass.

The next morning, I awakened to hear Tony sitting beside Jody on the bed, calmly telling my fourteen-year-old cousin that his mother had died. I lay still, my eyes closed as they spoke. When Tony left the room, on his way to give six-year-old Liesi the same news about her mother, Jody and I began to speak, he methodically calculating the mathematical odds of himself, me, and other family members being prematurely struck down until he gave up and began to weep. I wanted to comfort him. "It will be okay," I told him. "I haven't got a father and it's okay."

"But he's *alive*," my cousin cried, and the irrevocable totality asserted itself.

In June, I returned to Croton, where Jody and I spent every day of that long, horrible summer playing tennis for hours, walking two miles across hills into town beneath trees drooping in the humid heat to the clay public courts. I beat him every time, which I did not want to do because his mother had died. His strokes were clean and polished while mine were unkempt, but I would somehow win more points. He said once that what he liked most about tennis was the chance every shot gave you to express yourself with perfect form. For him to win without correct execution would have been a false victory. Each afternoon, when he tired and his shots began soaring long or colliding with the net, his frustration would mount, and he would fiercely mime the proper form, and still the shots would spray in all directions, and I would feel culpable although I knew that all he wanted from me was my companionship, not my pity. Each morning we went back and played again. It was all we did, running and hitting on the hot dirt until clay stained our socks the color of rust, clung to the runnels of sweat on our calves. After breakfast, we didn't ever eat during the day, and we drank only from the large bottle of lemon-flavored Pepsi Light we always had with us. Finally, at night, we gorged ourselves with meat at supper and fell exhausted into sleep. There was never any question of just hitting for fun. Always we kept score. It was unbearable.

My cousin was a serious competitor. He had joined the debate team at school and was quickly a champion. Now the model airplanes were put away, and the surfaces of his room were crosshatched with index cards, scholarly books, journal and periodical articles highlighted in yellow Magic Marker, and bulky briefcases from which he was always extracting thick documents. His conversation was scattered with words and phrases like "counter-plan," "the turnaround," "crush the affirmative," and "the Depo-Provera argument," and his descriptions of the actual competitions made debaters sound like glorious gladiators of an intellectual gridiron, martial artists of the mind—an impression buttressed by the fact that most of the time I didn't know what any of it meant.

Once I let him win at tennis. On the walk home, sitting on a short retaining wall next to the sidewalk, midway up the steep hill on the Old Post Road where we always rested together and drank Pepsi Light, he turned to me and asked me if I'd let him win, and when I hesitated, fury and anguish passed across his face and he screamed at me for the betrayal. Something fell through my body and froze inside my chest, and I sat silent in my shame wondering why I'd done it.

Another time, on that same walk, sitting on that same wall, I asked Jody what he would choose if he could have anything in the world, and he stared at me in disbelief and said, "What do you think?" Horrified, hurriedly I tried to amend matters, told him, "No, no, not that, things a person really could have," which only made him more upset.

The death had taken a corrosive hold on me. Not only was the world a far worse place without Susi; I was a far worse person. It was as though my soul were fraying as our whole family was fraying. Tony spent his days in bed or eddying around the rooms of the house, floating in anchorless circles of grief. Nobody paid enough attention to Liesi. A succession of housekeepers hired to help Tony came and went until he married one of them. I saw my uncle less and less after Susi died, and each time we visited he was harder to recognize as I used to know him. He seemed scarcely to notice as we all grew up and went on into life without him.

My mother, in the grip of a heartbreak that remained fresh for years, put up a shrine of photographs to her sister on her living room dresser top in New Haven. My mother stopped going to church because she could not forgive God for taking her sister, and for a while she measured her friends by how sympathetic they were about her loss. "All they want is for me to get over it," she'd say. She seemed to measure me that way as well. That I had not cried right after Susi died I knew gave my mother pain. I did not understand why I hadn't cried. I wished I had. None of us knew how much we had loved her until she was gone, how much she had held us all together, how supportive and fragile a thing is family.

One day that summer I was in Croton, and opening a closet door I happened to come upon the fake down blue coat Susi had traded with me for her real one. I was surprised and then embarrassed; it was like encountering someone in front of whom I'd once misbehaved. Meeting eyes with coat hangers, slickers, windbreakers, and mufflers, I was unsure of what to do. The coat was bluer than I remembered. There was the simultaneous impulse to try it on and to close the door. I kept standing there looking in. Suddenly I could tell that Susi had never worn it.

The Christmas after Susi died, we were in Cambridge, visiting my grandparents, when deep in the middle of the night the telephone rang. It rang and rang until someone answered it. Then my mother was at my bedside, telling me to come downstairs. There was tension on her face. When I reached the first floor, I saw my grandparents standing near the telephone with sweaters over their pajamas, looking concerned, which made them also look very old. "Let him talk to Nicky," my grandfather told my mother, and I was handed the phone. I put it to my ear and heard screaming. It took a moment for me to recognize my father. Over and over he was ranting "I want to see more of my children." Terror shot through me. It was unbearable to visit him as often as I did and now I would have to go more often. Nobody ever said no to him. "Hi, Dad," I said. I don't remember what we talked about, just the howling voice, the bellowing demands. It was peculiar to me at times like that how he could seem both all-powerful and persecuted.

Even though I was going to a new school, in the late afternoon I still came to the Worthington Hooker schoolyard to throw a ball against the wall, get up a baseball game if enough players for one could be found. Lately this was more of a challenge. On the "play machine" jungle gym, kids huddled together, dragging on cigarettes, burning their initials into the wooden surfaces with lighters. Sometimes the play machine would be empty and plumes of sweet, sapid smoke arose from the hidden cantonment of the back porch. Most of the kids out on the back porch didn't play much baseball anymore, and the ballplayers tended to keep out in the open until, one day, a freckled kid who was an excellent infielder suddenly announced that he wanted to get stoned. Nobody could believe it, least of all the back porch regulars, who, you could tell, saw this conversion almost as a validation. They led him off for his first time with great ceremony, and something behind my ribs gave way and a hole opened up in me as I watched him going back there to light up.

A procession of hard new faces was gathering at the schoolyard in the evening, kids called Dino and Loot and Burn, all of them drawn to this sudden zone of disrepute. Some of them were toughs from the Saint Francis home for children with behavioral problems, others were up to no good from down by the highway, and several of them lived in the mansions of Livingston Street, including a pale, Luciferian figure who wore a long trench coat and had a lidded, untrustworthy way of looking people over that made me think of dirty work. Word had it he kept getting kicked out of the private schools his parents sent him off to every September. To amuse themselves, they all played with firecrackers. The most common firecrackers were the candy striped salutes that could blow off a finger, kids said. When the whole pack was lit at once, it sounded the way the background noises in news reports from Vietnam used to on the radio. More powerful than salutes was an M-80, a genuine explosive; you could hear them mortar-thudding deep into the night. Our neighborhood had become a force field of gunpowder and broken glass. On trash collection nights, no garbage can was safe. Paper bags and money were changing hands regularly in the schoolyard, and police cars began cruising by.

One day I came upon a group of the tougher kids having a football game on the schoolyard pavement. It took a moment to register that they were playing tackle football, smashing one another into the asphalt at full speed. They made primal noises, roaring and grunting and snarling, and their eyes had the fog of hot-shower-heated glass as they hurled themselves into the line, causing collisions that were so violent it was quickly apparent that they had no interest in scoring, they just wanted pain. None of them took any notice of me. Finally I understood that they were all high out of their minds.

Those kids rarely spoke to me, but there was the day one of them said, "All you ever do is play baseball." It sounded like an accusation, and, when I thought about it that night, I decided he was right: all I did was play baseball and read books, many of them about baseball, and I felt how limited I was, that I did not have adventures. Now when I hear his voice, what he is also saying is "You're not like us," and it was true, I was no longer part of the neighborhood. There I was privileged, the kid going to a private school—where I felt different because my family had less than most of my classmates. My position felt perpetually out of step; I didn't exactly fit in anywhere. Even after schoolyard curfews were established, a Block Watch created, and things calmed down almost as quickly as they'd flared into disorder, I rarely went there anymore. The grandeur of it was gone.

Everything was changing except for me. The telephone would ring and I'd answer it to hear someone on the line greeting me, "Hello, ma'am!"

"Sir!" I'd protest. "I'm sir!" Sometimes, especially when they had called with something to sell, I'd get an apology: "Sir! Of course. So sorry, sir." But as the conversation resumed, I trilled at such an acute frequency that a moment later they'd forget and I'd be "ma'am" again. It wasn't a stranger's fault that my voice wouldn't break, that I was "Little Nicky," a high school freshman with long, skinny arms attached to a torso smooth and narrow as a windshield wiper. When I turned fifteen that November, my mother hired a plumber to install a showerhead above the tub in our bathroom, explaining that "an active man needs to take showers," and I was both flattered and confused to be now considered a man, since nothing about me had changed to suggest to me that I was anything more than what I had always been.

There seemed to be so many different ways to be a man. Men camped, they walked their dogs, they tied knots, they built fires, they fixed toasters in their workshops and bent over car engines in the driveway. Men went hunting and trapping, received goodbye kisses and left on business trips. Men knew about the night; in books that was when they visited pool halls and bars, gave one another nicknames, talked politics, and "chased women"—which I imagined as a ritual game of tag. I had no idea about any of these things. Fuse boxes were a particular mystery to me—something about the shiny and intricate way they looked, what they seemed to promise. I didn't understand how to knot a necktie or carve. I wanted to test my skills, my courage. But who would guide me, prepare me for all that? It occurred to me that I was getting only half the data in life I was supposed to have. All these questions and doubtful concepts coalesced into my idea of what it meant to have a father at home. Then, many years later, when, in a magazine story, I read the clause "Dadly noises arose from the stair" I realized that I still had no idea how those would sound.

In a world filled with truths regarding things I knew nothing about, like topo-maps and oil pans and springer spaniels, I was always alert, tried to take initiative. At the drugstore on Orange Street I bought several bottles of English Leather male cologne and lined them up along my dresser top. I never wore any of it. I went and stood outside Archie Moore's, the bar on our street, and looked in at the men perched on stools, imagining them all talking in a gruff, guylike way, off-loading their distant, heavy memories. I climbed up to the attic and watched beside Mr. Sullivan as he refinished a piece of furniture, too held back to ask for instruction, just hoping the knack of it would sink in. When I heard someone describe a dead fish handshake, I firmly grasped the point. Soon somebody told me with approval that I had "a good strong grip," and I thought, the eye seeks what the eye requires.

New Haven in March was a dreary wind in your face, the gutters ponding with slushy water, dirty snow at the edges of lawns, precisely the conditions that had bred the baseball tradition of spring training in Florida. Spring training was the baseball time of possibility, the season of augur and optimism when even the difficulties, something called visa trouble, were nothing that a little front office pettifogging couldn't solve. In spring Tommie Aaron might become his brother Henry, losses were meaningless, unheralded youth made its name, and sportswriters, their typewriters sanguine in the tenor of things, dispatched soft, breezy notices that might—and did—introduce the week's promising rookie like this: "He embodies all that's special about the National Pastime and the American spirit." (Three weeks later that rookie would be sent down to the minors.)

In March of 1978, now fifteen, I was one of three freshmen to travel to Florida with the high school baseball team for a week of spring training at a youth baseball complex in St. Petersburg. All the way down from New Haven to the airport in New York, and then boarding the airplane, I was silent, in the thrall of the adventure. Once we were seated, our two coaches on the trip began talking baseball, and when one of them discovered that I knew such things as the starting lineup for the 1934 Detroit Tigers, the third baseman in the Cubs' famed Tinker-to-Evers-to-Chance infield, I was soon reciting them, so enjoying the opportunity to retail names I had only read like Marv Owen, Billy Rogell, Charlie Gehringer, and Hank Greenberg of the Tigers, and Harry Steinfeldt at that Chicago hot corner, it took me a while to notice that some of the older kids had different ideas about what a week in Florida might mean—had the uneasy expressions of people anticipating life spent in the close company of a music box with no off switch.

We slept as a team in a dormitory on bunk beds, awakening to eat in a dining hall and then play baseball all day together, at first hitting off batting tees and then building up to live competitions against other schools later in the week. I always liked being around the ballplayers, hearing the crude, manly hilarity of kids like Chris Cogguillo, a jovial pitcher who reveled in being called Pisswackman Cockswallow, and might himself conduct inspections to make sure you were wearing a protective cup in your athletic supporter by calling out, "What's the capital of Thailand?" and bestowing the geography lesson with a knee to the groin as he bellowed "Bangkok!" That week there was a trip to a major league spring training game where it seemed only half real to encounter the Mets of New York and the Cardinals of St. Louis in a quaint little downtown ballpark ringed by palm trees. After the first few innings, familiar faces like Lou Brock and Tim Foli gave way to players with high numerals on their backs indicating names we couldn't recognize. The best part was the chance to listen to the talk of the high school juniors and seniors who would comprise the varsity's starting lineup. They had nicknames like Milo and Deals and Woogie and a funny, squeaky, nasal way of talking to one another, and some of them talked to me that way too.

I came home tanned and thrilled, and when, on the first day back in the boys' locker room, I spotted one of the seniors from the trip, I bounced up to him, greeting him by his nickname, which was Gordo.

"Get away from me," he said. I thought I'd misheard or that he was teasing me. We'd all had such a good time together. "Hey, Gordo!" I said again, this time adopting the nasal intonation. He was tall with broad swimmer's shoulders, feathered blond hair, and the pouting good looks of a daytime television actor.

"I said get away from me. Get this kid away from me." He'd raised his voice loud enough that some of the other seniors now were turning from their stalls to look at what was agitating him. That I was an insect to him was not quite registering with me. In my mind there had still existed the idea that these boys who would start for the school varsity were special, like big leaguers, and that a coefficient of their baseball skill was a personal nobility. It seemed that I should attempt to revise his thinking, but I had no idea what I'd done, was too shocked to say anything. Later that afternoon, I ran into my friend Randy, whose older brother, Mark, had been on the trip. Randy couldn't resist telling me that among the seniors I had become known as WBP. So I too had a nickname. What did it mean? Randy wouldn't say. Finally, I convinced him. "After you grounded into double plays twice in a row off a batting tee, they decided you were the worst baseball player they'd ever seen. You know, worst baseball player, WBP."

Besides the wounding shock of it, a lot of other things went through my mind at such a moment. I wanted to find a way to get them to retract it, even as I wondered, did everyone think that? Then I tried to imagine what else was going to come around a blind corner and hit me below the knees. I remembered the part of *My Turn at Bat* where, after the young and gawky Ted Williams spends his first spring training in Florida getting a lot of riding from the older Red Sox veterans, he is demoted to the minor leagues by the team and, as he leaves, he sends the veterans some parting words: "Tell them I'll be back." Finally, out at practice and turning it all over for the fiftieth time, I just thought, "Am not." Because there, on a field, you could have some say in the matter, and after that I kept what they said in mind, using it.

On baseball fields my small size could be compensated for with enthusiasm and with effort. In New Haven, our seasons began under low, chilly skies the color of well-used flatware, with those grungy piles of old snow still ringing our outfields, and then ended in August on glass-strewn city infields burned to dust by the sun. My hands and feet seemed to crave infields. I'd play anywhere and I did, turning up all over New Haven with my spikes dangling from one bicycle handlebar, my glove looped over the other. The day back in seventh grade when I led my junior high school team to victory, got into the back seat of our car, wriggled out of one uniform and into another as my mother drove me across town, and then had several more hits in a Pony League game, felt like the latest climax of my life. My virtues then as a player were agility, cleverness, and such a boundless, unquenchable appetite that I became lost in the play. My swing was precious to me. To preserve its delicate mechanics, I now refused to play tennis until my baseball season was over or to play Wiffle Ball ever. After I saw a photograph of Pete Rose sliding, his low-flying body parallel to the ground with his hands extending before him toward the base like struts feeling for a carrier deck, I too slid headfirst on forearms whose scars I wore with pride like cuff links. Standing at shortstop, between pitches I'd tend the soil, smoothing it with the toe of my spike, sifting out stones and small rocks and tossing them away beyond the foul line. There was a logic to this groundskeeping; I'd read about the infield-pebble-inspired wayward hops that had turned both the 1924 and the 1960 World Series, but the truth is that there I was proprietary—this was my domain.

My summer league coaches were invariably the fathers of one or more of my teammates. Somehow, those teammates always played whatever position they liked, batted high in the order, even if they had failed to make their school squads, a casual nepotism that galled me. At fifteen, when I joined a new Babe Ruth League team that had three coaches, each with a son on the roster, our lineup also included several close friends of those sons, and early in the season I rarely played. One day, we were winning by a substantial margin and they sent me in to pitch. Heading toward the mound I felt insulted, resentful, so out of my head with accumulated griev-ance that when I began pitching I couldn't overcome it. I threw every pitch as hard as I could, growing more and more distressed out there until I was having a tantrum on the mound. I wanted to stop it, but I couldn't pull myself together. The catcher would return the ball to me, I'd hurry through my windup and heave it back at him. I'd never behaved that way, had never seen anyone else behave that way either. The field got very quiet. All you could hear was the sound of me disgracing myself, walking batter after batter. Eventually they removed me from the game. "Don't worry," one of our coaches consoled me. "Thirteen-year-olds don't play as much. You'll play more when you're fifteen."

"But I am fifteen," I wailed, and when he looked startled, I felt my eyes brim. Sitting next to me on the dugout bench was Reggie, my former Pony League teammate. "I'm not crying am I, Reg?" I asked him.

"Maybe a little, man," he told me.

"Reg, those are not crying tears. Those are tears of rage."

"Okay, Nicky, man."

The next week I was put into the lineup and I batted over .400. "As soon as I taught him to hit, Nicky's been great," one of our coaches told the team as he awarded me the game ball after we won a playoff round.

The shower area in the boys' school locker room was shaped like a capital E with a space between the stem and the unattached middle stroke, so that with several nozzles lining all five pale-yellow-tile interior wall sections, wherever we stood we were exposed to one another as we washed. If you were, like me, the only boy in the high school baseball program not yet to have reached puberty, this fact was conspicuous—visible to all.

I played third base for the junior varsity that ninth grade spring, and every day during practice, as a team we did our running together, circling all of the school's upper athletic fields at a canter quick enough to keep in condition, but not so brisk as to preclude conversation. It was during these transverses that I acquired another new nickname. A leading golfer on the professional tour in those days was Hubert "Hubie" Green, and one day a teammate was inspired to meld freshman and fairway so that from then on, to all but the softest-hearted members of the group, I became Pubie Green. As soon as the taboo of mouthing such an explicit word was overcome, it was a name that became irresistible to them. They never tired of saying it, lengthening the lubricious vowel, interlacing the Pubies with the occasional "Kojak"—after the television detective played by baldheaded Telly Savalas—so that very quickly I wanted to die. You heard about men who too soon lost their youth. Had there ever been someone who never came of age at all?

That team had two third basemen, the other a sophomore whose arms were hung with muscles the size of tree fruits. Alongside him at the position, taking practice grounders, I looked like his kid brother, but he already had a twin brother, our center fielder. For all his strength, in actual application, the sophomore's play lacked art, and halfway through the season he missed a game. In his place I made a couple of diving catches, and after that I became the starting third baseman.

That there was something vulnerable about me occurred not just to my baseball teammates, but to several others in the school who began to take recreational pleasure in "beating on Nicky." In the hallways and walkways, my lank shoulders invited them to wind up and deliver. Blue bruises flowered at the peaks of my arms and I became timid, a flincher. Somebody would cock his fist and feint in my direction, I'd duck, and laughter ensued. Childhood has very specific differentiations. Each age and each school grade have great significances all their own, and the days stretch out to hold so much experience. Maybe that's why the humiliations and reversals then seem to go on and on. In ninth and tenth grades, I felt perpetually singed; futile, foolish, cut-down, stuck with myself. Often I wanted to escape that self, but you can't escape what is still so unformed that it's constantly being reinvented. My response to being picked on was simply to take it. I never retaliated and I never snitched. Instead, I tried not to do the things they mocked in others, which is to say I sought to look and smell and speak as they did, to be like them right down to the shampoo they used in the shower—tubes of antifreeze-green Prell.

But to be like them was also hazardous. There was the day at school I was hurrying up the steep second-to-third floor steps of Baldwin Hall for class, and ahead of me was a kid who was also hurrying until he slipped and fell hard right on his face. I couldn't believe it. I'd never seen anyone fall on those stairs. What a goober! I started laughing. Three steps later, I slipped and fell. I remember the way the surface of those stairs looked when your face was pressed up against them, the paint worn away in the center from so many footsteps, how blunt and cold and colorless the metal was at the ridge, all the pairs of ankles rushing past my nose. It was an indelible experience and seemed kind of metaphorical. You could fall down at any time. And maybe, I thought, there was some connection: act like a jerk, you'll fall down.

On Sunday evenings, back from the panic of New York and

preparing to wade through the tar pit of another week of school, I began to be sure that, although they in the locker room didn't know my secret, they were responding to it. Thinking of myself as the hero of my own life story became increasingly difficult. I believed I had failed as a conformist because I was warped and blemished by my nature.

The parent who was raising me was the most independent-minded person I knew. My mother's enthusiastic opinions were expressed with such ferocious candor that after she'd proclaimed "Ye gods! You're not falling for that crap, are you, Nicky?" it was difficult to think how anyone could admire the Rolling Stones or Cheryl Tiegs or Woody Allen. She had vehement views on everything from Franklin Roosevelt—human perfection—to Jane Fonda—vapidity incarnate—to my erratic use of the proper pronoun—"It's 'my friend and *I!*' You sound so ignorant, Nicky"—to my comportment, which needed to be more chivalrous. I began to think of her as notoriously on time. I could be anywhere when the corrective voice migrated through my mind: "For crying out loud, son, that's no way to be," and I'd hasten to do the right thing because, for the most part, out of her hearing, I agreed with everything she said. Maybe I agreed too much. In her presence, something new in me found those staunch convictions intolerable, and at fifteen I'd reached an adolescent age where I wanted to argue with her, to take issue, find fault.

The dinner table was the Gettysburg field where week after week we wounded each other. As the clock neared six, cheddar-yellow plastic place mats would come forward from their barracks on the metal shelf in the kitchen, knives, forks, and spoons fell from their munitions drawer into position, glasses left the cabinet and took up watch along the ridge, and, at the whiff of what she was cooking, animus churned through me and I attacked. I'd lower my fork, catch her eyes watching me, searching for a reaction, and sometimes it took only the slightest grimace to tell her that once again she'd failed, that I still did not like her cooking. The dishes she served were assembled from cans and frozen packets by someone who'd been awake and working since five in the morning. Usually they were nourishing meals and they tasted, it seemed to me, the way anyone might expect a meal to taste that did not rely on fresh ingredients, or any seasoning beyond salt and pepper, or any study of the method. But this line of reasoning infuriated her. "Why do you always criticize me?" she wanted to know. "It's only food. Why can't you just be satisfied?"

Now I was incensed, had been waiting to be. "For dinner you pour Chunky Soup on top of egg noodles and you want me to call you Julia Child?"

As always, she began to shout: "Other mothers with husbands never cook anything for their children. They give them TV dinners. I cook for you every goddamn night after a long, hard day and this is all the thanks I get. You're ungrateful, Nicky. You've always been ungrateful."

"Why are you so upset if food doesn't matter to you?"

"Oh, Nicky." The voice was withering. "You're the expert around here. What do you think?"

Every night there was another meal, another opportunity to express my discontent—and to explore it. It was all an imponderable conundrum, only nominally about the flavor of frozen fish sticks and canned ravioli. She did not care about food. I did care. She cared that I cared. I came home the day I'd learned a relevant new phrase and over the dinner she'd cooked, which, as usual, offended me before I tasted it, I suggested that maybe our differences about the meals might simply boil down to my "delicate palate." Hearing myself say something like this to her embarrassed me, and a smirk crossed my face. She gave me a hard look and said, "When did you get to be so pretentious." Then she told me, "Susi always said you were a little actor."

We never got anywhere with each other. Out in the world, they were all kicking me. Why could she not give in, indulge me, soften the blows? Why was her reflexive response to any new proposal to refuse? Why could she never accept criticism of any kind? Why could I not be right sometimes? Why, on the other hand, could I not, as she said, "get all this out of your system," accept her as she was, understand how full her plate was, and ease off on the demands? Why did I persist in trying to change her? She would never change her ways, not even for me, and I would never stop trying to make her.

It made me frantic that someone so self-assured in her views as my mother could be so easily injured when I stated mine. Once, in a sudden whiplash of frustration, I turned from her, snatched the pencil cup off my desk and hurled it at my bed. The haloed slash it left in the wallpaper above the headboard was forever there to remind me of the way our voices could lacerate the walls. Another night I threw the telephone receiver and now the dining room too was scarred. I hated what I was becoming even as I continued to become it. Then all of it would empty out of me, and I'd curl up on my bed and fall asleep fully clothed.

The few times she did give in, she gave in to me so completely it was too much. "I'm such a lousy mother and I wanted so badly to do well by you kids," she'd confess, and, mortified with confusion and shame, I'd rush to reassure her. I was slowly understanding that she was fighting not only for her point of view, but for our sense of her as our one good parent. "You are a good mother," I'd say. And I meant it, more than anything.

My mother had always been singular in her habits and attitudes, a complex mesh of austerity and exuberance, but since Susi's death her great capacity for joy had been depleted, replaced by mourning. Her muscles still pulsed with readiness for all the tasks that an ironing board, a sewing machine, a dustpan, a roll book, a syllabus, and an unbalanced checkbook could offer. She still completed the reading of every book she began, and when I asked her why she stayed with a wide tome she'd announced twelve pages in was "godawful," she explained that "my sense of duty and order won't permit me to stop." As I watched her grimly scrubbing dishes in the sink, slamming the sopping cutlery into the drying rack, she seemed to have retreated under a carapace of anxiety—a need more pressing than ever to change the sheets the moment the day broke, get the thank-you notes written the instant the present was unwrapped. I had long both relied on and chafed against that gift for getting everything done, but now as she grieved, to see her deep ache exposed tipped the balance. Suddenly her deft economizing, her selfless asceticism, the doing without that had sent me to Florida, all of it felt like a reprimand. Because worrying was her weakness, now I couldn't stand the worrying, was tired of walking on eggshells around her so that she wouldn't explode. I wanted to detonate her, to make her admit that she was harsh and rigid and inflexible, that there were different ways to do things. I wanted a witness, an advocate, a man with an impartial perspective on the evidence who could help her see herself. If she wouldn't adjust for me, I imagined, she would for him. I just wanted our lives to be easier, calmer, for every day not to cost so much. It was exhausting.

In the morning, from my bed I listened while her new wedge-heeled slippers drummed against her feet as she rushed around in a compulsion of ordering fierce enough that from anywhere in the house I could hear her ironing a shirt. I wanted to know the conditions and the terms—to be prepared for who she was going to be; "Are you sweet Mom or angry Mom today?" is what I wished I could ask when she woke me up for school. Day after day brought another local crisis I felt I must solve, though about this kind of fixing, I had no clue where to begin. So attuned to her anxiety was I that now when she felt it, I did too, a parboiled stream rushing through my arms. For worrying was also my weakness, and, by resenting it in her I resented myself.

The year after Susi died was also the year I went to an America concert. Afterward I bought the group's *Greatest Hits*. The song that I liked best was called "Sister Golden Hair," a ballad about a man filled with regret about a golden-haired woman he let get away because he didn't think he was ready to love her enough. One day, when I played the song on the stereo I began to hear it in a more personal way. My mother was out of the house, off somewhere. When she came home, I cued up "Sister Golden Hair" on the turntable and called for my mother to come into the room. While it played, I looked at her. I didn't say anything because I didn't know what I wanted from her except that she should hear me play the song about the blond sister. After the verse where the singer says, "Well, I keep on thinkin' 'bout you, sister golden hair surprise, and I just can't live without you, can't you see it in my eyes," my mother looked up at me and then, without saying anything, she quietly left the room while the song continued to play.

Years later she told me that she'd spent that time in her life wishing that we had in the front yard of our house one of those white statues of the Virgin Mary that are often outside Catholic churches. "You know the ones," she said. "They have their arms spread open. That's what I wanted to see when I came home."

In my sleep I tilted. The floor planks of my bedroom had warped to such a slope that some nights I would have logrolled out of bed had my mother not enforced her Quantico standard of sheet cornering. Besides the bed, the room was now furnished with a night table, a shellac-brown dresser that had belonged to my great-grandparents Max and Sarah, and to which I once applied a "Keep on Truckin' " decal that had since proved impossible to dislodge, a secondhand desk with the first owner's coffee-mug-ring stains on the surface, a pine bookcase built by my mother, its top lined with my baseball trophies. Above the dresser was a shelf on which there were souvenirs from Susi's travels—a sandalwood jar she'd bought in Japan, a tiny Viking ship from Norway—as well as a photograph of my great-aunt Lydia in her beehive wig, a "Carter for President" button, and another button, courtesy of my Latin teacher, that proclaimed "I Take Latin."

My mother and sister still came frequently into my room. The telephone would ring for Sally or one of them required the bathroom, and necessity took its course. These passages through were so commonplace nobody acknowledged them as visits, making it as though we all were together in a railroad car and I just another anonymous traveler seated to their left or right as they hurried along the swaying corridor from one end of the compartment to the other. Now that Sally and I were older, privacy mattered more, and by ignoring each other we preserved our privacy. Even so, I always knew when there were women in my room.

I acquired a clock radio of my own. It was a Realistic Chronomatic 9 model, low-built and squared-off at the corners like a shoe box, with a faux-oak plastic cabinet, chrome and clear-plastic control dials, and rounded hour and minute hands that in the dark were backlit a dim lunar orange. These features had aspirations toward sleekness, but only a few months of ownership made clear that my radio was drab in the way the design ideas dominating mainstream consumer electronics in the mid-1970s were all drab. It was a look that was somehow between looks, one in which everything resembled everything else and nothing so much as the dashboard on the clumsy, rowboat-like LTD station wagons Ford was then producing. But if I stared at my Chronomatic 9 long enough, in the right mood it could seem, if not beautiful, almost handsome. My attachment to what came out of the clock radio quickly grew so intense I wanted an appearance to match.

What I was listening to in my room were Boston Red Sox baseball games. I hadn't been able to get the Boston games on my old transistor, and to discover now that reception was possible on the Chronomatic 9 was joy. By game time I would have spread my homework along my bed, distributing the books and papers lengthwise, so that when I positioned myself on the floor, knees to the rug, chest pressed against the edge of the mattress, head bent over my books, to Sally and my mother passing behind me, it must have looked as though I was supplicating myself to physics and *Lord Jim*. The radio was to my left, on the night table, and, as I worked, the team broadcaster, Ned Martin, said, "Welcome to Fenway Park in Boston," and right then a part of me zoomed down the I-91 highway entrance ramp and lifted out of New Haven. Martin and his commentating partner would discuss the game to come, building the anticipation until Martin cried, "Here come the Red Sox!" As he introduced the players position by position—"Jim Rice left field, Fred Lynn center field"—it was like having the cast of characters read aloud to you from the beginning of a Russian novel. All quieted as the crowd rose to listen while an organist played the National Anthem, and I stood too, put my hand to my heart, and with no flag in the room to gaze upon, instead stared fixedly at a red, white, and blue book spine on my shelf for the duration of the song. My mother began to come in and watch me standing there in still, patriotic tribute. At first I wished she would just leave me alone, but over time I began to like her observance of my observance, and when the door didn't open, I'd reach toward the radio and raise the volume to let her know she was missing the Anthem.

Early in the game, sometimes the reception would be erratic, clogged with static, and I'd have to jiggle the tuning knob, making such minute adjustments my hand trembled. It often helped if I stood near the radio in a certain position, invariably contorted, with one arm akimbo, another limb up in the air, a palm hovering inches over the speaker, trying to maintain position, barely breathing, as the sputtering details came out of the Chronomatic 9. Then the evening progressed, and the connection grew pure. Some nights when the Red Sox weren't playing, around the fifth inning, I could even begin to pick up broadcasts from Philadelphia or Baltimore or Pittsburgh. That had the appeal of combining the pleasures of baseball with the exploring of distant, unknown places. Between the Red Sox and me it was about something more.

After the Anthem, I was back on my knees as Martin told of the pitcher throwing his warm-up tosses—if it was Mike Torrez, he was "the big right-hander from Topeka, Kansas." Then, finally, the game began, and when the home team pitcher threw his first strike of the day, the crowd let out a roar as though they'd vaguely doubted he would ever find his mark, and I, who'd definitely had that worry— pitching was the team's perpetual weakness—felt a gust of well-being.

Ned Martin had a crisp, old-fashioned way of speaking, favoring phrases such as "harkening back" and "his batter's box ablutions" to embellish a cadenced flow of precise vocabulary he unfurled with exquisite enunciation: to hear him turn through all five syllables when describing the "auxiliary" scoreboard was almost as satisfying as his renditions of gaudy names of opponents like the Brewers' outfielder Sixto Lezcano, John Wockenfuss of the Tigers, and Paul Thormodsgard, who won eleven games for the Twins in his rookie year of 1977, and then only one more ever after. Martin took pleasure in embedding literary quotations in his commentary, once borrowing from Wordsworth's "The Excursion," for instance, to say this about the intelligent catcher Elston Howard: "Wisdom is oftentimes nearer when we stoop than when we soar." There was such a variety of different verbs, nouns, and metaphors used by Martin to convey a baseball in motion and a crowd in rapture that I got an impression of him as someone who prepared for his job by sitting in the hotel lobby during road trips, rereading Modern Library classics. It was a more leisurely and picturesque account than is favored today, and from this melodious man I learned a lot about the diligent labors of Red Sox groundskeeper Joe Mooney, what the wind currents were doing to the center field flag, the interplay of glare and shadow and the jagged dimensions of the lawn that made right field such a challenging position to master in Fenway Park. The outfield positioning seemed invariably to be "a step toward" right or left, and, when an inside fastball came close to a batter, it never failed to "straighten him up." In truly dramatic moments Martin fell back on brevity. "He's *got* it!" was his first response to difficult catches. When he was really impressed, Martin paused and then said simply, "Mercy!"

In those days, there was no cable television, no Internet, baseball had yet to become a field of broad statistical inquiry, and personal information about the players, including their salaries, remained mostly unknown to the public. And because I had no television or newspaper, I experienced the disembodied Red Sox only through the disembodied voice of Martin, which made it easy to believe they were the valorous figures we both wanted them to be. If initially he was formal with their names, as the game proceeded his references grew much more familiar. Rick Burleson was "Rooster" or "Burly," we knew George Scott as "The Boomer," Tom Burgmeier became "Burgy," Bill Campbell was "Soup" to us, while in a bit of policy inversion tailored to emphasize the heroic stature of the team's mightiest batsman, coming up now was "Jim Ed Rice the Gentleman from South Carolina." The descriptions of their feats on the field were buttressed from time to time with a detail of biography that, because it was all we got, seemed somehow comprehensive, the telling fact, such as the small-town New England boyhood of "New Hampshire's own Pudge Fisk" or third baseman "Butch" Hobson's elbow full of "floating" bone chips that at any time might, without warning, "lock up" on the stoical ex-Alabama football player, even during throws. From time to time Martin actually summoned the phrase "his deeds." In the gently partisan hue of all this, I recall no instance when a Red Sox player gloated or otherwise forgot his manners, except under extreme enemy provocation, and each Bostonian seemed to have a more abiding interest than the next in "community service." Martin enjoyed talking about rookies, got us excited about their youthful, seemingly limitless futures, which made it possible to think we might have them forever. Former Red Sox players traded to opposing teams from then on received the appellation "Old Friend" before he said their names. (This helped me to get over the loss of the players; I always wanted them to remain Red Sox forever.) Even we, "The Fenway Faithful," were cited for loyalty. I could never quite decide whether in Martin's view winning at baseball was a reward for just behavior or if just behavior was its own reward.

The months of baseball were a quest that took me to distant settings like Illinois and California and introduced formidable foes such as the Baltimore Orioles with their pair of pitchers named Martinez, Dennis and Tippy, and their couplet of batting lineup pests, Rich Dauer and Al Bumbry—the latter actually known as "The Bumblebee." The entire American League landscape was populated with fascinating characters. The Tigers had a base-stealing champion named Ron LeFlore who'd done time in prison for armed robbery. Later, fully reformed, he became, of all things, an umpire. In 1976, Detroit's best pitcher was a native New Englander named Mark "The Bird" Fidrych who talked volubly to the baseball on the

mound and convinced it to win him nineteen games. The next year
the ball abruptly ceased to listen. A Milwaukee pitcher named
"Moose" Haas weighed 180 pounds, while the Rangers infielder
"Bump" Wills was 175. "Beautiful" Royals Stadium was decorated
with sparkling fountains. Municipal Stadium in Rust Belt Cleveland
could have fifteen thousand fans inside and still seem empty as an
abandoned factory mill. You hadn't experienced heat until you visited Arlington, Texas, in July. At the end of the season, when word
was passed along of the small towns in distant states the players
were now returning to for an off-season of hunting, fishing, or work
in the family business, I could see Martin someday telling how
every winter I went back to New Haven to read again *The Glory of
Their Times* and *My Ántonia*.

Listening was ecstasy, it was bliss, and it was more: a fanaticism
so consuming that all other sounds faded away. I ate sunflower
seeds during the games, and I could get so absorbed in a close contest that I went through entire sacks of seeds at high speed, my
hand a blur as it moved from the bowl of fresh seeds, to my mouth,
and then to the bowl for spent shells, which got so full that eventually the huge saliva-dampened brown pile toppled over the rim
spilling along my blue quilt, soaking it with wet, brackish blotches
that I noticed only after the Red Sox were safe. I never would have
said that I could influence what happened to the Red Sox, though,
in fact, with my many compulsions I behaved as if, by some magnetic force, I could affect outcomes. When a rally began, I often
froze in position, holding my breath, fearing even to twitch lest it
ruin the promising momentum. Convinced that God would not
look well upon pagan acts, when I discovered my legs or fingers
crossed during a crucial moment, I hurriedly uncrossed them. I
believed that Red Sox success was a reward for good character, a
conviction that without question did improve my everyday behavior. To assist the Red Sox during close competitions, I went out of
my way to be helpful to my mother, kind to my sister, to put the toilet seat back down after I used it, to take out the garbage when it
wasn't my turn, and I made silent bargains about what I'd do if mat-

ters went the Red Sox way. No matter what the outcome, it never would have occurred to me not to follow through, to fail to keep up my end, because did not real disaster thrive on such invitations? Those were my happiest points in the broadcast, not when the hoped-for event had come to pass, but before, when it might, I reviewing all the experiences that could happen, all the possibilities. It seemed to me then that baseball could grow time, that its endlessly digressive nature made it not so much immediate as an activity in dialogue with immediacy. Each game might, in theory, continue forever—until it didn't. Naturally, I wanted the Red Sox to win, but, if I could have wished for anything, it would have been for this game that was played at a lifelike, real-time pace to last and last, to go ahead and become life, for it never to end and send me back into my room again, back to the world's deficiencies.

By now I'd gone to a second game at Fenway Park, and afterward had begun thinking back on that first time I'd been with my mother. There could not have been a more banal and disappointing game and yet now I wanted to ennoble it, for it to carry a memorable significance equal to my feelings for the Red Sox. It began to occur to me that the team's old brick ballpark was the special part.

How I had loved to be there. Fenway Park was out of another time, so different from modern Shea Stadium, so different from anywhere else. I thought of Fenway the way I did the Worthington Hooker schoolyard, all the weirdly girdered porches and overhangs, the asymmetrical green walls and corners encircling the field in strange, viridian crenellations of high, low, near, far, everything built to the dimensions of an earlier version of the city that was still imposing distinctiveness and unpredictability on all the games played there, and on all the people who came to see the games. I think now about the way I, who then always favored such regularity in my personal environments, was so drawn to these eccentric public contours, these skewed proportions, and I see the stark demarcation between desire and need, the love for the surprising patterns of the past and the wariness of present deviations.

At Fenway I was less guarded, more receptive than usual in many ways to the timbre of sounds, to the play of light and sky, to degrees of breeze and temperature, the smell of food, the foam-whiteness of the bases surrounded on all sides by very dark earth and very green grass. I sat in the center of the city with the feeling that I was far removed from it. The world at ballpark vantage felt explicit. Everything was more than itself, especially the heroic ballplayers: Yastrzemski, Burleson, and even Andy Hassler.

Poor Hassler! I followed his career closely. Despite all the incantatory forecasting about his left arm, despite the easy mastery he'd displayed that first Fenway day my mother and I had seen him, he never did become a great pitcher, though for many years he seemed so much to embody the part that he continued to water expectations. After he'd failed first with the Angels and then the Kansas City Royals, in 1978 he briefly joined the Red Sox, still faintly shining with promise. Less than a year later, his record at one win and two losses, they gladly parted with him. Hassler became almost a law of physics to me—that something can never be more than it truly is no matter how much you want it to be so.

Other boys had favorite players, and I couldn't ever figure out why I never did. I revered all the Red Sox, and yet my feelings had neglected to deepen into the particular commitment I was seeking. I had no idea what that might constitute other than my conviction that he existed. Just as some adults searching for a spouse or a new house or even a dress can come to feel overwhelmed by the belief that the ideal for them must lie somewhere in the big haystack of the world, but that everything they are likely to encounter will represent some form of compromise, what pulled at me was the notion that there was a ballplayer perfectly suited to me out there if only I could find him.

One night I had a dream in which all of the Red Sox players were spread along the foul line at Fenway Park and we fans were permitted to line up in front of one of them for an autograph. Most of the fans chose the famous players, with thousands of people waiting to get a signature from Carl Yastrzemski or Carlton Fisk. I chose a reserve player positioned way out in right field, and because nobody else stood in front of him, there was time for him to talk to me. The dream was so vivid that I thought about it often. I wanted something more personal from the players, something absolute.

I scarcely knew the Red Sox at all. The faint silhouettes limned by Ned Martin meant that beyond their play, they were blank to me, had no tangible inner qualities. That situation had advantages. There was nothing to stop me from filling them in myself, seeing them with the same mysteriously resilient clarity of perception in which in my mind I saw places I'd heard about but had never been to, images that, once formed, I retained for years, such as my Minnesota: dark green and hoar-frosted with a lot of cabinlike structures surrounded by fir trees. In my imagination the ballplayers were strong and friendly and kind and benevolent and much given to easy laughter, and I interacted with them, by which I mean that I half thought I could bring them into my room and learn from these men how to live by listening to their games. Because they were so skilled at baseball, I had the idea that the Red Sox knew all the important things, had mastered life, had secrets to tell me about existence that nobody else could. That I was close to them, in turn, made it easier for me to disclose to the Red Sox the emotions that in the rest of my life were not easily expressed. To me, in a small apartment I lived in with women, the Red Sox became the men in my house. There was a game every day, and that schedule created a mutual constancy of commitment. I did not feel fully alive until I had gone off to be with them and hear whatever story they had for me that night. There on my knees, I poured myself out to them, loving them as though they were one with me. When it was time to be under the covers, I set the "sleep" switch on thirty minutes and allowed these Red Sox players to be, with a little help from Ned Martin, the ones putting me to bed every night—the present but nonexistent men I wanted around me to make up for the absent but existing father whom I no longer wanted at all, except in ways that he could not be.

I shared the Red Sox with nobody, not even my grandfather. That they were his team had drawn me to the Red Sox, but I still rarely visited him, and the Gerschenkrons did not make long-distance telephone calls. The truth is that I knew him from a remove similar to the way I knew the Red Sox, and because those had always been the terms, I accepted them without question. That, and the fact that my grandfather lived in another city, made it easy to idealize him. It was in some ways enough that he was up there in Massachusetts with the Red Sox, all of them watching over me from afar, present always in my imagination.

Only once did I visit my grandfather on my own. One spring weekend the year I was fifteen, I took a train to Boston and I remember the excitement of coming out of the subway at the Harvard Square stop, the sidewalks full of college students, the streets clogged with honking vehicles tagged with red and white license plates, the pace of my walk hurrying into a run as at last I neared the house, the sight of him opening the door to greet only me, the wide welcoming smile under the thick crest of gray hair and glasses that pressed against my cheek as he drew me into an embrace. Up in my room there was a pair of royal blue Adidas sport socks waiting for me on the pillow. I visited for two or three days during which there was no discussion of the Red Sox. Instead he talked with me about Tolstoy and my schoolwork, took me to a cocktail party where I watched his colleagues flock to him with an enthusiasm that didn't surprise me because it matched my own.

The next fall I was visiting a school friend on the October day my grandfather died. The news seemed impossible, all out of rhythm from the new, more reciprocal friendship we had just begun. I remember, in the starkness of the moment, everything rushing around me, the feeling of trying to focus, hearing a loud ringing in my ears that lasted until I wept. I wept and wept until my mother looked at me and said in reproach, "You didn't cry at all when Susi died."

Most distressed was my grandmother, who could not live without him, and died herself within short months, though not before being flimflammed out of thousands of dollars by a young confidence man she had hired to help her with household tasks. To see what the loss of my grandfather did to her, the listless despair that she wore ever after like a scarf, it was impossible not to believe that a person could die of grief. For my mother, it had been a merciless procession of loss. She now had no husband, no sister, no father, no mother—no background. There was only Sally and me.

That summer of 1978, the year my grandfather died, the year after Susi died, was the apogee of my fandom. I was becoming aware of how summer was supposed to be for teenagers, the hot, fun, sweet, endless August days they sang about on the radio. But I didn't know any night moves, had never been under a boardwalk. Instead, in my room, I lay sweating beneath the sheet, motionless, in a thrall, as on my radio the Red Sox won night after night.

This was by far the best Red Sox team I had followed. By the middle of July they led the Yankees by fourteen and a half games, the fleet of Boston sluggers, Fisk, Scott, Hobson, Evans, Lynn, Yastrzemski, and especially Jim Rice, bludgeoning the opposition with Precambrian brutality.

Then, as the first day of school approached, the Red Sox began to founder. Such an enormous lead vanishing felt like seeing a glass bottle full of juice falling from a table to the stone floor. You could watch it all happening there, so slowly and in no time at all. There were injuries to several players and terrible pitching, but what in particular ate at me was the deficient fielding, so many errors that, if somebody had told me that the Fenway Park clubhouse was infested with leather-eating moths, I would have believed it, would have demanded to know why somebody hadn't hurried out to buy cedar. I was in nightly genuflection with my radio, encouraging, imploring, coercing, scolding, reproaching, and cursing as the Yankees over-took them. Anybody who read about baseball knew that nothing was so predictable in life as Yankee victories, and that was what was most hard to take, the inevitability. How I detested the Yankees for their smugness, their grandiosity, their chesty, insatiable greed, the

way they salted Octobers with opportunism. The very existence of
the Yankees and their monochrome flow of victories jeered and
ridiculed me—as though the Red Sox defeat was also my own.

Just as suddenly, the Red Sox revived. There were days when I
hadn't listened to the broadcast and felt the muscles in my arms
straining with exertion as I stood by the radio awaiting a result from
Boston and from New York. When the news was good I never felt so
happy as relieved, and the news was good just enough times that on
the final day of the season, Boston was behind by only one game.
And then miraculously the season ended with the two teams tied as
Luis Tiant shut out Toronto while Rick Waits of bottom-feeding
Cleveland was outpitching New York's Catfish Hunter. After all the
months of baseball, there was to be a playoff the next day, October
2, at Fenway Park, to decide who would qualify for the postseason.
One game, winner-take-all. That the Red Sox had been so down and
then recovered their spirit made me forgive them all the squandered days of August, made me anticipate the playoff with an
incalescent throbbing of joy that tingled because almost instantly it
was cut with pessimism and doubt.

It was an endless Monday morning of school, and then I had soccer
practice. When finally we were released, I came running into the
athletic building and down the concrete corridor, which was slip-
pery in cleats, skidding into the office where Mr. Porter, the athletic
director, had for the day installed a black and white television. I had
never seen a television at school and that Mr. Porter had gone to the
trouble of hauling one in, setting it up, manipulating the rabbit ear
antennas into credible reception underscored what a day of unusual
moment it was.

The office couch, chairs, and floor space were crowded with
coaches and sweaty boys and girls staring at a black and white
screen that looked bleached, so bright was the afternoon sun in
Boston. The Red Sox were winning 1–0 in the sixth inning when I
found a wall space to lean against near the doorway, and now the
lead improved to 2–0 as Jim Rice singled in a run. I remember

standing there, rigid with attention, my concentration so instantly focused that it was as though I were alone in the room filled with others, others who were all Yankee fans, for New Haven was a Yankee town then, and mine a Yankee school. I recall it so well, for after all the months of hearing them, there the Red Sox were in the flesh—and they were winning.

With two outs in the seventh inning and two Yankee base runners, the Yankee shortstop, Bucky Dent, was up. Catcher Fisk had been running back and forth from the plate to the mound to counsel our pitcher, Mike Torrez, through this crisis, and I think he visited again for another delivery of pep as they went to work on Dent. There were two strikes before Dent lofted a pop fly that seemed soft, tender, and vulnerable even after it plopped like a fallen tightrope walker into the net just above the massive wall in left field. It was to become a famously dispiriting home run, but I experienced it first as something absurd. *That* counted? A moment later the Yankees scored a fourth run and then, in the eighth inning, Reggie Jackson hit another home run to make it 5–2 New York. A fatal melancholy settled over me. Mr. Porter had periodically adjusted the rabbit ears as we watched, and here he did so again, or at least I remember it that way, and I remember the bright green of the floor tiles and also the sudden pungent odor of electric burning.

The Red Sox scored twice in the eighth. In the last of the ninth, the score 5–4, Burleson walked and second baseman Remy lined a hit to right. On the television, the screen briefly went a monochrome white as the camera searched for the ball. We couldn't tell what was happening and then it was clear that right fielder Piniella couldn't either. Blinded by the sun, his body tensed with the danger of an invisible hard object approaching with surface-to-air valence that might be taking it anywhere until, by pure chance, the ball came out of the sky right next to him. Piniella held out his palm and the rent money found it. Next, Rice hit a mighty but just barely insufficient sacrifice fly so that Burleson was at third base, Remy still at first, as Yastrzemski came up with two outs. When you are a child, a ballplayer in his late thirties seems incredibly old, and the memory of Yastrzemski's final swing remains as indelible an insight into mortality as the sight of my aged grandfather shuffling on his way to bed. Pitcher Rich Gossage's fastball came vibrating toward the player whose name my grandfather had loved to say, Yastrzemski's torso twisted with the futile effort of his swing, an agony of burdened recognition blighting his face as this pop fly did what they usually do.

I felt boned like a fish. The others in the office were celebrating, and yet as I walked out into the cement hallway, I knew that they were also gaping at my misfortune. My hopes, how much I cared, were exposed for all to see. It was embarrassing to feel so humiliated in front of everyone, and to be made foolish by baseball. The end was so precipitate, like a lamp clicking off. Suddenly there was no more Red Sox, and I was back on my own without them. I don't remember anything else except an old inadequacy—and the new sense that the inadequacy of the Red Sox exactly matched my own.

That game was the moment that codified a public awareness of a titillating historical baseball truth, for suddenly everyone seemed to know that the Red Sox had not won the World Series in seventy years, since 1918. Further, throughout that long malaise there was now a litany of expressive Red Sox failures to think back upon, in particular the near-misses of 1946, 1948, 1967, 1975, and now 1978, and here the name Torrez was added to the corresponding Foxeian catalogue of martyrs: Pesky, Galehouse, Lonborg, and Burton. My Red Sox had become the iconic losers, the team that couldn't win.

That I had unconditionally given myself over for life to a doomed pursuit was not news to me. Long before anybody talked about all the lamentable decades, just by following the Red Sox you could feel how imperiled they were. That I was asking for happiness and diversion from such a fouled-up institution made no sense to me then. But this latest garish loss only deepened my love for the team, and, as the winter of 1979 began, my first winter without my grandfather, I felt oddly consoled by their pursuit of failure. Could I have intuited that my full-hearted, yet distant grandfather would enjoy a baseball association appropriate to the lines of his own history of wandering and loss? Not likely. But I had sensed that they conformed to something deeper in him than mere habitual attachment, and that his approach to being a baseball fan had been passed on to me. There was a madness to the Red Sox, to be sure, yet they were also healthy and unthreatening, not crazy at all, but irresistibly forsaken—like the Chekhov plays I had begun to read where the impending sorrow was tolerable because it was related with such beautiful ennui. It had been a horrible year, and I was grateful to the Red Sox for taking me out of myself, giving me something to anticipate, for not being too happy themselves.

In each ensuing year of high school, the Red Sox fielded promising teams that lost in the end, and yet I don't think I ever truly felt ashamed of them. I was frustrated by their fuddled, fizzling breakdowns, just as I often was frustrated by my life, in which everybody close to me seemed either sick or dying or tormented with grief, and that commonality of experience made the wistful pleasures the Red Sox provided accessible to me. At sixteen I had come to believe that nothing worthwhile comes without great suffering; there was deeper meaning for me in catastrophes. It was because of the Red Sox that I began to understand about people and personal history, that while everyone wants a radiant history he can be proud of, he also wishes for an apposite past that he can imagine replicating his own true experience. That I now had a group of men to embrace in my life whose cause was noble, interesting, vital, and yet weighted by the long drag of failure made it easier to go forward. As a child, if your life story contains sordid elements, you believe yourself to be unique. It's a relief to discover that something you admire without reservation is also flawed. Because they were so conspicuously imperfect, the Red Sox were always there for me.

CHAPTER TEN

My City in Ruin

I grew up between two great cities in the seaboard purlieu of a waning port town, its drowsy streets laid out by Puritans below now crumbling twin monoliths of red basalt, one to the east, one to the west, my daily transits taking me past the crested gates of the eminent university and those chained outside the closed factories, I neither of the university nor of the town, the son of divorced parents with different faiths, a scholarship student at a school of privilege, my address the first floor of a two-family house where I lived juxtaposed in narrow rooms by two strong women, in the middle of things and completely out of it. As I went through the last grades of high school, more than ever I hoped people would think of me as an upstanding young man, and I strove to be obedient and well-mannered, following rules, telling the truth, trying to adapt to what others valued, but because different people valued different things, it was hard to keep up with them all, and I expended such effort in this pursuit, that wherever I went during my middle-teenaged years, I felt like an imposter, and in my shame I acted like one.

I did not have a driver's license, and, because my school was miles across the city, at the end of the day I became reliant upon others for rides home, schoolmates or their parents who had never seen where I lived, who required directions from me. Approaching from the west, there were a number of possible paths to numbers 290/292 Willow Street with its bruised face of chipping gray paint, clapboards chewy under the tar-shingled roof from the drip-drip of hundreds of vernal rains, the front yard a brief dusty scrabble of rhododendron, three tired front steps climbing past a splintered banister to parallel doors calipered so close together that at first ours, 292, seemed superfluous, a fistula, the gibbous ceiling porch light kept in darkness through the blackest January evenings because the on switch tracked to our power bill. I never chose the direct route. Instead, I wound my deliverer through a sequence of rights and lefts designed to put my surroundings to the most picturesque effect, avoiding the cadaverous lowland districts east of Orange Street, avoiding the prosaic rumble of Orange as well, if I could help it, setting instead a more scenic compass north along broad, stately Whitney Avenue, until a right turn, not down Willow, but before, at handsome Edwards Street or shady Lawrence Street, there to the Livingston Street intersection and then left onto that grand and majestic thoroughfare honoring in name an heiress, which I allowed to reflect grandly upon me right up to Livingston's corner with Willow, where I hopped out before there was any question of the right turn signal, insisting "I live only a couple of houses down and it'll save you going all the way around the block." Some days I guided a course that cruised along the higher ground of Prospect Street, and then made a right turn down Canner Street, where the car windows produced a glorious sweep of rambling Victorian and Queen Anne houses on either side and also out along the leafy perpendicular vistas of Loomis Place, St. Ronan, Autumn, and Everit streets, an enfilade of regal dwellings lasting right through to the corner of Canner and Livingston, where I alighted, over a block from humble 292. "It's no problem from here," I'd call, relieving an imposition no driver ever gave signs of feeling. "Thanks for the ride." Often there were other passengers to drop off, and since my destination seemed inevitably to lie farthest afield, it made small sense that I should be keen to be helpful, more than glad to be deposited along the near, Canner Street end of Everit Street, or the very top of Willow Street, at Whitney Avenue, even in winter, after sundown. And, indeed, with these abbreviating gestures nobody seemed to think me guilty of anything more than consideration. It was late, everyone was hungry for supper, eager to be home, and if Mrs. Gifford or Mrs. Lovejoy did wonder later about a boy so willing to walk long blocks to save them short seconds, something told them that I was probably more comfortable being left in the dark.

My harbor city, beloved city of my youth, city of faith founded by ministers, city of industry where a mass-produced firearm was invented and also the lollipop, "Model City" of the War on Poverty, learned city of light and truth, now somnolent, desiccated, city fled by whites, abandoned by governments, riven with hardship and its Pyrrhic consolations, the public common a penumbra, the sidewalks empty at eventide, panic grass between the cracks, miles of neglected porches, all the vacant lots, fleets of tumbledown cars mottled in body-shop maroon, the acid-green river feeding the oil-soaked currents, heaps of scrap at the northern delimits, hills of slag to the south, a property without value, my city in ruin.

Since the gun factories began shutting down, the streets were less safe. New Haven had been in slow decline for many years, but I had failed to notice. Now, at the end of the 1970s, I awakened to a city that had so many slums they'd become bisectors of all sections, long, barren, car-door-lock-lowering stretches on which I could see through our raised backseat windows that men who had almost nothing would spend it all on a secondhand Cadillac. The jades working their lamp-lit trade at one notorious intersection inspired my sister and me to shorthand the siren dressers at our school: that sophomore's look was, we agreed, "very Chapel and Howe."

Downtown we watched a lone glass-and-steel box-tower rise on Church Street, read the "Office Space Now Available" sign, counted the months before there was light on a single floor, counted high. By now I had studied the schoolbook history of my city, and on cold winter evenings I could look into the frosted glass of that empty tower and see history reflected, a history that had been quickly punctuated by aspirations when in the 1640s, shortly after the founding of the Colony, a Great Shippe laden with investment cargo was sent through the January ice to England, the future hopes of the new settlement resting on the wealth that would come sailing back to New Haven. The ship never returned, though year after year New Haveners spotted its fugitive masts rolling aloft in the clouds, an apparition with enduring resonance in a lost city that ever after always seemed to be waiting for the money to arrive, for its ship to come in.

Yale, losing applicants, poured resources into security, and we denizens needed to see no memoranda to know it, for now the gray limestone walls of the courtyards seemed to be grommets holding off the turbulent city, buffering even the faint Brahms melodies drifting down to the sidewalk from the music school practice rooms.

A man named Gans asked me to guess where the four tall, rooftop, orange letters spelling out his name as signage for his eponymous suburban business had come from; after I gave up he told me, "I got them when Grant's closed!"

Not only Grant's, but Kresge's, and J. Phipps's, and Esther's and George and Harry's restaurant and Malley's, more and more sturdy mercantilists deprived of their apostrophes until we had a downtown that felt voided of transaction, a seventeenth-century Colonial grid updated in plywood-shuttered windows and empty display cases, all of it backlit by traffic signals still calibrated to a busier day so that on red we sat lengthily in still streets, waiting and waiting for green. The true quiddity of white flight was scorned space, a residue of empty time. Nearby on George Street was a gray-white concrete parking garage built with Neo-Medieval arches that was noteworthy among architects—a famous exponent of Brutalism had drawn it—though to us, who lived in the shadow, it was only a good place to get held up. And across the way, the rusty hulk of the Veterans Memorial Coliseum, a civic center that had emanated corrosion since the ribbon cutting. Beyond it, the aborted turnpike beltway where the road abruptly ended in cat-grassy swale—all of this lending new meaning to "We Bombed in New Haven."

In the dusk of a revival house screening of *All About Eve,* I

watched as Addison DeWitt briefed Eve for her out-of-town pre-
view at the Shubert Theater—the Shubert on College Street in
New Haven, which I crossed every day on my way to school.
DeWitt was explaining that "what looks like a very small city," is
really just a somewhere on the way to elsewhere. As he spoke, there
in my cinema seat I had the sensation of eavesdropping on my own
hometown.

That I lived in a place many people hoped to leave was my recurrent discovery. We had minor league teams and Yale students, all of
them soon to be moving on. Every spring I'd watch the station wagons line up on Chapel and Elm streets, all the undergraduate parents helping their children clear out for the summer. I had the idea
that they were glad to be going. For years I had wanted to validate
this place where I came from as it had once validated me. But perhaps now there came a divergent revelation—maybe I had begun to
feel that I wanted to get clear of New Haven myself, though without any alternative destination in mind. Adolescence is life on the
cusp of life. You crave options, but none are forthcoming because
you're not ready for them.

In a city with many unattractive public housing projects, among the
grimmest was the Church Street South Apartments, which stood
across the street from Union Railroad Station. The project was a
funerary succession of low-rise roughened concrete blockhouses
and unshaded courtyards ringed by a concrete outer wall, all of it
pinched and jammed onto an arid parcel between the highway con-
nector and the tracks. Less than a mile away were the Gothic clois-
ters of Yale with their wall friezes, belvederes, slate walkways,
crocketed gables and pinnacles, a proximity that was not proximate
at all, so pervasive was the isolation of the housing project. Though
it was teeming with people, Church Street South nonetheless felt
deserted, like a surrounded fortress that was slowly being starved
into submission, the population languishing in their strangely present exile. That was the problem with Urban Renewal in New
Haven, that the new buildings conceived as the concrete lodestars

of civic progress stood conspicuously separate from the rest of city life, so that to encounter them was to see idealism gone awry, the failure of optimism. Whenever my mother left off Sally and me at Union Station, like all the other travelers, we went hurrying toward the safety of the terminal doors, I trying to resist looking back over my shoulder at the throng outside the project entrance, all the restless men with nothing but time on their dark hands, I resenting them because the choicelessness of their lot made me seem small to myself in my own discontents. If I also saw in them the man I was on my way to visit, I was unaware of it.

With its clean brick exterior lines, inlay of soaring Gothic window arches, and handsome ceiling work, Union Station had once presented arrivals with a dignified face on New Haven. Travelers entered a corniced grand hall where there was dusty light shining down from the high windows onto long and sturdy wooden benches, everywhere an amplitude of space that made our town seem welcoming. But now the building had fallen into disrepair and had become too expensive to heat and renovate, so passengers bypassed the sealed-off station proper, entering instead to the left under a temporary porte cochere that led directly into the tunnel ramping to the tracks. It was a remarkable comedown, as though a lean-to had been asked to stand in for a padlocked winter palace. The current station served only to funnel us onward, a purpose emphasizing my circumstances: I had to go. Each time I made this ingress, I believed I was shedding all that was good in my life.

Sally and I went to New York at off times, in the middle of a holiday week or on the Sunday of a long weekend when the trains were a quarter filled, most people already arrived and burrowing into the occasion. Nobody on the train ever spoke to us. People who yearn for weekends, holidays, and summers to be over, who become suddenly upset on the Tuesday before Thanksgiving and at the mid-December sound of Christmas carols in department stores, tend to be quiet with such secrets. Month after month, year after year, we left and came back in this way, and just when the dog-faced eventlessness of the journey seemed most intolerable, I learned how much I liked taking the train.

My father discovered that a bus ticket cost much less. Now our visits ended in the swirling bedlam of the Port Authority Bus Terminal. To me, unable to tolerate my father in full view, here I looked instead at the bus station habitués lurking in the windowless fluorescence, so many sly, desperate, and disconsolate faces. It was then that my father had begun to have his own homeless periods, months in his life about which I knew nothing, for excuses were made until he had been hospitalized and treated and released, ready to be home and visited again by his kids. His face didn't look old, he hadn't any wrinkles, but it was impossible not to associate him with this mangled place I came to because of him, impossible not to think of him as a mangled man.

We boarded the Greyhound and sat directly behind the driver for safety, though no driver ever looked at us and the small "Your Driver" name-card slot above the windshield was always left empty. Perched on seats of durable, striped synthetic, trying not to irritate one another by crossing the DMZ of the armrest and brushing elbows, Sally and I rode north in restroom air, smelling also cigarettes and the tang of snacks born by our fellow riders—two hours of pounding along the turnpike with the restroom door whanging against its frame, drink cans rolling up and down the aisle, until the driver swung into his bay, released the lock with a hiss, and we were in a parking lot beside Chick's Auto Body in the shadow of the Coliseum. I never quite knew where I'd just been.

We were now in the purest form of our grotesque limbo, my father and I, I not wanting to have any thoughts about him, resistant to knowing anything, sure it would terrify me, yet always waiting for something terrifying to happen. Though I was getting older, my memories of New York from the bus years are in even shorter supply than those from earlier in life—which was by design. I remember the passes he would make at the saleswomen and waitresses we encountered during the course of the New York day, the arguments he'd get into with strangers in cramped public rooms where there was no way for me to melt into the wall, the dirty magazines scattered around his apartment. And I remember his circuit-breaking rages where his weirdly flickering eyes looked as if they were going to spring out of his face as he went on and on about how all the good women in our family were whores: "It's true, Nicky, all of them, and your Aunt Susi was the worst. A real flirt. She was always coming on to me." Every meal I sat eating with him I spent praying to hear the sound of my own footfalls.

I couldn't do anything about any of it, and there were still years to go before the mast, so when I got back to New Haven I just worked hard to dispossess myself. The situation seemed so impossible and horrible that where my father was concerned, mostly what passed through my mind were ruminations. One went like this: I have to go see him even though he never does anything good for me; not true—he gave me life. And another: he bears no responsibilities; given that, can he be considered irresponsible? In French class we were learning about Sartre's "other," and these musings likewise seemed too existential for me to engage with; I didn't know what to do with any of them. Eventually, I would learn that my father also was struggling to explain himself. His technique was to present people with copies of Saul Bellow's novel *Seize the Day*, the story of a man of high promise falling apart.

Back on the bus, I used to wonder how my mother could have married this person. It was frightening that such an able woman had made such a colossal error. I could not imagine two less compatible people than my parents, and there was, in these moments, something repellent about the whole thing to me. How could she have been so foolish, so careless? But I knew. The time I talked with her about it, she told me how deeply in love they had been, how "charming, and good-looking, and funny, and intelligent Don was, how much he loved me. You never knew him the way he was, Nicky." Then she said, "I thought I could make him happy and that with me he would be well. I was very young and very romantic and very hopeful." As for me, she said, "You got only the best parts of him, Nicky."

A light heart lives long," my mother liked to say, but only the rest of me was complying. My wrestling weight classes through high school progressed from 96 pounds to 105 pounds to 119 pounds as a seventeen-year-old junior—when the coach took me aside following another lost match to ask in consternation, "What's going wrong for you, son? Why aren't you getting better?" It's uncanny how all the hours of life you put into something can come to a head with such stunning compression. Day after white winter day in our low and narrow wrestling room that warmed through practice like a bread oven, I'd rehearsed the moves and counters he taught me, their names as vivid as chess combinations—openings, defenses, and endgames like the single-leg takedown, the fireman's carry, the Suplay, the Granby roll, the cross-body ride, the figure-four scissors hold, the several fractions of Nelson, the guillotine. His name was Kirchhofer. He had a cowlick, sideburns, squinty eyes, and enormous, hamlike woodcutter's forearms that he seemed to wear in the same way he did his sharply creased chinos. If something upset him he'd exclaim "Gadzooks!" When really exasperated, he'd add an intensifier: "Good gracious."

Wrestling wasn't fun the way games like baseball and soccer and touch football were. I did it because of Kirchhofer. What I liked best about wrestling was how much he wanted us to honor it. Every day when he walked into that stifling room with its crosscurrents of ammonia and old sweat, he was luminous with higher intent. "When you're in here with me," he'd say to us at the beginning of practice, "I don't want your mind on your math test or your girlfriend or your problems. Just have your mind on wrestling." Nothing was more important than our doing this spare, ancient sport not only well, but beautifully, and the hours I spent with him were so strenuous that during them I indeed couldn't think of anything else.

Kirchhofer was an excellent instructor because he passed along both the skills and a private sense of objective so urgent that kids who were not otherwise illustrious began to see themselves as champions and then became them. Although he never talked in a proselytizing way about God, we all knew that Kirchhofer was a religious Christian and it was apparent that to him there was an article of faith in wrestling. He asked people to draw from wrestling a kind of physical truth, and, when it happened, you saw the way wrestling could express what was admirably individual about every kind of person. I had hoped to be one of those boys, and now I had failed him.

The apparent reason was lack of strength. Mounted on the gymnasium wall was a climbing pegboard. Other wrestlers sped up and down, manipulating the pegs in and out of the many rows of holes with such ease and precision that they looked like sculptors up there with chisels, their feet in those striated shoes we wore seeming to walk right upon the wall. I couldn't do it. I would cling at the pegs, kicking my legs, thrashing my torso skyward, attempting to hurl myself toward the second row of holes, finally removing a peg and wildly trying to slam it into the higher hole in the split second before my right arm gave in and my weight swung me away, still flailing at the hole, until I drooped absurdly on one arm, inches from the ground.

Then one afternoon in wrestling practice, I took down the great Valente in a match for a spot on the varsity. Soon enough he reversed matters and pinned me. I was expecting to lose. Mr. Bakke, another coach who was refereeing, looked at me and said, "You know, Nicky, when you took him down, I would have thought you'd go harder after him. You seemed to hold back." Mr. Bakke was my favorite history teacher because in the classroom he could make you see great events in time as an algorithm—the step-by-step consequences for big actions that foretold the progress of man. I knew he was right about my wrestling, and for weeks I wished I had gone harder, because the moments life gives you to surprise yourself aren't predictive or frequent; you have to be ready for them to come up.

My solution was to remake myself: I would shrink until I was light enough to be strong for my weight. My wrestling diet allowed one tiny meal a day, an evening repast of a single slice of jam-spread bread, an orange, a glass of juice, and a bouillon cube. Immediately afterward I'd sink into a broiling bathtub to sweat it off. I was so famished I craved the acorns on the ground, but I was also inflamed with purpose. "What are you doing to yourself? Are you crazy?" my mother would cry. She'd once taught a wrestler who passed out in class. Already skinny, now I rapidly became twelve pounds skinnier, my waist as lank as my arms. By depriving myself in that way I experienced some sense of the body control other kids got on the peg-board, and for a time I won a lot of matches and a trophy in the year-end tournament, launching myself at opponents with a starved fury of aggression that was startling both to me and to at least one rival, who, after a first period on the mat with me, flatly refused to return for the second. I was indignant and also amazed at this; so far as I knew, nobody had ever been afraid of me before. But these self-denials were gamings of the system, false triumphs. Since the true essence of wrestling is its purity as a test of self, I could not get better because I was not yet myself.

One summer day in 1979, as sixteen-year-old I worked my mainte-nance job tending the grounds and grooming the red-clay tennis courts at the New Haven Lawn Club, I was sweeping the area along a baseline directly beneath the dining terrace where Gordo and his family were reclining over what looked to be the fresh berry and ice cream parfaits that were the kitchen's dessert special all summer, when my broom handle snapped with a rifle crack. "Did you get in trouble?" his younger brother, Stew, asked me later. In fact, when I telephoned my boss and confessed about the damaged broom, he replied, "Don't bother me at home with something like that."

Many families from my school were members of that club. I knew that even if we could have afforded it, we never would have joined. My mother hated exclusivity of all kinds, and she loathed the Lawn Club, which, she said, had a long history of discrimination in its membership policies against "blacks, Jews, Catholics—just about everybody." I understood all that, and, yet, when in my work clothes I confronted my schoolmates at their leisure in Speedos and tennis whites, I would have to struggle to remember that mine was the nobler course. As I raked and trimmed, I used to watch them on the tennis courts I had swept for them.

One day I requested the following Saturday off. Then I asked a schoolmate to bring me to the Lawn Club as his guest. Arriving there wearing tennis clothes, I felt awkward meeting up with people I worked with every day, and I wondered how I could not have anticipated that. I felt fraudulent—as though they could all see me passing myself off. A worry ran through me that I had violated a code, overstepped in some crucial way, and would lose my job. I spent the afternoon playing tennis, competing in such a rage of resentment that I overwhelmed whoever stood across from me, pummeling the ball past them with savage, unschooled forehands, playing as well as I had ever played, laboring for breath between points as my opponent tapped clay from his Adidas. Afterward, I sat at a table and ate one of the berry desserts. It tasted stale, too long refrigerated.

When I came back to work, I had not lost my job, but not many days after that I was switched to working alone, seven nights a week, as the club watchman. I sat by myself at a desk and made periodic rounds through the empty rooms, glad to be no longer a part of any of it.

Such a steamy, miserable time, adolescence. I dreamed of the girls I saw in furtive and smitten glimpses around the city. A redhead with eyes the color of hulled pecans standing in brow-to-brow conversation with a guy my age along Livingston Street, I wondering how he could manage the composure to form sentences, take adequate breaths, she gazing at him as he's telling her what he watched on TV last night. Up in the chair at the Lawn Club pool, the water-nymph lifeguard, the allness of her tank-suited self right there, tanned and alert in the heat, the soft hairs on her skin warmed to a pristine, dry bone-china white by all the hours in the sun. Wasn't she a twin? If so, maybe her other was turning out less pretty, within my hopes. But still pretty.

At school, every day surveying the Levi's corduroy asses shifting in compact rotations as they strode the corridors. Here was L.'s bullfighter ass singing "Toreador," prancing high. How impressive of P.'s to synchronize with the industrious to-and-fro of her ponytail. K.'s said sheriff; it was easy to imagine holstered six-shooters. But in the end nothing could match the grandeur of C.'s near-autonomous dual pockets swaying down the hallway in the heroic struggle to keep up with the rest of her. How fortunate they all were to have ownership of these asses. How lucky were the chairs they sat in. I knew about these asses because I looked at girls only from the reverse angle where no face could find mine.

I with my sheep's eyes, my first-Eucharist voice, such an unbearable innocent. When it came to blow-jobs, I imagined the involvement of puffing. A rim-job? I couldn't get past the bathtub drain. And nowhere to research the answers to these graphic and undermining riddles; everybody else just seemed to know already.

What did I think about when I thought about love? I thought about Laura Ingalls and Cilla Lapham and Ántonia Shimerda and Becky Thatcher. What absurdity, going into life relying on imagined descriptions of experience as my guide to experience. But Laura and Cilla and Ántonia and Becky were the only girls I really knew.

My Lawn Club maintenance-crew colleague, aged John, once had offered to sub-in any weekend shift for me if I had a date. "A kid should have fun on the weekend in the summer," he said. A date for me! At school, when Stanley and a dimpled, square-jawed friend secretly wagered to see which of them could win kisses from more different girls in a month, the first entry in their contest totals surpassed mine of a lifetime. What was love? Some vapor available to others, never to be breathed by me. Even when present, I did not exist. One day a kid named Arnold and I were chatting at the end of a school afternoon as Debbie came over to join us until her ride appeared. A car pulled up. She collected her books. "Goodbye, just Arnold," she said.

Over at a friend's, looking around the house for him, I walked in on his mother when she was changing. In bra and panties she grinned as I froze. A television flickered behind her. The shades were down. She said, "Well, at least you didn't catch me bare-assed naked!" That she didn't seem at all upset confused me. If she was not alarmed, why was I?

All these years since we left my father, my mother still never, ever had a boyfriend and I didn't even think about it. This was the way life was. At home when I encountered my sister's and mother's undergarments out on the clothesline, I averted my eyes. The sight of people kissing flustered me. It had suddenly become uncomfortable to be alone with a woman in an elevator. Why did I fear sex harmed nice women, believe that they didn't like it? Could I remember my father getting rough with her? I thought about divorce the way people said children of suicides couldn't get it out of their heads that someday they'd do themselves in. So many confusions. From the first, my courtship strategy would be to advertise the honor of my intentions by displaying my eagerness to do what girls wanted—just talk. The result was a lot of long conversations about other guys. I was not deterred. If I was loyal to my methods, eventually my virtue would earn me happiness. Or maybe not. In which case happiness had never been meant for me. I accepted it as a condition of my life that I was someone to whom love would not happen until I married. But how would I ever cross the gangway and become a viable groom? Did life have a schedule in mind whereby gravity suddenly relented? Would I someday develop a preference for classical music and golfing? How many billions of teenagers had there been in the world before me, and yet the ways life worked kept occurring to me as though I was the first one. So much of it seemed to involve figuring out what I should have figured out earlier. Perhaps my complete absence of experience was evidence that I was gay. I had never met someone who said he was gay. It was a different time; the word still meant light of heart. Nobody I knew ever talked about homosexuality except in derision, as life's most odious condition. When people called me a queer fag after I made a lame joke or misheard something because I was daydreaming, I just smiled, but I worried about what they knew. I just wanted to be like everyone else. If I really was queer, I reasoned to myself, wouldn't I think about penises all the time? That I didn't think about penises ever was some relief. Yet how would I prove to the guys in the locker room that I was not queer if they accused me? I tried to assemble escape routes for such an emergency. And just to be safe, when we ballplayers showered together, my eyes never tilted downward.

I imagined wooing women with something higher than desire. What would it be? Just what could I offer someone else? In a huge world filled with boys for girls to choose from, I believed I was irreplaceable only to myself.

My father had manic will and drive, and for a while, he concentrated it on legal prose. In 1973, he'd merged the great preoccupations of his life by publishing a book, *The Malpractice of Psychiatrists*, which he dedicated to Sally and to me. It was the first important analysis of the legal responsibilities of psychiatrists in relation to therapy, medication, hospitalization, suicide, and shock treatment. That my father could have risen from the abyss to write an accomplished legal treatise didn't seem miraculous to me because I scarcely looked at the book at all. I couldn't understand many of the long technical words he used, gave up after a page.

The book that stood there untouched on my shelf for all those years is itself a model of detachment. Nowhere is there any sign inside that the scholarly lawyer who is holding forth in such a disciplined way about "the utility for law of the nonscientific character of psychiatric evidence" may have been drawn to the topic through his own mental illness.

My father also wrote articles for law journals, letters to the editors of periodicals and newspapers, and rafts of personal letters. As my high school years progressed, he had begun writing to me frequently, copiously, and with varying degrees of sanity. I could always tell when the letters were going to make me upset just by the way he had addressed the envelope. The handwriting would shift from cursive to print letters. As his condition declined, the printed words would grow smaller; eventually they became almost microscopic. Weeks of silence followed. Then one day an envelope from New York addressed in a booming scrawl would be waiting when I came home from school, and the cycle would begin again. When he was healthy, his way with words made him witty. When he got sick, he quite literally lost his wits, and the wordplay went out of control. He punned compulsively and said things that were grandiose, lewd, bigoted, and cruel. Then he misplaced words, lost track of their meaning, forgot his own name. Finally it all turned completely incoherent. I didn't keep any of those letters, but I always read them.

To my knowledge, after I threw a letter away, I never afterward thought about it. When stressful thoughts came into my head, I reflexively dissociated from them, picking up and vanishing myself from the present—my image of myself in those moments was a boy in a hot-air balloon basket. People at school would do imitations of me with my slumped posture, my mouth half open, my dilating eyes fixed on a distant horizon. They gave me another nickname—The Fogman.

At our round wooden dining table there were four wooden chairs with machine-woven cane seats, and the three yellow plastic place mats. My mother sat to my left, Sally was across from me, and because these positions never shifted, for the fifteen years I lived in New Haven, the chair to my right was always empty, with no place mat in front of it. The cane straws in that chair retained their tight-strung gloss as the other three seats faded and grew slack and frayed. Now every night my mother, my sister, and I brought books to the dinner table. My mother's periodic solution to being "sick and tired of you kids ruining meal after meal with your endless carping at each other" was to ban conversation in favor of reading. Once reading at meals was instituted, things quieted except for the turning of pages, the chink of fork tines against plates and bowls, and the resonant sounds of my mother's swallowing; she scarcely ate all day and came home famished.

Silencing me was a good idea. Too often of late I had been compelled to visit disorder upon my mother's orderly rooms with bursts of sibling aggression. To listen to my end in these mealtime exchanges, you would think Sally to have been lacking for nothing in life but fraternal critique—a deficit that I was so up for filling it was at times difficult for my sister to do or say anything without my bruitous intervention, followed up with a mocking I-know-better laugh. Sally sat down to breakfast one day wearing new shoes. "You're going to wear *those*?" I asked her. At dinner the state capital of Rhode Island came up in conversation. Sally didn't know it was Providence. "How can you not *know* that?" I asked. Into her room she'd go to practice her flute: "Mom," I'd loudly warn from my room, "I can't get anything done in here with her in there *piping*." In my bandolier, "un" was the prefix of choice, as in "How *un*cool can one person be?" Again and again and again riding her, these harsh sorties, and what had she done? She could be perhaps moody and a little bossy. I was the Dodge Ram pickup roaring up behind a bicycle, racing the motor and then leaning on the horn just for hate. In the moment there was always the tissue of cause, the roweled spur of circular justification. She had to be provoking me, otherwise why was I angry? But here were her real provocations: she was near and she was safe—safe to impose upon with my precarious moods, safe to share the secret of my truculent discontent, safe because she understood I was unhappy even if I didn't, safe because I knew that she loved me in spite of it all. I inflicted my cares on her and on my mother, allowing what I disliked about myself to seem like their doing, and they forgave me. We three were a little family.

That was the real novelty of my adolescent discontents, that I was so unaware of them. I had moods that could shrink the house, and I never had any idea. When in my presence somebody began to talk about a couple getting divorced or I overheard Joan Baez singing "Daddy You Been on My Mind," to my surprise I'd lose control of my eyes and throat. Immediately I'd focus on hurrying myself past it. Wretched as I sometimes was, I knew I must not seem down because things could always be worse. I was fortunate, had my own room, while in New Hampshire, my grandparents had known a local family that had numbered so many children five boys shared a bunk. And think of my mother, asleep in the living room, turning herself out so I could have a private space. I firmly believed myself to be having a happy childhood. "You were such a sunny kid," people tell me. How then to account for my miseries? I refused to think of them as miseries. I viewed them instead as wrongs committed by others, which fate would someday prosecute because in the long run life was fair. My mother did not know that I found it comforting to see the world as a place where ultimate justice was pending, but she encouraged my interest in delayed gratification when she told me that it was okay with her that I was not "one of those people who is peaking in high school. Most of them never go anywhere." That my time would come had abstract appeal. Then I'd get tripped up by the usual snare of how unprepared I would be to face my moment when finally it arrived.

Out behind our house was our forsaken backyard, the grassless firmament sinking lower and lower beneath exposed tree roots that arched from the dried-out topsoil like ruptured tendons. I wanted to fix it up but didn't know where to begin. When I thought about how to solve such deficits of knowledge, I now often pictured somebody in a plaid shirt as the one to guide me. He would be there to talk me around a tool belt; to teach me to—I had an ever-increasing list—fly cast, chop wood, train a dog, keep a treehouse aloft, drive and then to lend me the car on the condition that I'd wash it Sunday afternoon; to lead me out back for lessons on how to put up a tent before taking me camping; to show me where I was going wrong with my math homework; to come to my games and diagnose my swing afterward; to tell me the way to behave around women; to fill the empty chair at dinner; to make an after-bedtime murmur of adult voices with my mother. I was mortified by my manly inabilities. Could it be so difficult to master a fuse box, learn to fix a flat bicycle tire, or lay down fresh seed and fertilizer? I didn't learn because—how can I explain this?—there seemed to me a wrong way to know.

I wanted help so I wouldn't need the help I wasn't going to ask for. I wanted help to keep me from messing up my life and ending up broke, friendless, alone, and strapped down. Yet if you'd asked me then what I wished for most in the world, I'd have said with

complete candor, "I want the Boston Red Sox to win the World
Series."

The inability to see myself distorted my vision of others. I knew
that suffering had visited the homes of many of my classmates. A
house burglar killed one boy's father after which the boy seemed to
me to grow so increasingly fair and fragile that by the time we were
seniors he spoke in a sweet childlike contralto, and his delicate
blond lashes lit his face in angelic forbearance. A second boy's dad
had been crossing a city street when a car struck him down. That
boy was among the most popular members of our class, though
around me he always acted scornful. Another kid's dad died and the
kid quietly left our school. Divorce was not uncommon. When a
separated mother returned for visits to the house where one of my
friends and his siblings lived with their father, I saw how life was
transformed by her presence right down to the more upbeat rock
that went onto the turntable and the baked goods that appeared on
the kitchen counter. I never knew any kids who talked about the
unpleasant parts of their lives, and I would not have known how to
do so with them, would have been too fearful of visiting that kind of
pain, would have distanced myself by all means possible. I wanted
everyone to be unaffected by their hardships and disappointments,
and I found it possible to imagine that they were all taking what life
brought them in perfect stride, just like me.

Once I stood in a New Haven backyard as a good friend and his
father argued. I was paying scant attention. In this year when the
father bought himself a steel-blue Porsche, wrecked it, and went
out and got another, my friend and his dad had been quarreling a
lot. The impetus for this latest squabble was nothing so remarkable.
Then suddenly I watched astonished as the father struck out with
his arm at my friend, who captured the arm and judo-flipped his
father head over shoes onto the turf. The father bounced, then lay
on his back so still he could have been sunbathing. I was marveling
at this, marveling at the sight of my friend panting over his van-
quished progenitor, when I heard a maternal voice breaking

through the weird calm, "Nicky, go home," and out the garden gate I floated, the whole incident begun and ended with such blurry celerity I wondered on my way back to Willow Street if it could have really happened. Then I got to thinking what a gorgeous flip it was, that I didn't know my friend had it in him. Soon enough I was back over there at the house, joking in the convivial kitchen with both parents, none of us acknowledging that something surprising had happened, something that might have suggested to me that the world out there was a place much stranger and more tragic than I pretended, and more forgiving.

One of the kids in my neighborhood passed along to me a new record he'd come into and didn't want. On the cover was a knock-kneed, splay-legged, pigeon-toed man in cuffed jeans, skinny necktie, and a blazer, holding a guitar in a way that made me think he was concerned about dropping it. The man had on a pair of eyeglasses with the thick black frames popular among Treasury men during the Eisenhower administration, a lumpy pomp of black hair and such a pale face that his glowing head appeared to be levitating free between his collars. He was seething. The laid-back Eagles did not look like this. The stadium-filling, blow-dried members of Yes, Kansas, Foreigner, Van Halen, Journey, and Styx didn't either, and not the merciful James Taylor. Nobody pictured on the front of the black souvenir T-shirts with the scrolled list of tour cities down the back that kids wore to school the day after going to concerts bore any resemblance to him. This lone misfit without a band was either torturously ashamed of his own geekdom or enraged about it enough to want vengeance. Maybe it was all a joke to him. He was calling himself Elvis Costello, he'd named his record *My Aim Is True,* and over and over across the album cover in small, manic type he was proclaiming himself king. What the hell was this?

I put the record on the turntable and the voice came squalling out "Why, why, why, why," coarse, jittery, and echoey with strain as though Costello'd got himself locked inside the laundry room and was deeply pissed off about it. What exactly did he have on his mind? Well, he was frustrated ("I can't do it anymore and I'm not satisfied"). And he was trying to get past it ("I used to be disgusted; now I try to be amused"). And he wasn't having much luck with the result that he may have been boiling over ("I don't know how much more of this I can take"). The man was a complete malcontent, swarming with bitterness, emasculated by faithless women, longing for revenge against all the fools, deceived, lost, hurt, the angriest guy in the world shouting "I'm not angry anymore." All this, and the added pressure of trying to stay safe by keeping everything under wraps ("If they knew how I felt they'd bury me alive"). I found this hostility vastly reassuring.

I had the impression that I was touching a strange region out there, with a county road lined by telegraph poles disappearing into a horizon somewhere far away where the people more like me were living. I played *My Aim Is True* over and over, singing along with Elvis—"I could tell you that I like your sensitivity when you know it's the way that you walk"—sometimes guessing at the slurred lyrics. Even when I did get them right for sure, they tended to have such a pithily opaque finish that I had no idea what they meant. ("Red dogs under illegal legs"?) But I understood everything. Here stood one bold man unafraid of showing his hand to the cruel world. He was combusting with fierce desires and sneaky feelings, and, guilt-stricken as he might have been about some of it, he felt worse that his undesirable self just wasn't going to get satisfied tonight, this month, or probably ever. Listening to the record, I was not specifically conscious of why I might be drawn to Costello. But the general fact of it was this: I, a person so frequently unaware of my own state of mind, so doggedly disconnected from my true experience of life that I didn't even know that I was especially angry, was not angry anymore. I was ecstatic.

If rock 'n' roll really could, as the rock stars promised, offer a young guy deliverance, set him free, the Red Sox seemed to have the opposite effect on me. When the Red Sox wasted a scoring opportunity with a base-running mistake by Rick Miller or a clumsy swing by Butch Hobson at what the broadcasters told me was "a hanging curve that Butch *really* wishes he had back," it would take me a while to get past the unnecessary failure. Sometimes I thought on and off about it for hours. I could become enmeshed in this kind of lamenting even when the Red Sox were leading the game, because I couldn't forget that they ought to be ahead by more. These regrets were most tenacious when the Red Sox broke down and lost a game they'd been about to win. Only then could I ever admit that I'd expected a win, and the way I knew was because of the reluctance involved in divesting myself of what I'd prematurely begun to savor. One method for coming to terms involved a little internal sermonizing—thinking to myself how "unforgivably careless" it was of them to squander something so difficult to achieve. Yet even after I believed myself to be reconciled to the game that was frittered away, I would display signs that were to the contrary. For days, chirring through my mind was what the team record "should be" along with what it actually was.

Where the Red Sox walked, I foresaw only danger. When the Red Sox got many runs ahead of an opponent, I would wish for them to cease, not plate any more, for there seemed to be a moral risk to scoring too much, whereby if you were gluttonous this one day, it would cost you in the future. It was a logic of sin and economy, for it also stood to reason that there were only so many runs available in a season, and I hoped to make the supply last as long as possible. I was the sort of worried fan who went out of the room only when my team was batting, when nothing terrible could happen. If the Red Sox lost to a weak team, and even when they won imperfectly, I fretted, certain it promised ill for later in the season when the schedule would grow more challenging. Baseball being, after all, a game of simple justice where teams must earn their ups—merit the privilege of hitting—I wanted the Red Sox not only to win, but to deserve to win. When they lost, part of what consoled me was the righteous sense that on this day they were unworthy. Curiously, I did not hold other teams to this fierce, punitive standard. If Red Sox opponents made even egregious mistakes, I had no problem regarding them yet as fully puissant. Indeed, when I would think through the names of all the Red Sox American League rivals, I detected latent menace in each club, endowed all of them, from Toronto to Milwaukee to Texas to California, with lethal guerrilla powers. I nurtured a proactive fatalism even though year after year the Red Sox had a winning record. And yet, inconsistently, I also always had aspirations. Ready as I always was to be disappointed by the Red Sox, when they went ahead and did disappoint, I was dimayed in a way that suggested I had not been ready at all.

On days when, for some reason, I missed listening to the Red Sox game and didn't know whether they'd won or lost, as soon as I returned home I hurried to my Chronomatic 9. The most expedient way then to get a score was by turning on WCBS 88 and waiting for the twice-hourly sports report at 11 and 41 minutes past. When the news anchor said "time for sports" and threw it to the sports update man, who began to run through the results, I was clenched in suspense, gauging his inflections for clues, trying to know before I knew, looking over at the spines on my bookshelf across the room to see if the first letter that caught my eye was an L or a W, buzzing with negative clairvoyance, expecting a loss and yet hoping anyway for a win. If the Red Sox opponent's name was said first, I flinched as though my bare foot had landed on a protruding floor nail, though I knew that sometimes the sentence would unfurl in a happy way, with "Oakland lost to Boston 6–3," rather than the dreaded "Chicago 7, Boston 1." Even when I already knew that the Red Sox had won, if I happened to turn on WCBS and hear the results being announced, I'd still get a little tense until the winning score was repeated and I was reassured that nothing had somehow changed with the information venue. When the Red Sox lost a few games in a row, it crossed my mind that they would never win again. When they did win again, I would wonder: why was it so hard all the other times? I was always sadder after a loss than I was happy following a win.

The morning after listening to a Red Sox game on the radio, during a free period at school I would go to the library, sit down with the newspaper in one of the soft chairs over by the rear window, and read the Red Sox box score, the tabulated numerical summary of the previous day's game. There was something soothing about revisiting the game in agate now that the results were not in doubt. The streamlined box scores of the 1970s were nothing like the plump rectangles of today with the generously compiled up-to-date batting averages, earned run averages, and other premium statistics. As I read, I would often think how simple and clear a box score was, such a cunningly concentrated representation of truthful events. Every day came another tidy installment of new numbers to puzzle over, and, by reading them faithfully, I could try to decode what the game had meant.

Along the way there were the pleasures of watching individual Red Sox players accumulate spectacular statistics. When Dennis Eckersley won another game or struck out a farrago of Baltimore Orioles without walking more than a batter, that he was setting himself apart in this way, making himself remarkable, gave me a surge of satisfaction. The satisfaction came in noticing right along, appreciating the achievement as it became itself. And likewise, if Jim Rice was on a hot streak, each day when I looked at the jagged transcription of letters and digits that made up the box scores, my eye first found Rice's line, and should it be filled with threes and fours and fives, images would bloom in my head of long-traveling home runs, of the opposing pitchers executing fouettés to see what Rice had done to them this time, of all the base runners he was driving in getting a little fatigued by so much cardiovascular activity. There was also the whimsical uplift when they did something out of character: a home run for diminutive Jerry Remy, a triple for Gary Allenson, who ran—and looked—like his nickname, Hardrock.

The list of Boston names made me happy—most of them. As I read Renko and Rainey I would think that the men operating the Red Sox must be as aware as I was how the fatal paucity of pitching always doomed the team, and I would wonder why these administrators didn't try harder to address the annual flaw. Even so, I knew that each year there was the possibility of a miracle, though a narrow possibility. This is how much I was with the Red Sox: I expected them to fail in the end, and yet every day I gave them my attention.

Baseball is a game of failure and it's those who can endure failure who succeed at it. By then I knew that the constancy of my commitment to the Red Sox would weather whatever loss and disappointment I might experience with them. The real pleasure of following the Red Sox came from the sense of how each game fit in the season-long unfolding of events. It was a private investigation I was conducting, in which my constant ambition was to see the past in terms of the future—all the games and all the numbers gradually justifying a narrative that by late September would solve the deeper mystery of the troubled nature of my team. That the Red Sox might be attractive to me because they were disappointing was something I did not linger on. There was, however, a sense of accomplishment in having chosen a team that made itself challenging to support and a satisfaction in knowing that I could stand it.

Later, I would regard these Red Sox immersions as a discovery of meaning, my first realization that the best relationships in life are those into which I could put more and more of myself. By virtue of my commitment to the Red Sox, I could see my understanding of baseball deepening. I was gaining expertise, which made the game more enjoyable. I also felt closer to the team, a familiarity that was something like intimacy insofar as one aspect of intimacy is making yourself vulnerable, revealing your vulnerabilities. When the Red Sox played badly, I became angry with them, might even act badly myself, shouting at the radio, glowering at the newspaper, brooding. I held them to high account, and if I learned that their play had been not only undignified, but inept, even farcical, or that a player had misbehaved—abandoned his civility—I felt outrage, the familiar implication. But even for those upsetting moments I was grateful. Being able to express disappointment is such a vital element of love.

Even after twenty years in the classroom, in September my mother still had an annual teaching nightmare. Sally and I knew them all. In one, she saw herself standing before her new classes completely unprepared. Another year, she dreamed of being forced against her will to be in the school basement as her students sat upstairs in her third floor classroom waiting for her. A voice in a third dream told her she was too structured and must refurnish her classroom with modular sofas that would spread the students out across the room, some with their backs to her. Then one year she dreamed she was made to teach advanced mathematics, which she knew next to nothing about. After she'd successfully bluffed her way through the first class and her students were filing out of the room, she thought, I don't have to suffer like this, and woke up. The morning following her dreams she would be shaking her head in relief, laughing, enthusing "reality can never be that bad," telling us how the dream had "scared the daylights out of me" and how "it went through me like wine through water," shrugging off the intruders, reassuring herself, gathering her resolve for the long year ahead.

We never saw her on Mondays. During the school day, her students handed in the papers they'd written over the weekend, and then in the afternoon she returned to her classroom and read them, covering the margins with red corrections and comments and arrows and exclamation marks, keeping her third floor light on deep into the night, even if snow was piling up outdoors, as she made her way through every submission so the students would get these stories and essays back on Tuesday while they were still fresh in their minds. I never glimpsed any of her work on these papers, never saw the papers at all, because they never came home. "I tell my students that their writing is a private thing, and I mean it," she said. "They have to trust me that those papers will never be seen outside of that classroom unless they decide to show them to somebody." It's easier for a parent to gain the confidence of other people's teenagers, but not much easier. My mother was the toughest person I knew and also the most frangible. She was stern, touchy, and tenderhearted, a person who could seem aloof and strict until her heart went into her mouth at something and she had to wipe her eyes. At school my mother was all business, nobody's pal. She expected the best from her students because she wanted the best for them. She did not banter in the hallways like some teachers, cool teachers, the teachers to whom yearbooks were dedicated. Yet when it was time to ask for college recommendations, more students requested letters from her than from anybody else. The students were aware that she understood them with the same penetrating grasp that she displayed when she told them about characters in literature. As she would have said, "All of them mean the world to me." Years later, I would learn that she was also frequently the teacher in whom students would confide behind a closed door when they were really in trouble, needed somebody who could be trusted to listen and then offer advice without judging them.

For as long as we can remember, my sister and I have been running into ex–Mrs. Dawidoff charges who want to tell us that she was the teacher who changed their lives. Her work didn't pay her well compared with what the parents of most of her students earned, and that modest remuneration confused me. It seemed so arbitrary what the world valued, whom it rewarded with large sums of money. And yet I believed that it was not arbitrary, that there must be a moral explanation for why some people had grown up to be wealthy and comfortable and why my gifted, driven, exacting mother was poor.

My mother didn't think the world owed her any favors. Truly on her own, without any meaningful community of support that I could see, she carried on, meeting every obligation like a Russian. That she could discover clothes she liked on the racks at Goodwill was a victory of thrift. When it was pointed out to her that as a divorcée holding a job she was a true Liberated Woman, she had impatient words for the Movement: "Those Women's Libbers with all their talk about careers are doing a beautiful job of undervaluing what it means to be a good mother." Her conversations with me contained references to those who were far worse off than I, children in India, children in Dickens, children during the Great Depression, children named Joad. I aspired to her example, but in some helix of emotion, I could also not stop myself from feeling disappointed in the world, being at once hurt by the woes of my adolescence and yet aware of how petty they seemed to be.

With a friend and his father from New Haven, I attended a summer evening game between the Yankees and Red Sox in New York, my first time at Yankee Stadium. The enormous ballpark was gray and unruly as a storm at sea, filled with squalling waves of people. At first it all seemed exciting, the big game between the two famed adversaries, but after Jim Rice stroked a home run for Boston and I cheered, somebody behind me smeared my head and back with hot dog mustard. I looked behind; there were only adults, their faces blank with contempt. As the game continued, it was as though they were all salivating for victory while the spit turned. There were many fights between fans broken up by policemen who bundled huge angry men from the premises. At one point, everybody around me craned his neck to watch as a spectator was saved from falling out of the upper deck. A friend who went to a Red Sox game against the Yankees in New York at the time reported that he saw a group of Yankee fans tear off a Boston fan's trousers: "They depanted him!"

These brief, random events confirmed an impression: the Yankees and their fans were bullies, brutes, something dangerous, humiliating, and out of control, and I conceived for them a raw and primitive hatred. And what made it all much worse was that the Yankees were now always better than the Red Sox.

The relentless year-in, year-out futility of it all was enormously frustrating, and there were times I'd think I couldn't get away from the malign weight of the Yankees. When once more the Yankees overtook the Red Sox for another lost game in another lost season, although I'd expected it, I couldn't believe it, and a powerless fury would rip through my body: devoured again.

Since the Red Sox couldn't beat the Yankees, it was enormously important to me that the Red Sox and I be more virtuous than the Yankees and their fans. To this end I worked out elaborate, Manichaean, Yankee-invalidating proofs in which the Red Sox personified goodness and the Yankees and their boorish, free-spending owner George Steinbrenner were the inimical force. The Yankees might win every year, but only because they needed to win too much. They were unfair, the instruments of a supernatural doom that destined them to prevail no matter what the Red Sox did. The Yankee and Red Sox players were men unknown to me, hailing from towns all over America, only wearing shirts that said Boston and New York, and yet by now my feelings about them were becoming stronger than my feelings for many real people in my life. Sometimes I became so emotional on the subject I could scarcely recognize myself; they were making me a different person. Or was it some other effect they were having?

There is a strange resourcefulness to childhood, an ability to find solutions to the overwhelming problems in your life, problems that often you can't begin to understand. While it was destructive to spend so much time reviling the Yankees for taking away my hopes and making me helpless, it was also useful to despise them. It never occurred to me that when I thought so hard trying to explain what made the Yankees evil, I was working on this as a way of avoiding other dreads, the dread of going to New York, the dread of what New York could mean about me. There was something festering down there, a family malediction in my father whom I'd once loved but who now terrified me and made me ashamed—and then ashamed for being ashamed because it wasn't his fault. Once he glanced down at my wrists, unusually thin and elongated, and showed me his, said I had "the Dawidoff-man wrists." That I was of him and might become him was too much to bear. I was holding it together by not thinking about that. Except every month, just when it would seem to me that I had my own life up in New Haven, I'd go boomeranging back into New York and remember where I came from. Then I'd return home and New Haven with the wind in my face wouldn't look very good either. The Gerschenkrons were dying. My uncle was lost. My cousins were sad. Everything I came from was rotting. Better to ward off the uncertainty by trying to be so good and so normal nobody could mistake me for something else. But damping down all the emotions was exhausting. That the brutish and ill-intentioned Yankees were annually refuting my need to see the world as a place where goodness would be rewarded terrified and infuriated me. It was comforting to be so angry at them.

Now it seems impossible to me that, through all those years, it never crossed my mind that my feelings for the Yankees might be affected by my feelings about anything else in New York, but it didn't. I just hated them. With my Yankee rages, I could reveal the inner self I never showed.

CHAPTER ELEVEN

Next to Love

It was the end of a mild Tuesday in the middle of May. All through the morning and afternoon at school I had been contemplating doing something that would require such strong purpose I tried to make myself unaware that anything was on my mind. I attended my eleventh grade classes and a baseball practice, went through my daily routines. Afterward, hurrying back across town for a new baby-sitting job on Linden Street, I stopped off at home. Coming through the living room, I put my books down on my desk and then I stood there in the quiet room with a blue rug on the floor. Whenever that day comes into my memory, the rug spreads aqueous and still, and I am looking down upon it from high, high above. I opened the door, walked out of the room, and found my mother. I heard myself say to her that I was thinking about inviting a senior named Annette Hamburger to the school prom. As I spoke, some throttle in my chest opened up and through the window beyond the curtain rods, clouds began accelerating across the sky in rapid formation. I had never before asked a girl on a date, had never asked one to dance. It was to be everything all at once. I felt the possibility of becoming someone else, and as I resisted the telephone, there was an inevitability both intolerable and electric.

Annette and I had attended the same school for five years, during which what I knew of her blurred indistinct from what I knew of her group of friends, a circle of viola players and cross-country runners and debaters, most of them studious, many named Sue. Our paths had seldom crossed because they were all a year older, such a vast interval in the early grades of high school. Yet there had been a long chat about high school cliques with one on a lunch line, a tradition of greeting another by his unusual middle name (Southerton), so that without much effort I now took for granted a shared outlook. For that morning, Annette and I had fallen into a conversation. She laughed as she stood there in Levi's, a Shetland sweater, and sneakers telling me how foolish I was, couldn't I see? What fun to be teased! How wonderful to be the object of sly little quips—quips made by someone with flashing dark eyes and a laugh like a clear chime. On what thickly misted longitudes had I been dwelling not to have noticed her before? She would graduate in short weeks and become a Yale student. I had nearly missed her.

My mother was taking care not to look too overjoyed as she told me that inviting Annette Hamburger to the prom was a good idea, but she said "good idea" with such conviction that for an instant it crossed my mind that this had been her idea, that I was acting at my mother's suggestion, that I was doing it for her. I had known she would approve. Just as the minister's children can tell who in the congregation their parent is most pleased to have knocking at the rectory door, high school teachers' kids grow up aware of how their mother sees the faces in her classroom. My mother always contended about her many students that, "I love all of them equally," and while nobody ever doubted she was fair and impartial and really did care about every one of them, it seemed impossible to me that someone who had such strong feelings for the characters in the books she taught wouldn't also have a soft spot for real people who had the qualities of Horatio, Prospero, Isabel Archer, Emma Woodhouse, and Jo of the dust pile at Tom-all-alone's. In rare instances she had shown her hand. Two of them were Annette's clever older twin brothers—"that Philip Hamburger" and "that Jeffrey Hamburger," who sometimes also became "those adorable Hamburger boys!" Another was "that Annette Hamburger."

I went back to my room and busied myself. Time went by. My mother called, "Sally and I are going out!" A moment passed. I heard her again: "Nicky, we're leaving now and you'll have the house to yourself!" Another pause, and then a singsong, "Before we get back I want you to have called her!" Finally I heard, "Faint heart never won fair lady!" and at last the heavy echo of the front door meeting its frame, followed by the slow hydraulic release of the storm door before it too bumped shut. In the sudden silence I imagined that people must see my mother as the parent of a child who was falling behind in life.

I went into the dining area, looked up the number, and stared at the telephone on the wall. A band of something was restricting my chest. Everything was slowing down and speeding up again. Maybe Annette was already going to the prom with somebody else. Who was I to be proposing this? I could just leave now. But it was a chance I felt doomed to take. I lifted the receiver off the hook and dialed the number. In recent weeks, my voice had begun without warning to make alarming, pitched treble sounds, like a radio veering erratically between frequencies. I feared an episode. A grown-up answered and I asked if I might please speak to Annette. Who was calling? I confessed. I heard "Netty, it's for you," and then at the sound of my name being announced, sensations described so frequently in books—weak knees, a roaring in the ears, shortness of breath—achieved sudden purchase. Annette came onto the phone, we greeted one another, and she sounded just as friendly and poised as she had in the morning. I went into a deep body bend. From somewhere down near the blue dining room floor I invited her. "Oh," she exclaimed, "but that will mean I'll need another dress and we just went through so much buying one for graduation." That there might be practical impediments had never occurred to me. I had not known that a new dress would be necessary. Then she said, "I'll have to ask my mother." I thought she would go and speak with her mother right then, but she meant that she would need to call me back. I explained that I would be baby-sitting and gave her the number where she could reach me.

On my way out of the house there was an elation to have done it and also the anxiety of now being in the balance. It was dusk. I remember the tree branches, how in the fading light they seemed sharpened with heft and texture, somehow more present against the air than usual. As I walked, I imagined a discussion of fashion beginning in the Hamburger house, a conversation involving a yellow silk ball gown, sleeveless, with a big yellow bow at the rear waist, saw Annette crouched at her mother's feet like Maroosia from *Old Peter's Russian Tales* pleading with her grandfather for another story. My mother usually said no at first to unexpected requests. Days later she might come around.

The father of the couple whose child I was baby-sitting was a young Yale English professor. I remember nothing about the family or the home except, after the child's bedtime, too restless to study, getting up and beginning to roam along the many handsome bookcases where *The Age of Johnson* caught my eye. I could think of no Johnson of such consequence. Surely not Andrew who took over for Lincoln and was soon all but removed from office in disgrace. I took the book down and began reading about Samuel Johnson, who by himself had written the first comprehensive English dictionary, authored essays and poems, and was eighteenth-century London's most revered figure, the man who knew the most—something to be in what was described as a palimpsest of art and history and pamphlets and conversation. I read further. Johnson was hideous to look at, pockmarked, ursine, squalid in his grooming habits—and beloved because he was so human. His own flaws made his understanding of the flaws of others more penetrating. He had the strength to look at the world and see it as it was, and the compassion to feel sympathy for wayward and undone people. In that moment, it seemed to me that I had discovered not only the most interesting man ever to have lived, but that there was a whole refulgent world out there waiting. The telephone rang. Her mother had agreed to a dress. We could go to the prom. But we didn't know one another very well, Annette continued. So in the interim we should do things together. We agreed to Saturday evening. My good fortune seemed endless.

When I came home, my mother had gone to bed, so to get to my room I had to walk sideways through the tight channel between the coffee table and the pullout where she lay on her back under a green, blue, and white quilt. If Sally or I was out at night, my mother never slept soundly until we came home, and now, though I tiptoed, she stirred. "Did you call her?" she asked drowsily. She was propped on her pillow, looking at me. I told my mother what had happened. She closed her eyes, smiled, and said, "There! Oh, that's wonderful, honey." Then she congratulated me, told me how much she liked Annette, that "Annette is a lady," and "a person out of Jane Austen," and I went on to bed completely glad.

The next morning I awoke to air that was radiant and warm. Filled with vigor, I got into the car to go to school and looking out the window as we passed across town, I found myself absorbing far more than I usually did of the natural surroundings I went by every day, the damp bark of an oak on somebody's Westville lawn, the crenate shapes of leaves, the painted-egg-blue wash of the sky, the last sprays of the forsythia, and the willow and dogwood osiers bending in a pinkish blaze along the West River gullies down in Edgewood Park. All my life since, when I have thought of spring colors, I have reclaimed the shades of that day, perhaps because of the way they seemed to me at that instant to reveal both what they had been and what they were about to be, the tentative yellows, watchets, and creamy pinks of April steadily gaining brilliance until now the once diluted hues had reached the verge of luster.

For much of the morning I didn't see Annette and was beginning to wonder if she was absent from school, when there, across the crowded student lounge, I caught sight of her brightly colored skirt glinting through the throng like a shard of glass catching the sunlight. Tense with dishevelment, I turned away before our eyes could meet. Something about the skirt made me uneasy. I had been expecting the usual Levi's. Had she considered me as she put it on?

Late in the morning, I spotted Annette sitting by herself out on one of the benches along the patio between the two main classroom buildings. The baseball team had a game at another school that day, and I was soon due to board the team bus. It was ridiculous to have avoided her for so long. I went out onto the patio. The bench was a large solid block of unpainted wood stamped "Gift of the Class of 1976," and I looked mostly at the stiff, weather-beaten surface as we made it through the conversation. She did not tease me this time, I did not laugh, and neither did she.

On the bus, I told one of my teammates that I was going to the prom. The news went down the aisle, and soon a couple of them began to make fun of Annette's name, calling her Annette Cheese-burger and Annette Funicello. A senior named Sully interrupted them. "No, no," he said. "She's quiet, but she's really pretty and nice. Nicky, that's great. You're lucky." It was as though she were my discovery. As the conversation turned to other things, I expanded in my seat with gratitude.

I called Annette to make plans for Saturday night. When she suggested a student performance of something I didn't catch down at Yale followed by pizza, I immediately agreed. When she learned that I did not drive, I heard her pause for an instant before saying she would see if she could borrow the family car. She could.

On Saturday, I confronted the problem of what to wear. How did people dress to go on dates? I had the idea that I must present myself differently, that I should put on clothes that reflected the occasion. I didn't want to involve my mother anymore, but the need was urgent enough that I compromised, mentioning in an asking way "I was thinking about wearing good pants." My mother was in the middle of a chore. She said, "Just choose something that makes you feel comfortable." I went back to my room and surveyed my wardrobe. My brown sweater seemed to call out to me.

Right on time I heard a car horn. "Have fun and be a gentleman," my mother said as I headed for the door. In front of our house was a large, dark green, American-built station wagon. It looked like a big, haunchy animal that wasn't sure about how it felt about my coming near it. I climbed into the passenger seat. We continued down Willow, turned right at Orange. Even as we chatted, I was too shy to look at her and instead gazed intently out the window where what I saw brought over me again the protean tension of being two people—me as I knew myself to have always been and this reinvented person I had just become, a boy in a car with a girl. As I kept lurching back and forth between versions, through the window all the familiar New Haven places had somehow become monuments of a past life—the barber shop where, while waiting for my first haircut, I opened a comic book and read a Charles Atlas advertisement featuring a weakling getting sand kicked on him at the beach; the law firm that had once been the meat and produce shop owned by stern old Paul Baer with a pencil behind his ear; the shabby porticoes where now rested former living-room couches; the firehouse with its pumpers and hook and ladder painted white; the dentist's office where I always refused Novocain because afterward you weren't allowed to eat for hours until it wore off; the museum with its dinosaurs; the Lawn Club driveway; an attic apartment window near the Yale School of Music where I had once taken cello lessons. My heart was going out to all of them, to life itself, life so grand, so full of slow-revealing centripetal bliss. After a right on Grove Street, we were parking near the cemetery. In line at the ticket window, I saw money in Annette's hand. The sky darkened. "I'll pay," I said quickly. "No," she told me. I tried to insist. It was my role. "No," she said again, and there was firm purpose to the way she reached forward and put enough money for her half in front of the ticket seller. As I replaced the bills for her ticket back in my wallet, I felt that we had abandoned the world of protocol, and I did not understand.

The performance was a medley of songs by Cole Porter and other professional songwriters who had gone to Yale. In my memory, the program cover had on it an illustration of a sophisticated man and a woman dancing close, and all of the songs sung that night were about love.

Afterward, we drove east toward Wooster Square, the old Italian section of the city where there were New Haven's famous Neapolitan pizzerias, Sally's and Pepe's. Annette said that which of the two restaurants you preferred defined you as a person. She'd heard that Frank Sinatra favored Sally's. Hers, she said, was a Pepe's family. In that instant I too wanted such affiliations. I had never been to Sally's and only once to Pepe's. The Wooster Square streets were lined with low buildings, many of them emblazoned with old neon. We parked, then waited in line for a long time. At last we were given a booth, ordered an extra large, and when it came, enormous and oblong on a dented tin tray, we were so hungry we both burned our mouths on the molten puddles of sweet tomato and cheese. We ate at great speed and had no trouble finishing all of it.

I said, "You're not going to let me pay for the pizza, are you?" and admitting she wasn't, she smiled, and I smiled too. We walked back to the green station wagon, got in, and Annette began to talk. "I don't think I can go to the prom with you," she said. The shame was immediate and crushing, as though a crate had dropped from a gantry crane onto my chest. I stared at the dashboard. Tuesday it had been yes. Now four days later it was no. What had I done wrong? What ugly quality had slipped out and revealed itself for her to see in me? I looked through the window to my right. The parking lot was blurred and shadowy. Traces of tangerine light glowed from a distant and flagging street lamp. All at once I was furious. I had never heard of someone rescinding an acceptance. Where were the rules? There should be rules. Otherwise, what was the point of taking the trouble to ask? I wanted to climb out of that car, get away from the catastrophe. But I had promised to be a gentleman, and she was still talking: "I'd like to keep doing things with you, but if you want to go to the prom you should ask another person. I'm afraid that I'm just really not a polyester dress and corsage sort of girl." Now I aspired to see it her way, to be as she was, not to be a boy who went to proms. "I know," I said, still looking straight at the dashboard. I wanted to tell her I was like her, to tell her about yellow silk. Instead I said, "Fanning goes to the prom." Fanning was a tall, blond, handsome, self-assured student government leader, and now, for me, because I was none of those things, Fanning was also a prom king. Sitting there, I saw generations of Fanning men in their black velvet britches and gold doublets at the lead of dance lines, confident and expressive in their easy mastery of polkas, waltzes, jigs, and quadrilles. When Jim Burden described dancing with

Ántonia, the steps to a new outlook seemed so simple. But here, finally in the reality, I did not know how to dance—had no idea what dances they did at proms, what else they did besides dance. My sweater felt hot. "You wore that brown sweater a lot," Annette would tell me years later. "You hadn't filled out yet. You were a shrimpy little uncombed fellow." I said to Annette, "It's okay." It was not okay. Why had I told the baseball team? I hated being me even though I did not want to be anybody else. She drove me home.

The next morning I liked her more. I could not explain it. I was wilted with defeat and yet somehow humiliation had kindled worship. I had just acquired *Days of Future Passed,* a Moody Blues album that melded their rock 'n' roll with classical intervals of the London Festival Orchestra. The record described a day in the life of an Everyman, and those songs so drenched in yearning with their gusting strings and melodramatic lyrics—"I'm just beginning to see, now I'm on my way"—were with me wherever I walked, as was Annette. She and the record became connected; whenever I heard my favorite songs, "Nights in White Satin" and "Tuesday Afternoon," I thought of her. I played the record over and over, descending each time into a moonstruck rapture of melancholy as the singer crooned "And I love you / Oh, how I love you." Annette and I had constant imagined conversations, I telling her all the humdrum events in my no longer humdrum days, for she was the figure perched atop all my thoughts. She became my source of inspiration and purpose. Everything I did, I did for her, everything I experienced I experienced through her, saw through her eyes, and suddenly life was no longer itself. I was sleepless, anxious, miserable, and the most alive I'd ever been. Nobody had ever felt this way before.

The school yearbook was distributed, and I broke the spine of my copy by turning every day to her page. In the photograph she was lying on grass. You could see the faint scree of freckles on her slender face, her features so graceful that after a moment of looking at them I would lower my eyes. Demolished with love, I assumed everyone was now seeing her the way I did. When I spotted Southerton talking with her once by a door at school, I hated him as a rival. Her flaws and blemishes would have moved me terribly, except that she had no flaws, not one blemish. I pined over her so much that when I actually talked with her it was surprising not to enjoy it. Because I knew so little about her, on my own I was forever supplying the facts. In her presence, I was thrown off by the reality, would flush and stammer with burning ears.

I did not know any of her habits, but because her mother was English, there was Britain in Annette's elocution, and now as I found myself favoring phrases and words I'd heard Annette say like "meant to" and "don't be foolish," and "chocolate chip cookies," and "Bitensky," I'd also catch a little London slipping into my voice as I said them, I tasting those words like balms. I felt exposed to a blizzard of love, to torrents of love, bursting with love, wanted love to take over my life. That she should respond with indifference seemed unsurprising, not an obstacle, but the opposite. To me shame was a natural ingredient of the condition.

I didn't tell anybody at school about my prom volte-face. A few days later, Annette called to invite me to play tennis. One of her Sue friends joined us. A chaperone, I thought bitterly. They took one side of the court, I the other. Sue played careful baseline strokes. Annette swung at every ball as hard as she could, some of her shots hitting halfway up the fence behind me on the fly. Once in a while, one of her balls landed in. I had never seen anybody play tennis that way. She had long legs and long arms, and when she struck at a ball, her limbs were saplings in swirling winds.

Afterward, Sue went home, and Annette and I walked back to her house for a snack. We found her father sitting in a turquoise kitchen watching the Mets on a small, countertop, black and white television. He was a political science professor at Yale, a jovial, ruddy-faced man with a spray of white hair and bright button eyes who, Annette now told me, played tennis the same way she did. "Tennis is a game of velocity," he said. The ballplayers moved on the screen. Her father waved to me. "Pull up a chair," he told me, motioning to the stool beside him. I took a step in that direction. Then I looked at her. "Oh, Daddy," Annette said, "you're stealing him!" He widened his eyes. I made a motion to turn back and she said, "No, no, I know when I'm overmatched. You men watch the baseball." We sat in that large kitchen cozily cluttered with cookie tins, pie plates, and dog-eared cookbooks, lit with the kind of thick, still, heavy light found inside barns, I hoping more than ever to be loved by Annette. If you were loved by a girl, her family too would love you.

I wanted to tell others about her to make her present in my moments as much as possible. The first person in whom I confided was a man. "She's not interested in you; she's trying to let you know in a nice way," he said. After that I waited a long time—weeks!—before I told a female friend about Annette. All my friend could do was hope for me, but hopes could be discussed over and over. To have an object of adoration filled the heart with possibility. Maybe her feelings would change.

That summer we continued to do things together, and, when I was away, she wrote me careful, good-humored replies to the epistles I'd drafted and redrafted. Around her I had begun to feel cultivated, like a mascot. We had a picnic one day on the lawn in front of a Yale library, and I was glum to be going back to high school while this would be her lawn, her library. But the next fall it was exciting occasionally to visit her at college, see the interior of buildings all my life I had only passed by, to meet her glamorous roommates—not a Sue in the bunch; they all had clipped, impossibly hip names like Dana and Jana—to whom she introduced me as either "my high school friend," which made me bristle, or "sort of my little brother," which didn't.

Gradually, over those next few years we became close. Once, on my birthday at college, I opened my mailbox to discover fifteen envelopes postmarked New Haven, all of them scented with perfume. "I wanted to improve your reputation," she told me on the telephone. When she graduated from Yale, I sat in the audience with her mother, her brothers, and her father in his mismatching suit. It was a lengthy ceremony held outdoors in a cold, steady rain, and halfway through, her father announced that he needed fortification. The next thing I knew, led by her father, her family was getting up, filing down the aisle, and abandoning the commencement for a nearby Burger King. I followed, flabbergasted. At Burger King, we sat in orange bucketed seats at a corner table, everyone happily feasting on Whoppers, looking out at the empty New Haven streets through fogged windows. Her father proudly explained his attire; he'd worn his best suit jacket but opted for trousers from an older ensemble so as to preserve the good pants from the rain and mud. Everyone thought this was very practical of him. Afterward, when Annette learned that no Hamburgers had seen her graduate because they were off eating, well, hamburgers, she was indignant. "I can't believe my family would bag out on my graduation for a snack," she huffed. "Well, I can believe it of my father, but you, Nicky, should know better." I hung my head, and as I did I saw to my surprise that she wasn't really upset, that, yes, she was annoyed, but mostly she didn't care. I wanted her to care. It came to me that this was the way they were, and that she knew it, and that she was secure in their love.

CHAPTER TWELVE

Leaving

The summer of 1980, by myself I went to see *Breaking Away*. I'd never gone to a movie without a companion before, and being in that sunken chair alone in the dark made it only easier to feel I was right there, in the story. It told of Dave Stoller, recent high school graduate, a stonecutter's son who'd grown up in the university town of Bloomington, Indiana, and was trying not to figure out what he was going to do with the rest of his life. Dave lived at home, didn't have a job, rode his racing bicycle long distances every day, and had convinced himself he was Italian. His walls were covered with posters of Italian cyclists, he listened obsessively to Verdi and Puccini, and every time he joyfully greeted his dad, "Bongiorno Papa!" his father hated "that Ity talk" from "that *got*-damned lazy deadbeat" a little more. Eventually, wearing a shirt that said "Cutters," Dave entered the big local bicycle race at the university stadium, and defeated all the college fraternity teams with his father showing up halfway through to watch, belatedly proud, cheering him on, encouraging him afterward to go for it in life too, to apply to The U. In my seat I got all excited, got so swept up in the one great sports victory and all of Dave's other victories and reconciliations, that, back on the sidewalk, it was like walking out of *The Big Sleep*, a movie so good that for ten minutes you were talking like Bogie and feeling all tough and hard-boiled and invincible yourself. In the high of the moment I was thinking that it could be me moving on, except that it was only a movie and not me at all.

The point seemed to be that this was a movie about class, and my class, like so much about me, was ambiguous. I wasn't truly deprived or truly advantaged either, wasn't quite a New Haven townie, wasn't a Yalie, wasn't exactly anything. I was a kid with a reasonably promising future; by most standards I had plenty. Whenever I'd catch myself doubting it, I'd think about the South Bronx or the lives of some of the kids I played baseball with who carried food stamps in their uniform pockets. So what was it that filled me with such insistent need? Could it truly be about clothing and food, or was the inexhaustible craving, the intense desires that fixated on such small things about something else? I think it was the lack of a sense that I was really part of anything that felt solid. I didn't quite belong anywhere, orbited around the periphery of all sorts of communities, instinctively floating free and apart—and of all the things I desired, what I wanted most was to change that. But I was unequipped, had no idea how to do it. Then, slowly and just a little, with the tentative and erratic progressions that are youth, life began to do it for me.

My eighteenth year, all durations seemed to speed up. I grew several inches, my voice finally deepened and so did my social resources: I became friends with boys and girls from all the various constituencies of our class, and as the cooler kids began to invite me to their weekend house parties and I went on outings with them to Grateful Dead concerts and Yale bars, it was a little startling to hear people who had given me a hard time for years now calling out "Hey, big guy!" as I came down the corridor. I wondered if our class was coming together or if it was me, and a part of me wished they hadn't liked me so late, when I didn't need them anymore. That's the problem with high school; you never know who you are and yet you expect other people to know who you are.

To be the child of a parent of fierce convictions made sharing my mother's opinions almost as complicated as disagreeing with them. I wanted to find a way for the opinion to be mine. Television, like baseball, was the American mainstream, and for a long time I had wished to have one in our house not only so I could see *Planet of the Apes*, but also as my ally in not feeling like an outcast from the culture, not seeming like a freak to others. That last year in New Haven, I could go out to friends' houses more or less when I wanted to and watch television as often as I liked, only to find that now I agreed with my mother about TV. I had begun not to like what happened to me when I watched. Given the chance, I stared like a guppy, immobilized for hours in somebody's den on an increasingly itchy wall-to-wall carpet, intent on things I didn't even enjoy, passive and yet also anxious, too aware of how soon the hour would be up when the little world in front of me would evaporate and I'd have nothing left but an uneasy regret and another new show beginning that I couldn't get up and walk away from. It was so easy not to resist because television was doing all the work for me, making all the decisions. That was especially true, I noticed, when I watched baseball. The field became reduced to the fragment that fit on the screen, minimizing the game into a fraction of itself, implying that everything happening off-camera was irrelevant. The players were minimized as well, because they did not exist unless the ball came their way. Then the lens swooped into their faces and there was too much of them—which weirdly created distance. Following on the radio, by contrast, what I saw was up to me, and the basic rhythms and landscape of the game remained intact. Soon I was developing a cherished idea of myself as a radio partisan as well as a sense of distinction about having no television—glad that at school I could shrug and look baffled when a *Gilligan's Island* or *Brady Bunch* reference was made. "He doesn't have television!" people then would exclaim, and it seemed I was now being rewarded for an old liability. Mystique had found me.

Except for one problem. When given the option of whether to watch or listen, I always watched. It was like being a vegetarian who can never pass up the veal—horrible to be so susceptible. I'd recently discovered Raymond Chandler. He said, "You can always tell a TV detective. He never takes his hat off," and there it was: television was a charlatan and made me one too, made me someone

I did not like to recognize. And yet how much like life was the situation, life always so different from how you envision it, and you always somebody other than who you imagine yourself to be. Growing up. Everybody does it. How was I supposed to know.

I began to pay attention to kids at school who were less cautious about the way they presented themselves. Among them was Tom, a boy who'd let his hair grow until it hung thin and greasy well past his shoulders. As he passed along the hallway outside the student lounge, people in letterman's jackets called out "wash your hair!" but he ignored them, kept moving at the same measured pace with eyes straight ahead, carrying an unintimidated ease that eventually made them give up. He wore a blue coat to school every day and kept it buttoned to the neck at all times, even indoors, like soft body armor. When the school yearbook was published, one of the quotations by his photograph was a line from the late nineteenth-century English poet laureate Alfred Austin that I found jarring, as though he'd had me in mind when he selected it: "Public opinion is no more than this, what people think that other people think."

Another classmate, Nick, loved to lie on a couch in the student lounge and talk about trout fishing. He was genial, plump, and easygoing, unhurried about everything. On his yearbook page I would discover a long passage by the author Robert Traver that compared expert fishermen to drug addicts and philosophers, saying: "Under his smiling coat of tan there often lurks a layer of melancholy and disillusion, a quiet awareness—and acceptance—of the fugitive quality of man and all his enterprises." There was the sense that Nick had decisively defined himself by his passion. It was the same with dimpled, cheery, "Big" Steve, displaying the measure of his gustatory powers to acclaim as our newspaper's pizza columnist, and my close friend Evans, a briefcase-toting future financier who had already been watching *Dallas* for a full season before anyone else had heard of Ewing Oil. All of a sudden I was sure that what had enabled each of them to endure adolescence was that they could see so far past it.

I too would have liked to show myself freely and not care what others thought. Or was it that I would have liked to show myself to myself and not care what I thought? Of all the diffident parts of me, it was my inward revelations that bloomed the latest. My youth was now completed, but I was still a child because the oldest and most suppressed fear still held, the fear that I was not just different, but incurably different, that there was deep inner warpage, that somebody would find out how I was and then that I would have to know. My secret was that my secret was always in the hands of others. I held them responsible for my sense of well-being and, as a result, they could not be trusted to know anything about me. When you are young there is the terrible inability to understand that it's your deficits that will make others not only like you but feel close to you.

One of the prettiest girls in the class began to come to me to discuss her troubles. She would mention her sort-of boyfriend, Stanley, and her best friend, but in a way so cryptic that I had no idea what she was talking about. While she spoke, her dark eyebrows would come together in concern over sad brown eyes, and everything I imagined of her life would go straight to my heart. I leapt blind to the cause, spoke with her for hours, trying to soothe it all—whatever it was. I'd listen, and then I'd think and think and think for her, my brain churning to find solutions to these obscure wrongs she was enduring. Were they talking behind her back? But how could I advise, how could I fix, I so easily shocked, so haplessly removed that only years later would I discover that an entire demimonde had existed casually around me at school. Kids were making out in the shadowed basement corners by the emergency exits and then scorning one another in the light. They were stashing booze in the chemistry lab cabinets for a late morning pick-me-up. The parking lots and the woods were alive with smoke and mirrors and sex. At night the phone lines trembled with rumors perverse and heartbreaking, some of them true. One day Stanley came sidling down the hall, saw my friend, gave all of us there a smile, slid an arm around her and led her outside. Guys were shaking their heads.

"Both of them," someone said with admiration. I gaped, foolish and a little stunned. Why ever had she been listening to me?

John Lennon was killed and the radio filled with his music for days. On the weekend, while putting together the school newspaper, led by the arts editor we took time out, sat in a circle, and had an informal Lennon memorial service, a moment of silence and then people, one by one, saying how much he'd meant to them. But he hadn't meant anything special to me. Over and over now I heard "Beautiful Boy (Darling Boy)," his song to his son—"Close your eyes / Have no fear / The monster's gone, he's on the run and your daddy's here." The heartfelt lullaby of this now lost father crosscut me, because what if your father was what frightened you? Over the years, my father's musical brother, my Uncle Robert, had given me a few country records, and I began to listen to them more and more because I liked how direct, matter-of-fact, and permanent lines like "There's a dark and a troubled side of life / There's a bright and a sunny side too" sounded. Bob Dylan said that the first time he heard a country record as a kid in Minnesota, it made him feel "I was not born to the right parents or something," and I heard that. The forlorn intimacy and Saturday night high spirits of the old Carter Family and Hank Williams songs moved me in a way that was different from the heightened desire of rock 'n' roll. These songs about shattered hearts and broken bottles and faith, family, and sorrow were music that came from somewhere far away, places named Brown's Ferry, Old Kentucky, Flint Hill, and San Antone, and it took me there, took me into these public yet private spaces of music for a few afternoon hours and made me feel that here was life as most people lived it. Those were sounds that would hold you. The music went right at emotion, said that out there in America, a lot of people were going day to day and feeling as though the world was filled with consequences, ordinary little ambushes all designed to remind them that this too would pass, and then more would come. You just had to keep on, like everybody else.

At that point in my life, I was drawn to things all the time for good reasons that I rarely recognized. For my birthday I requested the book about Samuel Johnson I'd seen while baby-sitting and was presented with something better—a copy of Walter Jackson Bate's recent biography. I opened it up and discovered that the saddest part of Johnson's life, according to Bate, was how disappointed Johnson could be in himself—hostile to the point of inward laceration. An enormous man, all but the larger-than-life embodiment of the Age of Reason, Johnson brought himself to his knees with his diminishing self-doubts. Again and again he reviled himself for his weaknesses, his vanity, his sloth—was frantic to know and to improve himself. All the self-loathing eventually told; Johnson's brain, the clearest of all brains, became clouded with despair. Bate described Johnson's attempts to fend away insanity by reasoning himself out of it, and his lifelong need for the constant company of others to stave off his crippling distress. The fear of going mad was Johnson's terrible secret, a horror so real in him, said Bate, that at age twenty, Johnson crossed briefly over the line. Falling to the floor he began weeping and calling for his understanding, begging God so ardently to make him sane again that a friend bent toward Johnson and closed his mouth. Thirty years later, the ordeal repeated itself. Each time Johnson fought back with a courage so moving in Bate's description that even now, when I look back at it, I have to struggle not to weep. At the time, though, I read right over it, noticed instead how witty and brave and strong Johnson was.

My baseball coach that spring was a young teacher with a weed patch of curls and skewed shirt collars named Doyle, who sometimes appeared as though he wished he were still one of us, especially when his mischievous face went wistful at the sight of senior girls or when he did things like pose himself for the yearbook reading the Monarch Notes for *A Midsummer Night's Dream.* Doyle seemed too recently our age and restless in his own life to be our mentor, but he'd turned down Yale to go to the University of Virginia on a baseball scholarship, and he knew hitting, knew the game, and could talk about it in ways that resonated for me. One day, early on, he described himself standing in right field at college knowing very few balls that mattered would come his way, but that there would probably be at least one, and how he spent the entire game out there hoping for his chance, planning not to waste it. That was just the way the former Dodger outfielder Pete Reiser described his thinking in that old book I'd read. When this sort of conjoining happened a few more times, it seemed to me that all my reading about the game was at last merging into my life. All at once I felt not just prepared for anything on a baseball field, but now capable of responding. "Hit it to me! Hit it to me!" was still what I whispered to myself out in the field, and I meant it as never before. In our first game, I rapped line drive after line drive directly at opposing fielders, after which the coach told me in front of the team, "You keep doing that, you'll have a great season," and from then on plenty of hits fell safe. On a day when I felt sick before our game, I remembered the story in a Willie Mays biography of a feverish Mays dragging himself to the ballpark and hitting his record four home runs, and then I hit one that day myself. In *Sports Illustrated* I'd read about Tim Foli, who once spent the night after a game in uniform at second base, using the bag as his pillow, and now after six years at the school, I was so glad to be batting third and turning double plays at shortstop that there were days when, at the end of a game or practice, I'd be standing out there in the bend of solid dirt between second and third bases and have to resist the impulse to stay right where I was, to curl myself on the ground, press my cheek to the peaceful, quiet loam and just rest, never leave the best place to be.

A follower of our team was a sophomore with a low voice and high, undulating curves, a mermaid already a little bored with New Haven. From a distance there was nothing captivating about her, but as you moved closer and she kept her mouth closed so that the braces on her teeth didn't show, she was better than captivating; her gaze was level, bold, and magnetic, and there was an unsettling confidence in the way that, after you had said something, she seemed to decide whether or not to laugh before she did. I became sport for her. The game we played was that we were newlyweds, and she used to ask me "What do you want for dinner, honey?" and to joke about our dessert to follow, about all the ways we could enjoy treats topped with whipped cream together, and I'd be keeping up until she'd look me in the eyes and drawl, "Darling, why won't you ever just really kiss me?" She also liked to walk up to me during the school day, verbena-spiked in her wardrobe of pinks and reds, and ask "Are you hungry?" just to watch me get so flustered and worked up I'd have to scurry away.

After a promising start, the school baseball team lost game after game by that telling margin of one run. Our camaraderie never quite prospered either. I wished that we could be achieving a significance, that I might finally be a member of a close-knit group resembling the old clubhouses and Gas House Gangs I'd read about, the photographs of early-century collegiate and town teams, the players, with their long moustaches and short-billed caps, locked in fraternal embrace as they calmly regarded the camera. I wondered if life really could match what was in books.

One day in the school library, a chum of mine, a shambling, heavy-lidded, rubicund boy who'd embraced the cruel nickname of Vache (cow in French), began teasing me in the way he always teased me, calling me a "gap-toothed, walnut-shaped, square-headed, mongoloid, black sheep of a circus freak family," going on in this way until he saw that suddenly it was no longer hilarious to me. He wanted me to play. I wouldn't. A docile plaint came into his voice that made me wince because I hated his need. He lurched forward as if to shake me, make me revert, force me to be like old times, but in his awkwardness my coat was torn. He hadn't meant any harm, and he knew I knew it, but I decided not to know it, and coldly to hold a grudge, because all at once I resented the responsibility of always being nice to everyone. He was wounded, never understood my sudden shift, and, much as I soon wanted to make up, that would have meant explaining, and I couldn't explain. Instead, guiltily I worried that now with so many fashionable people being friendly to me, I had become a jerk. Was I the old story, a guy who frowns on the poor behavior of popular kids and yet wants to be them in spite himself? The freight of every spontaneity was always concern about what kind of a person I was turning into.

As the season and high school neared its end, I began to surprise myself with how much I wanted it all to be over. I was tired of seeing everybody else's father out there watching us play our games, weary of concealing my New Haven life from New York, and concealing New York from New Haven. When our team photograph was taken, the photographer shot one image for the yearbook and then a second photograph for team members to order as prints. Very few of us bought that photograph though, because one boy in the front row was on his feet to leave as the shutter clicked: I had ruined the picture.

One day in the boys' locker room, a kid named Mark gave me the sort of hard intramural punch in the shoulder I'd been absorbing from him and many others for four years. He was, in several ways, the epitome of the hopeful youth in the school's motto: handsome, studious, popular, athletic, the pride of administrators who were now suffering a bit as, with his long years of upstanding service completed, Mark was letting go by spending most of his free periods with one of the school's most enticing Tretorn wearers on his lap. The moment he punched me, I snapped. I grabbed him and threw him down to the ground between two rows of lockers, holding him there and screaming at him "Will you stop hitting me?" over and over as a crowd gathered. Here on the cement floor, I watched the event slow into a cinematic pan that took in the press of male faces, eager to see what would happen next, and then Mark, surprised and indignant, larger than me but unable to get me off with his one free arm, he struggling and struggling as I tried to figure out what to do now—did people really say "cry uncle"?—until finally he manipulated his fist around my hips and punched me square in the balls. I fell back as a low groan passed through the crowd, and from the ground I saw them all backing away. I felt their objurgation of me. Then from out in the hall, I could hear an

excited voice passing along the news: "Nicky fought back!" Nobody
at that school ever hit me again. I knew then that I had passed over
some threshold, and I remember thinking with a flood of consciousness, Is that all there was?

Mark and I had always been friends of a kind, and we went right
on in our former way, as though nothing had happened, a phenome-
non that made the expression "high school is hard for everyone"
pass through my mind whenever I thought of him. That's the way
the end of that school was; I was participating at some up-close
remove.

Graduation approached with the question of whether my father
would insist on attending, the worry that he would show up even if
asked not to and make a scene where my mother worked. In the
end, my grandmother stepped off the train from New York alone,
which was only a partial relief since I knew how very much she had
wanted him to be invited. She had told me that she considered it my
obligation "as a son and a graduate to include your father." I wanted
to tell her that maybe it was my father who should have been worried about obligations, but, even behind his back, I felt he couldn't
take any criticism. After the graduation ceremony, my mother gave
me a watch, and my grandmother treated everyone to a celebratory
lunch at an Italian restaurant suggested by Big Steve. We passed
between a small pair of sagging Ionic columns with worn volutes
into a sky-lit room where opera music played as my grandmother let
me know again how disappointed she was that I had traduced my
father in this way. I lowered my head. Then, as if now that she'd
extracted remorse her duty was done, her brusque tone changed
and she told me to order anything I liked from the menu, and that
she was proud of me. I had clams.

That night, Big Steve hosted a party at his family's beach home
on the shore. Disentangled from the school at last, we all walked
around wobbly and a little befuddled at the end of a long day of
being told we were changed, feeling the way people do when they
reach a milestone birthday and are asked how they feel so many

times they begin to wonder how they should feel. The sophomore was there, and when she pointed out that I'd promised to kiss her by graduation night, I found myself following her along a path into a large shed and leaning against a rough wooden wall as we held each other and I bent toward lips for the first time. After a little bit I began to think about not wanting to stop, but needing to stop, and then finally stopping. In that calm, smoldering voice of hers she asked what was wrong. "Your braces are cutting up my tongue," I confessed. Her eyes still only half open, she drawled, "Nobody else complained."

The mother of one of my old elementary school friends was out on the sidewalk near our house walking her fluffy white dog, and when I came by and said hello, she stopped me and asked, "You gonna go to Yale, Nicky?" I hadn't seen her in a long time. When I was younger, while I was visiting her son, she used to ask me questions about my mother, why she never bought us snack foods, why we had no television, why I had to be inside at a certain time. I could tell that the purpose of those questions was to let me know that she thought my mother was too strict, that my mother was a frump, that she believed I should have more fun. Encouraged, I used to report back from the woman's house to my mother what a good time I had watching television and eating ruffled potato chips, how "with it" the woman was. "Good, Nicky," my mother would say icily. The woman didn't like my mother and was unctuously friendly to her in a way that sought to emphasize her disdain, but, because my mother so plainly didn't care what this woman thought about anything, the disdain wouldn't hold and inevitably wavered into timidity—which used to frustrate me about the woman. I wanted her to stand up for potato chips. Now there was a resigned sound in the woman's voice as she asked about my college plans. I told her that I had been admitted to Harvard. As I said this, I felt an expression falling across my face that I knew she would misinterpret as hubris, as evidence that I thought my mother's methods had been proved correct in the end.

But what was happening was that a Sunday had suddenly come back to me from my boyhood when my father had been in New Haven for a visit. Sally and I were with him in the backyard, where the woman could see us over the several fences from her yard to ours. The next thing I knew, she was joining us. She had never been in our backyard before and I had the feeling that she would not have come if my mother had been there. At the time, I hadn't known about flirting, and had wondered why the woman was smiling so much at everything my father said, why she kept touching her freshly dressed and powdered face, and was putting such exaggerated care into her words and gestures—behaving so differently from the way she did when I came by to play with her son. My mother wore only lipstick.

That day, my sister, about eight at the time, had on a pair of brand-new gum-soled tan suede shoes, and at a certain point Sally asked the woman if she liked the shoes. "They're beautiful," she said. The woman had never shown any interest in Sally. I was suddenly sure she had none now either, that everything she was saying was intended for my father. I looked at him. As the object of this attention, there was something about my father's posture that made me think of zoo cats yawning and flexing. With a quick breath I realized I was seeing him as my mother's man, and that maybe the woman was too. Soon enough they were discovering that they both had grown up on Long Island.

Now, out on the sidewalk, I was hearing the woman hear Harvard as my father's school, hearing her think that I was following in his footsteps. I did not want Harvard to be his school. When I'd sent off my application, I'd worried that they in Cambridge who, no doubt, still knew his secrets, might hold them against me, and I had regarded my acceptance as their judgment that they felt they were in for no future trouble with me, that I wasn't any risk of becoming another him, that I was more like my grandfather. But here on the sidewalk I was seeing that others would regard my going to Harvard as evidence of how alike my father and I were. Because some part of me knew this was an irrational way to think, I became more upset, began to be afraid I was growing irrational, that I too would crack up in my dorm room, would rave at people, would give away everything I owned, even my beautiful brand-new high school graduation watch.

For years now I'd known that my father would never fulfill my parents' divorce settlement, would never pay for Sally's and my college tuition, that he had no savings, that he would never help me with anything. My mother had been anticipating this as well. By sewing her own clothes, by forsaking pleasure, it turned out that she had managed to bank thousands of dollars for Sally and me. On her tiny salary it represented such a sacrifice that I was as overwhelmed by her thrift as I was by my father's failure, found them equally upsetting.

To earn money for college, that summer I found a job as an inspector at Lehman Brothers, a factory that printed custom-quality paper products. The factory was a succession of low white buildings only a few blocks from my house. I had passed those buildings all my life and never noticed them. Lehman Brothers did their work using engraved metal plates. Type was cut into the plates, and then the plates were bolted to a machine press that inked the surface and thrust them down onto the paper that was fed through—up-down, up-down, up-down. An order might be hundreds or even thousands of sheets. After each piece of paper was stamped against the plate, it came out along a conveyor belt as I stood at the far end, waiting to remove the just-printed business cards and letterheads, looking carefully at each one to see that the quality remained perfect. If the ink had run or spurted on the paper, I fixed it with a razor blade.

It was hot in the factory and loud with the slam of machines, the industrial fans, and the music on radios turned up high. The close air smelled of ink and motors, except in the late morning when Jimmy B. shuffled by. Jimmy B. was a tall, lean-as-leather old black man, up from the Delta I imagined, whose job was to remove the empty ink fountains from the press after a print run and take them away on his metal cart to clean them in a boiling chemical bath. He always wore a chest-to-ankle rubber apron, and his face had a watery glaze even when it wasn't pooling with sweat, as though he'd spent so many years perspiring it had become a permanent condition. In late morning he'd wrap his plate of lunch in a layer of foil and put it on his cart, right on top of the fountains, which were still searing with heat. Often the foil held something like a squirrel that he'd shot himself, and as the meat cooked on the fountains you could smell the gamey stench long before he came near. Sometimes you also smelled him. Every month or so he'd show up drunk on corn liquor. His eyes were red as embers, and he'd be screaming about "muckin' ass whitey," and "the no good muckin' muckety ass white man," until Harvey, the all-business foreman, sent him home to sleep it off. Everybody feared Harvey, but some guessed he had a soft heart, and everybody loved Jimmy B., loved to talk about the slick way he dressed when the workday ended, and the flocks of good-looking women they said he stepped out with.

All summer I counted the hours. It was tedium, actually watching ink dry. And yet I knew others had it much worse. We were manufacturing premium merchandise for some of the country's leading corporations, banks, and investment houses, and people worked hard to do it well. But in making these diplomas, business cards, and certificates, we at Lehman were flywheels to these testaments to other people's progress, and the contrast between the lives of people with expensive diplomas and business cards and those who made them hung in the air. There was no way to think that most of my colleagues had once walked into a third grade classroom aspiring to spend their lives feeding thousands of sheets of paper into a press all day, every day. They did it because they had to.

That's what would be on my mind at night when the telephone rang and I heard my father's voice asking how work was going. I'd tell him about it with hard pride, thinking to myself that he was goldbrick-lazy, that if all of us could do this, why couldn't he? I was disgusted by how peppy he sounded. I wanted to lay into him, but, as I spoke to my father, I'd be thinking of what my grandmother told me every time she set out to convince me that I shouldn't hold anything he did against him, that I was his and it was up to me to make his life better. "He's a sick man, he can't help it, he's not himself," she'd tell me. That was one of the hardest things about having such a troubled father: because he was unwell, he wasn't accountable for anything. Whatever he said to me, it was always the illness talking, not he, and I was expected to forgive him, to let him off in a way that left him his dignity, that protected him.

I didn't want to protect him. As I told him about my job, I wanted to draw blood with my descriptions. I wanted my father to sound ashamed because for anybody but a grifter it was normal to want to work, to want to provide. If he loved me, why would he not work for me? Why was he never by my side? Why did he never sound ashamed? If he had been ashamed, I would have felt pity for how helpless he was, felt sorry that he should be so disliked by the world, and I would have kept hoping for him. I wanted to keep hoping for him. I'd spent so much of my childhood hoping and hoping and hoping for him, but it never did any good. You could give and give and give to a person, and it could make no difference. In the end, I never knew whom to feel sorry for, him or me.

What I heard in my father's voice on the telephone was a stubborn, relentless faith that what he had been he might be again, that he would rise to claim the illustrious career in America that had rightfully been his. They were telling him his life was over, that all he had in front of him was the grave? Well, don't believe it, bud. I wasn't the only one embarking on something new. It was his new beginning too; we were beginning together. His certainty about all this seemed ominous, and it was also chilling to me that he was hitching his hopes to my experience. As the sharp feeling of danger coursed through me, I also found it motivating. I knew exactly how I didn't want to end up.

The summer went on and I noticed that increasingly everyone was nice to me at the factory. They recounted their weekends, the fifths of Jack Daniel's they'd put away without effect at the motel bar out by the interstate, the new girlfriend who was an assistant manager at Caldor, the outings to county fairs. A mechanic with

feathered red hair named Mike kept telling me about the connection he had who was going to get him some Coors beer. Coors
wasn't then available in the East, which gave it an element of forbidden mystery because nobody knew what it tasted like. Mike
knew. He made Coors sound like some kind of ambrosial nectar.
When his shipment finally came in, he gave me a can to take home.
It really did taste sweet. "You paid your dues," my mother said.

Yet I was a Harvard freshman, and every once in a while I would
act like one. Two of the machine operators near me were women,
including a beautiful Puerto Rican who dressed well and swung her
hips to dance music on the radio as she fed her press. Sometimes in
the afternoons she used to pop shiny pills she told me were black
beauties—speed. I liked her and worried about her, and one day I
told her very earnestly that the drugs would get her sick. She froze,
rigid with resentment. Then she burst out, "This dull shit is what I
have to look forward to every day of my life, and if these things
make me feel good and get me through the afternoon, how the fuck
are you gonna tell me I shouldn't take them?" I didn't have an
answer for that, nor did I when an alert young black woman whom
I'd grown very fond of suddenly said she wasn't going to miss me
after I went to school. When I asked her why, she said, "You ain't
gonna miss me. You're going to college. So why should I miss you?"

By then I had begun to dread that standing at the end of a conveyor belt would be my life. Later, in university libraries, I would
think of the factory and study harder. For years I made myself work
every day at least an hour longer than factory hours, fending off the
hand of fate that could pick me up and drop me back there to lose
my eyes reading thousands of sheets of paper embossed with the
name of the same J.P. Morgan vice president, a razor blade in my
hand.

After work, some nights I'd put on a shirt that said "New Haven"
across the chest, and I played shortstop for the city's Senior Babe
Ruth team in games against surrounding communities like Oxford
and Cheshire and Seymour. There, on burned grass under the
green and white bill of my cap, the idea of being a member of the

town team thrilled me, for this was what I liked best about baseball, how flexible it was in time, another generation of the local nine playing the same game as previous generations, making a visible connection between my team and our forebears. The New Haven reality, however, wasn't much like those early town teams I'd read about from Lucasville, Ness City, and Wahoo. I had no stories of sleeping in fields and barns on my way from game to game, filling up on apples borrowed from some farmer's orchard, making friends for life. I had, in fact, no stories at all. That is the only team I ever played on where I can bring back none of the names. I remember diving to catch a fly ball in short left field during a game played out under a big country sky, and I remember coming very close to killing myself and some teammates with an ill-timed second gear merge onto a crowded highway in the red Dodge, but what was most remarkable to me about the experience was how unremarkable it seemed. It also felt a little pathetic to want so much to come from somewhere even as I was leaving it. There was altogether too much negativity and what I'd really finished with was all that.

I spent a lot of my evenings that summer in a gym lifting weights with my cheerful friends Passarelli and Merchant. Those evenings passed the way my mornings and afternoons had, with endless up-down mechanical repetitions. I was glad for the company of those friends because otherwise it was a dull, menial time of pure preparation. I had spent my youth projecting life, waiting for life to happen, envisioning high school as the slow rehearsal for the act of becoming myself, believing that right about now I would finally get there—that this post-graduation summer would be an afterglow of resolution. But the past months had instead been shot through with anticlimax, which puzzled me. You imagined the horizon, you moved toward the horizon, and the horizon moved away from you. Realizing certain goals and aspirations settled nothing. Perhaps life's succession of days involved no true vanishing points until the final one. And maybe preparation was not preliminary but the essential gesture—all you could wish for. Life was possibility and it was desire;

the imagination required no more. Everything was out there to be endlessly rediscovered.

In bed at night, I did the summer reading Harvard had assigned, *The Education of Henry Adams,* and saw that Adams had arrived at my moment in life only to realize that the education he had received bore little relation to the one he needed, that he had no education yet at all, that he knew not even how to begin his education.

And then it was time to leave. On my early September visit to New York, my grandmother bought me a striped tie to take to college, and soon I was back at home in my room, packing it in my mother's old student steamer trunk. I was going now to where my grandfather had lived, where the Red Sox played, where my cousin Jody was a sophomore, and I was looking forward. Never had I looked forward to something so much. In many ways, the looking forward had always been the best part for me, and I wondered if that would always be true.

Listening to a Ballgame, I Hear My Life

Another lifetime later, in July 2004, visiting my mother for a week in New England from my home in New York as she recovered from cataract surgery, we followed the Red Sox together on the television she'd acquired for herself the week after Sally left home for college. We were annoyed by how complacent the Red Sox seemed as they lost game after game to the Orioles. During one broadcast, when the name Cal Ripkin, the former Oriole who played in more consecutive games than any other player, was mentioned, my mother said, "Oh, him, the guy people made a fuss about because he came to work every day." The Red Sox's next opponent was the Yankees, and when the Red Sox squandered a three-run, mid-game lead, my mother stood up, said, "Maybe they've all got some kind of disease," and went to bed. I stayed immobile in my chair for the whole game, an 8–7 Red Sox loss. Afterward I felt like a pollarded tree. It took me a while to get to sleep. The following morning, I looked out on grim, overcast New England weather and reported to my mother that I was tired of the Red Sox. "I have to question why I spend so much time thinking about them," I said.

"They're exasperating," my mother agreed mildly. "That's what you get with the Red Sox."

"Too exasperating," I said. "It's like something out of Irish literature."

"Yes," she agreed, suddenly engaged. "Those attractive characters filled with potential and then they fall apart. Why does it happen? Why? It's deep. The Red Sox have flawed human personality. They're not a well-oiled machine. You want that, fine, go be a Yankee and win. The Red Sox are about something to hope for, something to look forward to."

"Sometimes I feel worse than I think I should when they lose," I confessed. It felt ridiculous to hear myself talking that way. She was the one who had just come out of the hospital. It was only baseball.

"But you haven't failed, a team has failed," she said. "All a team can give you is what any entertainment can give you, good stories. They try and they try, but they can't pull it off. That's interesting." She was looking genuinely excited. "Why can't they pull it off? What happens to them? Your grandfather believed it was a morale problem. Who knows. Whatever it is, it's a fascinating mystery." Then she felt compelled to defend them. The Red Sox were her team too; had been for more than fifty years. "They are not ridiculous," she said. "They are never ridiculous. Even the poor guy whose name has turned into a verb."

"Buckner," I said. "Bill Buckner."

"Yes, Buckner. They rise again and again. They give you so much in character. Baseball satisfies more than your desire to win. You have moments when you think 'Why am I doing this?' but then you are part of the crowd walking down Commonwealth Avenue after a game at Fenway Park and you've got something out of it even if they didn't win. All the good stories aren't about winning," she said. "The good stories are about struggle."

My irresistible team. They were artists of doom, a member of the pantheon of heroic debacles, from *Hamlet* to the Russians to Robert Scott's South Pole expedition during which one of the fated explorers, Lawrence Oates, provided an epitaph for stoic lost causes everywhere by saying, as he made his final exit from his tent into the Antarctic freeze, "I am just going outside and may be some time."

Now, in the new century, the Red Sox had a new management group that slowly had been reconfiguring the team with a more limber and progressive outlook heavily grounded in the unemotional, scientific projection of performance—a search for order. Gradually, that August, the Red Sox began to play better, and then much better.

At the beginning of October they reached the playoffs and crisply defeated the Angels in the first round. In the American League Championship Series, a four-out-of-seven competition, they opposed the Yankees, who immediately beat them once, twice, and then three times. I wanted to get away from the annual vortex of bitterness and gloom. Leaves were falling. Soon it would be November and the first frost. I was born in November, but disliked the month. It felt arid to me, wind-scarred, the loneliest month of the year. As a child, my holidays divided, when I'd gone riding on the train into New York from New Haven for Thanksgiving, the last stop before Grand Central Terminal was 125th Street. One Hundred and Twenty-fifth Street was November. The expectation of winter was colder than winter itself.

The previous year, when the Red Sox had squandered a three-run, eighth-inning lead and lost to the Yankees in the decisive game of the playoffs, Henry, one of my grandfather's favorite former students, had called to tell me in his own Slavic accent, "Courage, boy!" Henry was a Red Sox fan who always sounded a little happy when things went badly for the Red Sox. Then my Uncle Robert, my father's brother, telephoned me from the West. I was ashen when he reached me and he could tell. "After they lost it never occurred to me that you'd feel anything but grief," he said. "In our family, grief keeps us connected to ourselves. Do you know what I'm talking about?" This was my father's brother. Of course I knew. They could not win. Failure was the team's distinction, what made them unique—and it was the same with us. If we won, we'd lose our true selves.

One day in the year she died, my Aunt Susi took me alone with her on an errand to Brooklyn Heights, a New York City neighborhood of low nineteenth-century roofs, flower boxes, handsomely forged ironwork, and sedate streetscapes. Montague Street, the main boulevard in Brooklyn Heights, was dense with cafés and we went into one for lunch. We were right across the river from Manhattan, but I had no idea of my coordinates, had never been to Brooklyn, had never been in a café. Susi led me down two or three steps, found us a table, and told me I could choose my lunch from what was listed on the chalkboard. Then she suggested an omelet. I didn't know what an omelet was. She urged me to try it, and suggested that, if I didn't enjoy it, she'd eat it and I could order a hamburger. At close-by tables, other people were drinking wine even though it was the middle of the day. Up on the sidewalk, I could see feet passing at a leisurely gait. I had the sudden sense of not only having fun myself, but that everyone around me must be sharing my mood. When my omelet came, goldenrod yellow and browned to a crisp on the edges, Susi turned a pepper shaker over it until the surface was well dusted, and I liked that omelet before I tasted it. That nothing else really happened was the point. Susi elevated ordinary time. Later, in college, I fell in love with someone who had grown up in Brooklyn Heights, a romance that was never happy for me, never fulfilling, though for years it always felt as though it was about to be, and never more so than when I came out of the subway and went hurrying up Montague Street, more convinced with each passing block that now, finally, when I got to her house, I would be loved.

There was some of that in Susi too. Her enormous desire to live and experience the world struck me on some instinctive level as coming from a place of suffering. As a child I could somehow tell that grown-up painful things had happened in Susi's life, that her sorrows had given her life an urgency, that she carried a memory of sadness with her always, and drew on it in search of joy. She was not a brooding person in the least; it was that intimacy with disappointment informed her enormous desire for happiness. This understanding of feelings had been what led her to psychology, just as it motivated her rich sympathy for the misfortunes of others. That it had been she, not a father playing catch with me, who had led me to baseball, now, all these years later, made perfect sense.

After college I was offered a good job in New York. In my first office, I opened my first box of business cards and gazed at my name. The letters were bright and bold; there was a well-etched texture to them. I ran my finger across the good paper, then looked at the box. Lehman Brothers, New Haven, it said. I didn't know how to feel about this. Suddenly I had the idea that somebody might have left me a note inside the box. It had only been a few years. I looked to see, but there was none, for so many reasons there could not have been.

It had been a difficult decision to come and live in my father's city and I worried that I might not be able to handle it. Each time my father and I got together, something always seemed to go awry. He asked me to meet him one day at the Yale Club, where he was still a member "for professional reasons," and I was talking with him in the middle of the lobby when, suddenly, his eyes went strange, and he began screaming at me, telling me—and the cocktail hour throng—what a horrible person I was. I ran out of there. I always needed days to prepare myself before I saw him, but at times I didn't have the chance. Some nights, I'd arrive home to encounter my father standing in front of my apartment building, waiting there to let me know what a pathetic excuse for a son he had. He sent enraged letters to me, wrote them about me to my employer, left screeds on my telephone answering machine, which I always erased before roommates and other people heard them. Almost always. Once, I walked into the house with my friend Austin, and I remember the surprise registering on Austin's face after I saw the blinking red light, forgot myself, and played the new message. Austin was my first adult friend to hear my father's voice, and what he heard was my father yelling into the tape that I'd never make it in the world, that I better give up, try something else, better hurry too, because you never knew what might happen. The next time I saw my father he asked me for money. "He takes all the help he can get, and it never does any good," my mother said. "You have to decide if you want to help him. You have your own life to lead."

He was my only father. I continued to see him out of some combination of guilt and also fear at what he might do if I refused. In the world he was ill. To me he had always been threatening, someone who knew where I was and could come after me. It was more. There was the knowledge that whatever he did to me every month or two could not compare with what the typhoons inside his head were doing to him every day. For thirty years he had been a guy whose life was behind him, a guy who stayed too long at community center coffees, ate in lousy restaurants by himself, stopped along city sidewalks to strike up a chat with strangers who looked back uneasily. Even when I was lying exhausted on my bed after a gruesome telephone conversation, I thought about what it must have been like to be a young man of such intelligence, talent, and promise and to have it all washed away like sand on the beach; to confront me, this person formed in his image, and to look at me beginning to make my way free of the impediments that had taken him down.

By this time, I knew that my father was always comparing us— our looks, our intelligence—and I used to hate that, but in a way he was doing only what I had been doing for a very long time. I had formed myself in terms of him. Not becoming my father became a daily act of will. Through my twenties I remained mostly single. I worked every weekend. I studied people cautiously before I showed them anything of myself. I ate and exercised with care. From the age of twenty-two, I built a savings account for my future children's college education. I felt I wasn't entitled to fall in love until I'd proved I could handle the long-range responsibilities that came with it. With women, I tried to be the perfect boyfriend— generous and devoted. All along, it never occurred to me that my self-sufficiency was making it hard for other people. A woman I went out with for a few years told me afterward, "You were so loving and sweet to me, but you were always slipping out of my grasp."

My grandmother owned a photograph of my father running in a road race, his head thrust back, mouth hugely agape for oxygen. Out running myself one day, I caught myself with that mouth, that carriage, and had to stop.

My hair began to thin. I found myself checking my reflection in shop windows, hoping and praying not to see any change. Sitting in the barber stool, I kept my eyes closed. But there were tufts around the drain every time I took a shower. I knew Graham Greene's view in *The Third Man:* "There must be something phony about a man who won't accept baldness gracefully." But I was upset at this all out of proportion, in a way that other people couldn't understand. It was that there was nothing I could do about it. I would look like him.

In 1991, my father came to my grandmother's house for Thanksgiving. During the meal, there was a conversation about the Supreme Court confirmation of Clarence Thomas. After we'd eaten our turkey, my grandmother brought out a cake for my birthday, which was to be a few days later. My father burst out into a loud chorus of "Happy Birthday." During moments of celebration, my father often wandered off into puerile or antagonistic terrain. Sure enough, instead of "Dear Nicky," he sang "Dear Stupid." His second verse concluded with a crescendo, "Stand up! Stand up! Stand up and show us your ugly face!" I rolled my eyes and blew out the candles, and we resumed our discussion until my father recalled that one of the boys my sister had dated back in college was black. In a sudden fury, he glared at Sally and warned her not to marry "a nigger." Then he snarled the same instructions at me. I asked him to cut it out. His eyes gleamed with anger and excitement. He said it again: "Listen, Nicky, if you ever marry a nigger, don't expect me to show up for the wedding." The futility of investing so much time and thought for so long in him came over me. Lost time was his tragedy, and now it was becoming mine. My friends were all settling down, advancing in their fields, making families, going on with their lives. In many ways, I was nowhere. I didn't want to be angry; it just wasted you. I got my coat and left. My father followed me out of the building, calling in a soft, almost keening voice, "My son, my son," as I walked away.

Those turned out to be the last words he ever said to me. Since I could remember, he had been my duty. Now I decided I couldn't see him anymore. It was an impulse decision made across a lifetime. I let everyone in my family know my intentions, unlisted my telephone number and hoped for the best. At first, every bald head I saw approaching me on the sidewalk made me want to turn and run. When I came home at night, I half expected to see him waiting for me again in the foyer. I learned later that someone had given him my address, but he never came.

When I saw movies or heard songs in which relations between fathers and sons were central themes, I would find myself overwhelmed. Father's Day for me was like Valentine's Day for the brokenhearted. It would catch me by surprise every year, and I would slump.

Once I had made him invisible, I found I could begin to admire him. The reason my father been such a successful college lacrosse player was not that he was unusually gifted; he was a plodding runner in a fast game who tried harder than the others. When the Harvard lacrosse team took showers after practice, there was always one member of the squad missing. That was Donald Dawidoff, out on the darkening field, running extra miles, my father preparing himself.

I don't know how many breakdowns he had, how many new prescriptions he submitted to with all their devastating side effects, how many times he put all his possessions out on the curb, how many months he spent in mental hospitals, what he did with all his days and nights, but through everything he regained his hope over and over. It had taken real courage to return to Harvard, the scene of his first public breakdown, and courage to get through every hour of his life. In a letter he wrote to my great-aunt Ann after her husband, Sid, died, he warned her of "the vast abyss you will find. This is not to usurp your experience," he continued, "nor to pain you more than the present. Only to tell you that I've been there, for years and years and more years. Only now, awakening to what is in and around me, I can look back to what a great sense of loss is." My father never stopped telling people how good the future was going to be. On one level he was spinning straw, but on another he was merely saying that he would keep on.

On the morning of November 3, 1999, I was finishing breakfast when my sister rang my doorbell. She said, "I have to tell you something. Dad died last night." A massive heart attack had thrown him to the floor. He was sixty-five.

We went over to my grandmother's house, where my father's sister, my Aunt Judy, sat with me on the couch. She watched me trying to be stoic, and she pulled me into a big hug and said, "Nicky, for God's sake, child, let it out." And for the first time since I had left Washington thirty-three years before in the rain, I began to sob for my lost father.

A memorial service was planned, and I knew this would be my last chance to introduce my father to the people I love. I invited my friends and former girlfriends, none of whom had met my father or knew a thing about him. Then I set out to write a eulogy, a tribute that was both kind and true—that told how things really were with him. I described his struggles with mental illness and the things he hadn't been able to do. I also wanted to show that there was a way in which my father had always loved me, and I searched for a way to explain it. I kept coming back to the last eight years, when we'd lived in New York together, and how he'd let me alone. I had the sense that this was a great gesture on his part. If my father had never been what I'd wanted him to be, in the end he had found a way to take care of me. That seemed eerie, a father expressing his love for his son by avoiding him, but I believe it.

Confronting the 2004 elimination by the Yankees in four consecutive playoff games, the Red Sox won the fourth game and then the fifth. The games were contested at night, and each lasted more than five hours, the play so intense that one needed the pauses in between every pitch to regroup and ready oneself for the next one. Pacing, shuddering, calling out to my old Chronomatic 9 that was relaying to me the actions of men who could not hear me, I lost track of time; it could have been morning or afternoon. Afterward I'd lie in bed trying to come down, running through the events just passed, possibilities for the game to come, my eyes finally closing through fitful sleeps.

By day I was warlike, giddy, enervated, irritable, and superstitious enough to believe that my irritability might somehow cost the Red Sox. I made a habit of volunteering for other people's chores. I became an over-thanker and an over-tipper. Was I neglecting my elderly grandmother? One morning, standing over the sink full of coffee mugs and cereal bowls that I wished I could leave until later, I turned on the water, began to scrub, and had an image of myself as a hunter lost in the spinney—a man doing just what he wanted yet disoriented by his pleasure. I felt drenched in baseball, caught up too much in the extremes of vicarious endeavor, the optimism, the dread, the proximity to ecstasy, misfortune, calamity, and despair. The Red Sox won the sixth game.

During the afternoon, I would think about the players. As an adult, one inevitably saw ballplayers and ballgames differently from the way one had as a child. It was impossible to ignore the limitation, the avarice, the cupidity of the modern game. Yet with a little effort all this could be overlooked. They could remain the cardboard soldiers from my youth that I still enjoyed playing with. Despite the familiarity of their faces, I did not feel I truly knew them, nor did I want to. As a boy, to build strength, the magnificent hitter Manny Ramirez had run up hills dragging behind him an old automobile tire roped to his waist. With his earnings from pitching, the brilliant, soigné Pedro Martinez built homes for the poor in the Dominican Republic. On the mound, Martinez's lashy, oval eyes were all full of pride and spark and blue notes. And Ramirez, such a serene and enigmatic flyswatter! The fun was that I had these scraps of their biography and no more, just enough to make up the rest of them—to make them into a separate reality known only to me, to make them mine. The experience enabled the creating of a private relationship with something colossally well known. Being a Red Sox fan depended upon what kind of meaning you could make out of them. I still wanted not only to know the players in my own way, but to love them, and the smallest fragment of truth could ensnare me. In those I did love, I saw possibility for myself and others.

As the afternoon wore on before the seventh game, I was thinking how very much it felt like a holiday to have the Red Sox still playing games at such a late time in the year. It was a windfall, lagniappe, and really I should not expect anything from them tonight. My team was the unrequited team. I loved them for what they were. I refused to imagine them winning.

The seventh game was not close. The Red Sox batters pummeled the Yankee pitcher Kevin Brown, an aging star, and a succession of relievers. The Red Sox had won four consecutive games against the Yankees. It was the comeback of comebacks, a sporting miracle that brightened even the days of people who didn't like baseball. "I just wish I could have been the guy I used to be one more time," said Kevin Brown. How astonishing to hear a Yankee sounding so vulnerable and human. All despots seem infallible until they topple.

There was immediately the worry that overcoming the Yankees had been such a heroic accomplishment that there would be no energy left for the World Series against the St. Louis Cardinals. Yet the Red Sox players had a nonchalant, sunny, carefree collective personality that seemed immune not only to physical duress but ideally constituted to withstand the whole Boston legacy of doom and loss. They were self-proclaimed "idiots," "a bunch of earth-pigs" according to relief pitcher Curtis Leskanic, and "borderline nuts" in the view of team manager Terry Francona. Francona meant this in an affectionate way, aware as he was that his players were also surprisingly reasoned in their responses to struggle. "When you slump, it's like a cold: it has to run its course," said the unflappable first baseman Kevin Millar.

No danger of slumping now, as the Red Sox won the first two games from the Cardinals in Boston, traveled to St. Louis, and won the third. It was all happening with an alacrity that had nothing to do with my life with the Red Sox. My sleeps were thick with dreams. I dreamed of my grandfather, wanting to help him watch the games too, telling him "look, look there," and then weeping when I could not make him live again and see. And I dreamed of myself in a train high over a field on which the Red Sox were playing, I struggling still to see them through the window as the train pulled me out of view.

My grandmother Rebecca was losing her memory. "Who was your father?" she asked me one day when I visited her.

"Donald," I told her.

"My Donald?" she asked.

"Yes, Grandma."

"He weren't easy," she said, and we looked at one another and smiled ruefully.

On the morning of the fourth game I awoke laughing. I ate a bowl of cereal that tasted uncommonly good while enjoying the newspaper. Outdoors, the New York air smelled fresh, better than what was breathed in the mountains. That night there was to be a lunar eclipse, what Russian peasants called a heavenly portent. All day I tried to stave off optimism and then gave up. Today we would not bend. Today we would prevail. Did baseball help you face emotional truths or was it a way of not confronting them? The answer fluctuated over time. Baseball was a way of looking at things, and the way you looked was not fixed, nor was it random; it was up to you.

The old reverie of a thousand childhood nights resumed. What would it really feel like for the Red Sox to win the World Series? Would it be a bliss equal to life's rarest epiphanies? The way I'd felt during my second week with my auburn-haired first girlfriend? The feeling of my first day in Paris where everything looked and tasted better than I had known ordinary life could look and taste? But there was no comparable ordeal followed by redemption in any of that, no overcoming time and memory, no emerging from dense wilderness to find oneself at last in the true Arcadia. Maybe it would be a happy golden day of yore, those celebrations long wanted that had never been. Thanksgiving in my home sweet home at a long table filled with an ensemble of family faces, all of us together, the smell of woodsmoke and orchards. Or a Christmas in holly-decked halls, tidings of comfort and joy, all calm, all bright. Life in the imagination, so different from life. The truly killing melancholies cut closer because they were closer. How would life have been for all of us if there had been no war in Russia or Austria? If my father's father had not died so young? If my father had not fallen apart? If my aunt had lived? If my mourning uncle had not lost himself? If my mother had found love again? What was it like to come from a happy family? Was that not always what I envisioned when I contemplated the Red Sox victorious?

When they won the fourth game, I was thrilled, of course. I drank champagne. I answered the telephone to hear the euphoric voices of many friends. It was almost as if I myself had done something. One of the callers was Henry, my grandfather's student, who told me that he didn't know what to think because "I am attached to tragedy, but I am also attached to triumph over adversity." Then the telephone stopped ringing and my apartment grew quiet.

The longed for moment seemed to linger not at all. It turned out that victory defeated the imagination, that the Red Sox had always fallen short for me in all the right ways. Year after year, my flawed team, my lifelong lost cause had provided me with a sustaining form of suffering. Now that they were winners, I saw that happiness cannot exist without sadness. I felt a male regret. Never again would I hold my glove while wearing spiked shoes.

I had the feeling I should be elsewhere, should be doing something, going to a special destination. But where would I go? Once, after my father died, I had a conversation with my friend Austin in which he described his childhood spent moving from city to city all over America. "We moved at least ten times," he said. "A new school almost every year. But every summer we always went for a vacation to this little cottage in Rhode Island, so that became the homestead that I'll always return to. In some way for you, everything was so confusing in your life, walking on glass, your crazy old man screaming at you. I heard him on your answering machine that day. He was completely nuts. In some way you'll always be inordinately attached to the Red Sox because when you needed them they were there for you. Maybe they were your homestead. Maybe they saved you."

The end of the baseball season always came unannounced, like traveling in the car and having a radio station you were listening to vanish in a sudden instant as you drove out of range. Precipitately uncoupled, you were left alone with yourself, and there was the impulse to slow down the journey, to turn back and hear more, but you never did.

I gazed across my room at the pictures of my family on the wall. The faces looked tender and peaceful. The black and white print of my father on the lacrosse field was the picture that had been published in *Sports Illustrated*. Harvard had played the Naval Academy that day, and in the shot the photographer had captured a line of uniformed cadets marching in formation beside the field as the game went on. All of the cadets were in precise formation, eyes forward, rifles on their shoulders, except for one who had turned his head to watch number 42 in the midst of making his beautiful pass, my father giving the glory to somebody else.

Speaking of my father, my grandmother told me once, "It's better to lose with a smart person than to win with a fool." I hadn't known what to make of that then, and didn't now. It was men who called themselves "the idiots" who had finally won for Boston.

I turned off the light. Sitting there in the dark with my old radio, did I miss the story? It had been a beautiful American story, the team that could never win. In many ways it was the story of man, forever fallen, always striving to overcome his demons, doomed in perpetuity to succumb to the drag of failure. I did not miss the beautiful story. What I missed was what I had missed every year when the season ended and abruptly the radio was quiet. I missed them.

Source Notes and Acknowledgments

While this is a book of personal history and recollection, in addition to my diaries, many institutions, individuals, and publications assisted me in confirming my memories. I am grateful to The New York Public Library; the *New Haven Register,* where I thank Randall Beach; the A. Bartlett Giamatti Research Center at the National Baseball Hall of Fame in Cooperstown, New York, where the skilled and generous director is Tim Wiles; the Boston Red Sox and, in particular, Mark Rogoff; Lehman Brothers, New Haven, Connecticut, with gratitude to David Perkins; the Esther Raushenbush Library at Sarah Lawrence College and especially to Sha Fagan; the New Haven Colony Historical Society; the New Haven Free Public Library; Sterling Memorial Library at Yale University; Yale University Department of Manuscripts and Archives; the *Sports Illustrated* research library, with many thanks to Natasha Simon and Linda Wachtel; the Bobst Library at New York University; the City of New Haven Department of Parks, Recreation and Trees; Worthington Hooker School, where I'm grateful to Roberta Camera and the ever-wonderful Elsie Nast; Hopkins School, where I thank Mary Ginsberg and Deena Mack; the City of New Haven Police Department; The Library of America; The Miley Collection, Inc.; The Community Builders, where I thank Michael Patterson; the American Folk Art Museum; the Topps Company; *The New York Times; Boston Herald; The Boston Globe;* the Sons of Sam Horn, where I thank Eric Christensen.

I am appreciative of the correspondence, advice, and information I received from the following people: Andre Aciman, Stanley Arkin, Harriet Balay, Harold Bloom, H. W. Brands, Susan Feinberg, James Gibbons, Randy Harrison, Richard Howard, Jim Leighton, Richard Lingeman, Douglas Merchant, Steve Palluotto, James Passarelli, Nicholas Passarelli, Rachel Passarelli, Douglas Rae, David Raskies, Nancy Sinkoff, Alexander Taft, Stephan Thernstrom, Harry Wexler.

This book began to take shape in my mind after I wrote a piece entitled "My Father's Troubles" for the June 12, 2000, issue of *The New Yorker.* I remain indebted to David Remnick and Jeff Frank for their guidance and encouragement. My thinking was sharpened by subsequent related projects I worked on with Emily Botein and Dean Olsher at WNYC Radio's *The Next*

Big Thing, Gerald Marzorati and Ilena Silverman at *The New York Times Magazine,* and David Shipley at *The New York Times* op-ed page. I'm grateful to them all.

I am very grateful as well for the generous support of the American Academy in Berlin, Civitella Ranieri, the MacDowell Colony, and the Corporation of Yaddo. When my New York apartment began to feel too small, Lisa Howorth, Richard Howorth, Susan B. Howorth, and Andy Howorth, in Misssissippi; Betsey and David McKearnan, in Massachusetts; and Patti Scialfa and Bruce Springsteen, in New Jersey, generously gave me quiet places in which to think about New Haven.

David Halberstam's encouragement meant a great deal to me, as it did to the many, many younger writers he always had time for. He was a generous friend to this book, and how I wish he were alive to read it.

I couldn't have written this book without the many supportive and helpful conversations I had along the way with friends. In particular, I am remembering talks with Roger Angell, Donald Antrim, Armin Baier, Kevin Baker, Patrick Bennett, Emily Botein, Kathy Chetkovich, Ted Carman, Ted Conover, Nancy Dorfman, Ingrid Ellen, Jeffrey Eugenides, Tali Farhadian, Patty Frank, Francisco Goldman, Douglas Gollin, Sue Halpern, Larry Harris, David Herskovits, Jack Hitt, Lisa and Richard Howorth, Susan B. Howorth, Ben Katchor, Harold Koh, Ed and Curtis Koren, Annette Levey, Greg and Jenny Lyss, Gerry, Guy and Luca Marzorati, Bill and Sophie McKibben, David Means, Barbara Mundy, Austin Murphy, Geoffrey O'Brien, Genève Patterson, Thomas Powers, David Rakoff, Henry Rosovsky, Max Rudin, Vijay Seshadri, Charles Siebert, Bruce Springsteen, Lorin Stein, Jean Strouse, Melanie Thernstrom, William Wade-Gery, Anne Wenzel, Mark Winegardner, Colson Whitehead, and Kevin Young.

The fortifying enthusiasm and sparkling intelligence of my agent, Kathy Robbins, are wonderful things to have on your side, and I feel so much gratitude to her. David Halpern, Coralie Hunter, Rick Pappas, and Kate Rizzo carefully and gracefully look after me at The Robbins office.

All these Pantheon years later, Dan Frank remains the editor of my dreams. Many thanks as well to effortless Fran Bigman, Altie Karper, and Anthea Lingeman, first-class professionals and kind souls of the highest order, and to meticulous Fred Chase, Evan Stone, and Meghan Wilson. Of sterling Vintage is the wonderful Jennifer Jackson.

Rebecca Carman saw me through from beginning to end with generosity, with imagination, and with love.

It would have been impossible for me to write a book about family without encouragement from the Dawidoffs and the Gerschenkrons. Robert

Dawidoff, Judy Fresco, Barbara McNair, Anne Rosenberg, Carl Sussman, George Sussman, and Peter Sussman all helped me to tell this story. I can't say enough about how much the loyal support of Rebecca Rolland, Lisa Wiener, and Jonathan Wiener and his wife, Ginger Young, has meant to me through my life. My loyal sister Sally Dawidoff has many gifts, among them a great, big, lovely heart.

When I think now of my father, Donald Dawidoff, I remember what Dietrich Bonhoeffer wrote from prison: "We must form our estimate of human beings less from their achievements and failures, and more from their sufferings."

My mother, Heidi Dawidoff, brought me up by herself with tremendous care and love. She was the same way with this book. I thank her for everything.

About the Author

Nicholas Dawidoff is the author of *The Catcher Was a Spy: The Mysterious Life of Moe Berg; In the Country of Country: A Journey to the Roots of American Music;* and *The Fly Swatter: Portrait of an Exceptional Character,* a finalist for the Pulitzer Prize. He is the editor of The Library of America's *Baseball: A Literary Anthology* and is also a contributor to *The New Yorker, The American Scholar,* and *The New York Times Magazine.* A graduate of Harvard University, he has been a Henry Luce Scholar, a Guggenheim Fellow, a Civitella Ranieri Fellow, and a Berlin Prize Fellow of the American Academy. He is currently the Anschutz Distinguished Fellow at Princeton University.

A Note on the Type

*This book was set in Caledonia, originally a
Linotype face designed by W. A. Dwiggins (1880–1956).
It belongs to the family of printing types called
"modern face" by printers. Caledonia borders on the
general design of Scotch Roman but it is more
freely drawn than that letter.*

COMPOSED BY CREATIVE GRAPHICS,

ALLENTOWN, PENNSYLVANIA

PRINTED AND BOUND BY BERRYVILLE GRAPHICS,

BERRYVILLE, VIRGINIA

DESIGNED BY ANTHEA LINGEMAN